Good Trouble

Good Trouble

Good Trouble

How Deviants, Criminals, Heretics, and Outsiders Have Changed the World for the Better

Brian Wolf

LEXINGTON BOOKS
Lanham • Boulder • New York • London

Top cover image: Jacques Louis David's "Death of Socrates" (1787). Image used under license by Shutterstock.com.
Bottom cover image: Courtesy of Montgomery County Sherriff's Department. Photo taken February 22, 1956.

Published by Lexington Books
An imprint of The Rowman & Littlefield Publishing Group, Inc.
4501 Forbes Boulevard, Suite 200, Lanham, Maryland 20706
www.rowman.com

6 Tinworth Street, London SE11 5AL

British Library Cataloguing in Publication Information Available

Library of Congress Cataloging-in-Publication Data

Names: Wolf, Brian Christopher, author.
Title: Good trouble : how deviants, criminals, heretics, and outsiders have changed the world for the
    better / Brian Wolf.
Description: Lanham : Lexington Books, [2019] | Includes bibliographical references and index.
Identifiers: LCCN 2019009407 (print) | LCCN 2019011394 (ebook) | ISBN 9781498563451 (Elec-
    tronic) | ISBN 9781498563444 (cloth : alk. paper) | ISBN 9781498563468 (pbk. : alk. paper)
Subjects: LCSH: Deviant behavior. | Criminology--Sociological aspects. | Social change.
Classification: LCC HM811 (ebook) | LCC HM811 .W64 2019 (print) | DDC 302.5/42--dc23
LC record available at https://lccn.loc.gov/2019009407

For Grace,
May you always have the power to swim against the current

Table of Contents

Acknowledgments

As this book has been over a decade in the making, I would like to thank several people whom I owe an intellectual debt in crafting this book. Most critical to this project, I want to thank Phil Zuckerman, whose lecture notes on deviant behavior sparked the premise of the sociological understanding of *Good Trouble*. Ed Levy provided important editorial and substantive assistance in the development of the final draft of the manuscript. Several anonymous reviewers also gave important feedback that helped sharpen the focus of this book. Lastly, I would like to thank my wife, Melanie, who was steadfast in her support and encouragement as I embarked on and completed this project.

Preface

Courses (and books) on crime and deviance are among the most popular in the social sciences. For many reasons, these topics are interesting and compelling to both academics and untrained observers. From a spike in bicycle thefts on college campuses to the officer-involved shootings of unarmed blacks, nearly everyone seems to have a point of view on issues of crime and justice. Similarly, most people can readily conjure images of "deviants" and "criminals." Such individuals are almost always seen as bad people, a menace to society. However, consider the moral argument espoused by congressman and civil rights hero John Lewis during a commencement speech at Washington University in 2016:

> When you see something that is not right, not fair, not just, *you have a moral obligation, a mission and a mandate*, to stand up, to speak up and speak out, and get in the way, *get in trouble, good trouble, necessary trouble*.[1]

Rarely, if ever, are the "disciplined nonconformists" and "good trouble" John Lewis refers to included in these images. Yet, this book argues, these are some of the most important deviants and criminals to consider in any academic discussion of the topic.

Good Trouble is a tribute to the criminal—a special kind of criminal who is motivated not by personal gain but ethical altruism. This book conceptualizes such an individual as a "deviant hero." The premise of this volume is that deviance and crime are a vital source of progressive social change. Consider Martin Luther King Jr. Almost everyone considers his (and his compatriots') work and actions heroic. However, the figures and actions of the civil rights movement were (and in some cases still are) typified as deviant and even criminal. This is also true of well-known figures in other movements, such as the women's movement (Emma Goldman), the labor movement (Mother Jones), gay rights (Harvey Milk), anticolonialism (Gandhi), science (Darwin), and religion (Joan of Arc), just to name a few. Both history and contemporary society provide similar examples useful for probing within the theoretical frameworks proposed by the sociology of deviance. Yet, heroic or altruistic kinds of deviance are almost never considered in the literature on crime.

Resistance to such a conceptualization arises because "commonsense" understanding seems to contradict the proposition that crime might lead to transformative change. Most people, including scholars and academics, typically think of deviance and crime as behaviors that are either morally disdainful or at least a bit odd. While sociology may consider examples of deviance that might be morally neutral (depending on the context), such as tattooing, polyamory, gender nonconformity, or perhaps nudity, criminologists overwhelmingly tend to focus on behaviors condemned by law, which are typically unquestioned and assumed to be "immoral behaviors." However, looking back in history at people who made a difference, who changed things for the better, it is not unusual to discover that such individuals were often considered deviant or even criminal in their own social context.

Crime has always served as a means to question unjust laws, effectively transforming society for the better. Certain types of crime and deviance may also catalyze collective sentiment to overcome social inertia, provoking broad movements that reconsider shared moral frameworks. Yet, few people regard crime and deviance as representing a necessary social phenomenon. To my knowledge, no book specifically examines "good trouble," though this concept may be easily derived from scholarly understandings of deviance.

Sociologists usually define deviance as a fluid construct, relative to given social circumstances and neither negative nor positive in itself. However, despite the widespread rejection of absolutist approaches, most texts and studies of deviant behavior implicitly or explicitly still present deviance as morally bad, wrongly conflating deviant behavior with villainous actions, or morally neutral. This book argues that some of the most important deviants have been at the forefront of positive social change and the creation of a fairer, more just, and more humane society. Deviant heroes violate unjust norms and laws and face the repercussions, effecting social change in the process.

This book has three central aims: first, to establish the theoretical viability of a deviant hero and provide a method for considering how deviance may provoke progressive social change; second, to provide a typology of deviant heroism and to document examples—contemporary and historical—that represent the praxis of deviant heroism; and third, to examine the problem of conformity and establish how deviant heroism in everyday life may be a remedy for injustice in any social context.

FOR THE OBJECTOR

The aim of *Good Trouble* is to demonstrate that by introducing new moral frameworks or provoking needed social change, crime and deviance have a positive social value. To many, such a tribute to criminality and rule defiance seems outrageous, perhaps even dangerous. Readers and critics may question how norm violation could be celebrated in one moment but condemned in another. Others may find the deliberate violation of law, whatever the context, morally wrong, especially in a democratic society. After all, there are mechanisms, such as elections and legislation, by which people can change the law. Others may contend that any notion of "positive crime" is a moral and ethical slippery slope: Doesn't advocating the violation of one law disrespect all laws? Doesn't homage to those who break laws to advance a cause, no matter how ethical or just, open a Pandora's box leading to complete disrespect for the rule of law itself?

These concerns are valid, but they fail to acknowledge the value and function of rule breaking in certain contexts. It is true that societies, even undemocratic ones, have legal means to change rules and address citizen grievances or desire for social change. However, this assertion does not recognize how legal means of effecting social change may be monopolized, especially in societies with high degrees of inequality or discrimination, by groups that possess political and economic power or have a strong influence on the culture and society. It also does not acknowledge how history has been profoundly shaped by norm violators. The very people who express commitment to the "rule of law" may also believe in institutions that were formed by lawbreakers. The Founding Fathers of the United States were in fact such people, as were the founders of major religious traditions like Jesus, Martin Luther, and Buddha—all were rule violators to one extent or another.

The question of treating the law as a strict moral code that should not be challenged through unconventional means deserves further consideration. Both criminology and sociology tend to dismiss absolutist interpretations of criminal laws, which hold all crimes up to an invariant moral standard; an act is defined as a crime because it is bad or causes harm. But such a perspective does not account for immoral acts, such as slavery, that were once fully legal, or for crimes, such as human rights violations, that are relatively new constructs. It is therefore crucial to understand that the definition of crime is temporally and spatially bound. Murder in the context of warfare or capital punishment may be perfectly legal while using cannabis or betting on the outcome of a sporting event can draw a criminal sanction. A woman sunning topless on the beach in the south of France is perfectly acceptable; the same act in the south of Saudi Arabia would be an unthinkable act that could result in a very long prison sentence, or worse. The point is that crime always exists in a social context, and this is not so much about what is considered good or bad, but what is deemed criminal at a given place and time. Certain laws, when challenged, may be an act of altruism that brings about a greater good.

Lastly, an objector to "good trouble" may rightly ask, "Why is one's person's action 'good trouble' while the actions of a criminal who expresses an altruistic motive are not?" The first chapter delves into this further. This volume does not take a strict constructionist position on this issue. While I do establish an operational definition of good trouble based on clear criteria, I fully admit that this book is a normative rather than an objective (or positivist) undertaking. I invite the skeptic to consider fully the biographies and historical contexts of the deviants and criminals presented in this volume, and the impact their rule breaking has made on society. The first chapter delves into this question further.

ORGANIZATION AND OVERVIEW

The book is divided into three parts. Part I, "Deviance and Good Trouble," consists of two chapters that outline deviant heroism from a sociological perspective, considering the theoretical role of the deviant hero within classical and contemporary sociological traditions and identifying directions for social research on the topic. Chapter 1 problematizes how crime and deviance, which are almost exclusively thought of as negative or neutral phenomena, can be a source and driver of positive social change. Chapter 2 probes into classical and contemporary sociological theories that support this thesis. It will also propose a methodology to consider heroic deviance within a framework, first established by C. Wright Mills, that looks at the intersection of individual biography (specific deviants) and history (the unjust social structures in which they found themselves).

Once the theoretical viability of heroic deviance is established, Part II will examine specific people who have been labeled either deviant or criminal who have effected positive social change through their actions. This section will primarily focus on well-established heroic deviants in history, but contemporary examples will also be considered. Chapter 3 will use Martin Luther King Jr.'s "Letter from a Birmingham Jail" to demonstrate how heroic deviance may be practiced in a specific context. Chapter 4 will give further examples, in Frederick Douglass, Harriet Tubman, John Brown, John Lewis, Rosa Parks and Claudette Colvin, Malcolm X, Huey Newton, and others, including Black Lives Matter, of lawbreaking heroes who fought racial injustice. Chapters 5 through 8 will survey specific types of heroic deviance—respectively, women fighting for human rights, labor agitators, what I call truth-tellers or "lamplighters," and peacemakers.

Chapter 5, "Outsiders: Women in Good Trouble," examines the adage that "well-behaved women rarely make history." This chapter will consider the biographies, words, and actions of women who disrupted the status quo through direct action and other forms of confrontation to change laws and effect social change. Individual deviants include suffragists such as Elizabeth Cady Stanton and Susan B. Anthony. It also examines key figures in the first wave of the women's rights movement such as Margaret Sanger and Emma Goldman, who led the fight for women's reproductive rights. Alongside these profiles is an engagement of feminism and feminist social science, work that was long excluded from the sociological canon.

Chapter 6 looks at good trouble in the labor movement, generated by heroes of labor rights like Eugene V. Debs, Albert and Lucy Parsons, Joe Hill, and César Chavez. Chapter 7 contemplates how "truth-tellers" overcame normative contexts to alert the world to new ways of thinking or gross injustices. Truth-tellers may be scientists the authorities labeled as heretics, like Galileo and Darwin, but so also are whistleblowers like Frank Serpico and Karen Silkwood. Chapter 8 looks at Peacemakers, Earthsavers, Lovers, and Dreamers—people who, like Chief Joseph, Ann Frank, and Malala Yousafzai, through various acts of deviance, sought a peaceful resolution to conflict against a violent aggressor.

While Part II examined historical figures and contemporaries who challenged unjust laws on a sociological macro-level, Part III addresses the problem of deviance on a micro-level. Chapter 9 looks at the sociology and psychology of conformity, at the relationship of conformity to fascism, and how deviant heroism may be an antidote to collective acquiescence in the face of inhumanity. The case of US soldiers in the My Lai massacre in Vietnam serves as an illustrative case in the dangers of "complicit conformity." To further underscore the problem of conformity, this chapter also revisits three famous studies of conformity and their conclusions—the Milgram Study, the Asch Conformity Project, and the Stanford Prison Experiment. Chapter 10 provides a way for the reader to practice deviant heroism in everyday life, in deviant acts of kindness, for example. This chapter describes norm-breaching experiments that may be carried out with students in an academic setting.

Because this book is organized as a survey of several notable deviants who have impacted social change, it engages literature outside the sociology of deviance and criminology, in particular literature of social movements and various histories of these movements. However, *Good Trouble* is not an attempt to explain or capture partial episodes of any single social movement, let alone the entirety of one. Nor is it possible in a work such as this to give a complete biography of any single deviant hero. Volumes with the specific histories, processes, and intents of these figures are noted in the bibliography. Rather, this book seeks to underscore specific acts of deviance that have advanced humanity and to give some of the social context in which the deviance occurred. In addition, many of these acts evoked a political or social reaction, resulting in attempts at political or social control. Therefore, there is always a political and cultural context to consider in each of these cases of good trouble. Many of the examples are from the United States, but some are quite historical (going back to Socrates). In other cases, a comparative or international perspective illuminates key acts of good trouble in other countries and cultures. This is probed in chapter 5 as various women in good trouble are examined.

Because this volume is focused on deviance, law breaking, and conformity, it draws heavily on sociological traditions. However, criminology and psychology are also useful in capturing the dynamic social, historical, and legal process involved in the construction of deviance and heroism. Therefore, this book, though grounded in the major theoretical traditions of sociology, is interdisciplinary.

NOTE

1. Full text of speech found at https://source.wustl.edu/2016/05/john-lewis-2016-commencement-address-washington-university-st-louis/ on December 12, 2018.

I

Deviance and Good Trouble

Chapter One

Deviant Heroism

The conventional understanding of criminal behavior and deviance generally associates these terms with what is bad, evil, or detrimental to society. However, history—and most scholarly definitions of deviant behavior—show that this is not inherently the case. In various contexts, rules and instruments of social control can represent unjust and oppressive social forces. Consider civil rights leader John Lewis's principled argument, quoted in the preface (and the inspiration for this book's title), that one has a moral duty to get into "good trouble." Thoreau advanced a similar argument 150 years earlier in saying, "If . . . the machine of government . . . is of such a nature that it requires you to be the agent of injustice to another, then, I say, break the law" (8, 1849). Throughout history, the notion that one has an obligation to break unjust laws has been put into practice by a host of admirable leaders and morally driven rebels. Their deviance may have been labeled criminal at one time but it ultimately served to increase justice or decrease suffering, often at great risk to themselves. Often, at first, their contemporaries—in particular those who wield power and influence—label these individuals deviant or condemn them as criminals, but eventually their nonconformist actions come to be recognized as profoundly good and, ultimately, even heroic.

Well-known examples of heroic deviants include icons of the civil rights movement like Rosa Parks, Malcolm X, and Martin Luther King Jr., who were treated as outcasts by the entrenched powers and instruments of social control in their own day, only later to be vindicated by justice and history. Other societies and historical epochs are full of examples of individuals who played a similar role, ranging from Mahatma Gandhi to Margaret Sanger, from Phoolan Devi to Harvey Milk, and from Frank Serpico to John Brown. Indeed, the activist, the civil disobedient, the whistleblower, the rebel, the

3

heretic, and the freedom fighter are often seen as both deviant *and* heroic, given the social context of their actions.

However, the sociological literature on crime and deviance has rarely considered the selfless acts of such individuals. Criminology has been even less willing to consider how law breaking may represent a social good or source of beneficial social change. Nevertheless, given most definitions of crime and deviance, noble, altruistic, or saintly actions could very easily be considered deviant or criminal in varying social contexts (Kanagy & Kraybill, 1999); Jones, 1998; Wilkins, 1965; Lemert, 1951; Katz, 1972). Violating the unjust laws of a system of apartheid or challenging an oppressive system like patriarchy represents a clear example of deviant behavior. Do such people and their actions belong in the literature on the sociology of deviance? Are they consistent with the theoretical underpinnings of the major traditions in the sociology of crime and deviant behavior? This book asserts that the answer to these questions is a resounding yes. It is further suggested that a comprehensive understanding of the phenomena of crime and deviant behavior cannot be fully established without including such actions and such heroic individuals. Expanding on the concept of "positive deviance" and drawing from classical theoretical traditions, this volume will argue that the deviant hero fulfills a social role as an important agent of progressive social change and that, consequently, heroic deviance warrants recognition in sociological discussions of crime and deviance. Accordingly, this initial chapter proposes a reconceptualization of the term *deviance* along with several new avenues for social research.

THE VILIFIED REPRESENTATION OF DEVIANCE

It is difficult to challenge the perception that deviant behavior is a social evil, given popular definitions of the term and examples of deviant behaviors in sociology texts. If one were to ask a nonacademic or someone not in the mental health field, "What is the first thing that comes to mind when you hear the word *deviant*?" one is likely to hear that a deviant is a "bad guy" or someone who is clearly a villain or deeply disturbed. Answers I receive when I ask that question range from serial killer and pedophile to tobacco smoker and rebellious teenager. On the surface, it makes sense that the study of deviance and crime would focus on the types of deviance that typically elicit a negative social reaction.

The negative association of deviance may be endemic to a larger bias within the fields of sociology and criminology that regard deviant behavior as villainous behavior. For example, a brief survey of the deviance chapter in fifteen commonly used introduction-to-sociology textbooks revealed that each of these texts covers similar topics, ranging from the disturbing to downright evil. Nearly every textbook lists similar items as examples of deviance—for example, FBI-indexed crimes, prostitution, drug use, mental illness, and white-collar crime. I conducted a further content analysis of the examples covered in commonly used deviance texts/readers and found that the topics and examples given are invariably similar to those in the introductory texts. Nearly all the books center on the bad or downright malicious things people can do to themselves and others. Even though initially stating that deviance is neither good nor bad, they all unambiguously frame deviance as socially wrong or harmful.

Nevertheless, some of the topics covered in these texts represent actions that even their authors would deem morally neutral. Deviant actions such as homosexuality, nudism, tattooing, religious cults, and certain types of substance use that are commonly considered neither good nor bad are usually included alongside white-collar crime, street crime, family violence, and sex offending. For instance, ponder Kanagy and Kraybill's (1999) introductory text, *The Riddles of Human Society*, which openly describes deviants as "bad guys" and informs us that deviance includes "anything from raping to speeding to burping in class" (7). This tendency to conflate morally repugnant activities with morally neutral ones results in an incomplete understanding of what crime and deviance represent in the larger sociological context. It implicitly constructs law and norm violations as unjust or bad while simultaneously giving the impression that conformity and law-abidingness are intrinsically good or just; it teaches students to think of rule breaking as intrinsically detrimental or sociopathic (Jones, 1998). By reinforcing in the minds of those who study the sociology of deviance and crime the notion that conformity is always a good thing and deviance always a bad thing, this approach leaves the dialectic of deviance and conformity only partially explored, ignoring deviance one could characterize as heroic, altruistic, or beneficial and failing to challenge the pervasive ideology that views crime and norm violation as affronts to society.

Nevertheless, several major theoretical traditions in sociology do not support this one-sided approach. How should sociologists talk about people—now labeled criminals—who are actually fighting against unjust regimes? As I have noted, most conceptions of deviance lend themselves to being understood as good and bad or as morally neutral. Violating or resisting an unjust law might be considered "deviant," but at the same time as heroic. *Good Trouble* advocates such a nuanced understanding of what constitutes deviant behavior and recognition of the reality of the "deviant hero" and "good trouble."

THE INTERACTIVE CONSTRUCTION OF DEVIANT AND CONFORMIST BEHAVIOR

As it is not possible to find specific actions that are universally condemned at all times and in all places, absolutist definitions of deviance are not particularly helpful to sociology (Tittle and Paternoster, 2000). The discipline has long argued that notions of good and bad, right and wrong, vary according to time and place, that deviance can only be fully understood within its social context (Goode, 2015). In a classic example, nudity, or being naked in a public setting, seems like a deviant act; however, more context is always needed including the social response to and cultural meanings associated with nudity. A street flasher would certainly be arrested for public exposure, but a nude bicycle race at the Burning Man festival or a naked parade at Seattle's Freemont Street festival is normative in those contexts (Curra, 2013). Thus, constructing deviance is an interactive process involving the interplay of cultural meanings and coercion. In the words of Ben-Yehuda (1990), "deviance is not an objective, eternally true, essence. Deviance is the product of complex and dynamic processes of interaction, power and legitimacy" (221). More useful to sociology are constructionist approaches that may be situated within a variety of traditions. For instance, interactionist perspectives are ideally suited for this task as they incorporate an understanding of the process of deeming a behavior deviant and acknowledge that definitions of deviance may change over time. The interactionist perspective incorporates contextual factors used in the defining and labeling of deviant behavior; interactionism also demonstrates how social responses shape the application of labels and meanings associated with deviance. This perspective helps demonstrate how a dominant group may label a behavior as deviant in a specific social context, while differing audiences or epochs may recognize the same behavior as altruistic and ultimately heroic. The flexibility of social interactionist approaches to deviance makes it especially well-suited to account for changes in normative structures and reactions across time, place, and audience. The concept of the deviant hero demonstrates this construction of deviance.

The label of deviance is the product of interactive social mechanisms that Adler and Adler (2015) call *attitudes, behaviors,* and *conditions* (ABCs). Behavior is a major type of deviance, but beliefs or attitude, as well as specific traits or conditions, may also be deviant (Goode, 2015). For instance, as Goffman notes in *Stigma* (1963) deviance is a part of a social process whereby an individual or collective is deemed blemished and discredited by a larger social whole. In line with Adler and Adler's conception of deviance, stigmatized attributes may be behaviors, but could also be ideas, or physical conditions. Likewise, entire ethnic groups may be stigmatized as deviant by an ethnic hegemon. Deviance may be achieved by embracing alternative belief systems or acting outside of accepted norms, or it may be labeled based on the normative structures or conditions of a society; it is a fluid or relative term and a product of changing norms, reactions, laws, and power structures. Deviant heroes may be social actors on the leading edge of these social transformations, challenging entrenched normative environments that ultimately prove at variance with new social conditions.

Deviance is often defined as behaviors or beliefs that create an adverse response or violate a norm or law that is presumed to promote a social good. Interactionist approaches, again, seem especially well-suited to appreciate the dynamic interplay between the deviant hero and a normative order that is constantly in flux. Interactionist perspectives, especially as promulgated by Becker (1963) and Goffman (1963), emphasize that ideas and meanings associated with specific behaviors change and vary over time and place. At the heart of the interactionist perspective is the idea that deviance is a social creation, the result of linking and assigning meaning to behaviors among a variety of social components: actors, acts, rules and norms, audiences, and social reactions (Dotter and Roebuck, 1988). Rules and laws are open to a constant state of negotiation between these various components and involve a multitude of iterations. The label "deviant" may be applied to a myriad of nonconformist behaviors that can be good, bad, or neutral.

Of course, not just any behavior, heroic or otherwise, is randomly or haphazardly labeled deviant. Rather, that label is the product of complex social interactions between various social roles including the deviant actor, the audience, rule enforcers, moral entrepreneurs, and society as a whole (Becker, 1963); the definition of deviance, or the application of the label "deviant" to a specific behavior, may also depend on the self-reflexivity of the deviant. For Becker and other interactionists, the process of defining and labeling deviance, and the consequences of doing so, are more important than the acts themselves. Like other interactive approaches, labeling theory asserts that self-identity is influenced through an individual relationship to the larger social whole. Once the labeling process occurs, a person may reject the label "deviant" (primary deviance) or they may internalize the label and accept it (secondary deviance) (Lemert, 1967).

Precise descriptions of what constitutes deviance are likely to provoke much debate among any circle of sociologists (McCaghy, Capron, Jamison, and Carey, 2010). Both inside and outside the academy, the term is broad and amorphous. Some sociologists prefer normative definitions, simply describing deviance as a phenomenon relative to the norms of a given society (Clinard and Meier, 2007). Others are inclined to take a reactivist approach, looking at behaviors that are stigmatized by a group (Goode, 2015). For the purposes of this text, in line with social constructionist approaches, deviance is best defined simply as nonconformity resulting in a social response. Nonconformist behaviors can be good, bad, or neutral depending on the social context. For example, Germans who, during the Holocaust, chose not to shoot Jews when ordered were considered by most normative definitions of deviance in that social and historical context to be nonconformists (Browning, 1992). Likewise, a black woman refusing to leave her seat in the Jim Crow South was deviant and criminal, which would evoke a strong social response. Both of these nonconformist behaviors, given the time, place, and audience, were clearly deviant. Nowadays, most people would regard these behaviors as brave and noble, positive acts. The interactionist perspective thus demonstrates how meanings associated with deviance may change with time and place. Seen from within this framework, the deviant hero represents a symbolic impetus for much-needed social change.

To be clear, the conception of deviance is not limited to strictly interactionist perspectives. Founding sociologist Emile Durkheim was one of the first social scientists to argue for the social relativity of crime, stating: "We do not condemn it because it is a crime, but it is a crime because we condemn it" (1966, 163). He argued that actions considered deviant are based on what the collective conscience says is a crime, and not anything inherent in the act itself. In fact, Durkheim makes it clear that deviant behaviors are not necessarily detrimental to group life and may strengthen social cohesion and challenge existing norms. Kai Erikson (1962) offers a bridge between structure and the individual in stating that "deviance leaks out where the social machine is defective; it occurs where the social structure fails to communicate its needs to human actors" (313). Erikson (1962) echoes many of Durkheim's sentiments, arguing that laws and norms are in a perpetual state of renegotiation during which beliefs about conformity are squared with changing beliefs and collective sentiments. Having acknowledged the relative and ever-changing character of deviance, the next task is to work toward a sociological definition of deviant heroism.

BEYOND GOOD AND EVIL: UNDERSTANDING AND DEFINING DEVIANT HEROISM

Heroes represent important mythologies and realities within almost any culture (Wright, 2001). The type of heroes it celebrates, or its lack thereof, reflects the nature of a culture. If you were to ask North American children who their heroes are, they are likely to give you the names of fictional characters as opposed to real people. Adult Americans may report not having any heroes at all; indeed, a Gallup poll found "a lack of major heroes among Americans," and that two-thirds of Americans did not think there were any living heroes (Saad, n.d.). In a normative sense, it is good to have heroes. In complex and nuanced systems of morality, heroes help people understand what they believe in. More broadly, heroes are indicative of larger moral and cultural values; their causes clarify ideals and embody personal traits a collectivity finds important and are therefore sociologically significant.

Many sociological accounts of deviance do not explicitly mention heroes, yet stories of heroes form subtexts that penetrate many aspects of social life. Crime narratives, like fiction, are often filled with heroes and villains dueling in a dramaturgical fashion for a conclusion that solidifies a public's perception of good and evil. Applying the insights of Goffman (1959), one can discern contentions between heroes and villains playing out as a two-act drama in which a weaker group is victimized in act one and vindicated through restorative justice bestowed by a strong hero in act two. Conformist heroes are easy to praise, as they work within existing social structures to champion a cause. Deviant heroes may be more challenging, as they violate laws and norms with actions that only later may bring awareness of their heroism.

The conceptual definition of heroic deviance used in this book is nonconformity that increases justice, decreases suffering, or violates oppressive rules with the intent of changing normative contexts. Further, these deviant acts are law breaking and rule violating and are done intentionally, altruistically, and without regard to either the personal benefit or detriment of the norm violator. Usually, the deviant hero also prompts an initial response in the form of some type of social control. Consistent with the constructionist approach to understanding crime and deviance, this individual may be a criminal in one context but not in another, stigmatized in his or her day but later vindicated and celebrated by history.

Advocacy for recognition of the deviant hero does have some support in other definitions of deviance. The concept of *positive deviance* has been proposed, and aroused some debate, as an antidote to overly negative conceptions of deviance (West, 2003). For instance, Spreitzer and Sonenshein (2004, 828) define positive deviance in a normative perspective as "intentional behaviors that depart from the norms of a referent group in an honorable way." In contrast, Dodge (1985) suggested a more reactive approach, defining positive deviance as deviant actions receiving a favorable social response. I advocate a social-justice-oriented approach to deviance that considers the deviant a virtuous hero, especially when he or she challenges unjust norms, effectively making deviance a source of social change.

WHAT IS NOT DEVIANT HEROISM?

Given a social constructionist approach to the understanding of good trouble, the following question inevitably emerges: Why is one group or individual who challenges norms or breaks the law considered "good" while another group is not? Take, for example, the Bundy family, who led the standoff with federal agents at the Malheur Wildlife Refuge in Oregon. Or a clerk refusing to issue marriage licenses to same-sex couples. Are they examples of good trouble? What about the Animal Liberation Front, which uses arson and the threat of violence to advance its cause? Or Oliver North, who was convicted of three felonies related to the Iran-Contra Affair? Each of these examples involved criminal acts, yet clearly, they also have a constituency that supports and believes in their cause. Using our operational definition of deviant heroism, however, it is easy to separate acts that inflict violence on the innocent, perpetuate exclusion, or are motivated by personal gain from the good trouble that is the primary focus of this book.

Social constructionism is criticized for clouding perceptions and obscuring questions of basic morality (Burr, 2015). While this book makes no claim to neutrality in describing good trouble or deviant heroism, it is still possible to determine what is and what is not heroic deviance. Three simple tests can discern the difference between good trouble and crime while engaging in a deviant act under the guise of a higher cause. These criteria relate to one's goals, motives, and means.

Regarding the goals of the action, does it aim at increasing fairness and equality? Good trouble challenges inequality while other kinds of crime perpetuate a crime cycle. Stealing a person's coat to protest that not everyone has one does nothing to challenge the underlying cause of inequity. All this does is unjustly deprive someone else of their clothing. Similarly, denying a legal certificate of marriage to one couple in protest of a marriage equality law is unjustly perpetuating exclusion. Therefore, the intent of the deviant action must be aimed at remedying an overarching unfairness, and not simply violating a norm for the sake of norm violation.

The second test considers the underlying motive of the criminal or deviant act. For example, was the motive altruistic? Refusing to pay taxes or occupying a federal wildlife refuge may very well rest on principled arguments, but if it was done to enrich oneself it cannot be considered a pure crime, a term Lovell (2009) uses to distinguish illegal acts of virtue from ordinary acts of crime. Musing that pure crime "is a curious characterization, to be sure, especially since criminal behavior is rarely described as a form of political expression, let alone one that is wholesome" (65). Lovell goes on to explain that pure criminals, those deemed disobedient by the reigning powers, are some of the most celebrated fictional, political, and religious figures in our civilization. Pure criminals openly defy laws and make no effort to conceal the behavior while openly accepting the punishment, and even welcoming arrest to expose the injustice of the state. Yet, like Socrates and Martin Luther King, the pure criminal makes no apologies.

The last criterion considers the means employed to achieve the goal. Behaviors that use threats of violence against unhardened nonmilitary targets or unarmed civilians cannot be classified as "good trouble." The question of violence in this volume does add nuance to this argument, and several deviant heroes profiled in later chapters do resort to violence—for example, John Brown in his raid on Harpers Ferry or the Polish underground resistance during the Warsaw Uprising against the Nazis. Herbert Marcuse made a distinction between violence and counterviolence, with the former being justified against a violent oppressor (Castro 2016: 167). For purposes of argument, good trouble may use violence against a military or armed oppressor, but not against civilians or the undefended. Therefore, arson against a civilian target, whatever the intent or righteousness of the cause, would not be classified as good trouble.

TRADITIONS IN CRIMINOLOGY

The ensuing chapters investigate the viability of "good trouble" as a reconstructed concept for the sociology of crime and deviance. While criminology or studies of deviance do not readily accept the notions of good crime or positive deviance, they do not entirely ignore the topic, either. For instance, there is support in both classical and contemporary texts for the idea that crime can be a positive social force (an argument detailed in the next chapter). Contemporary sociologists and historians have probed the organization of deviant social movements and the historical significance of key moments of resistance in periods of social change. Since Thoreau's *Civil Disobedience*, activists as well as scholars have pondered the process and consequences of law breaking for altruistic reasons.

Closest to this work, Jarret Lovell (2009) profiles actions of civil disobedience as "crimes of dissent" where laws are broken openly and altruistically. In his book of the same title, he urges an understanding of the process of dissent as a political strategy, employing criminality as a method of contention:

> In truth there are as many names for these acts of dissent as there are strategies, and there are as many strategies as there are actors. And although each strategy differs in its level of confrontation, risk, and playfulness, they all share one unifying component: each requires a modicum of criminality in its staging and execution, rendering these protest strategies what I refer to collectively as crimes of dissent. (2)

Besides risking formal sanctions, dissenters may be labeled as dangerous and subversive and may even be ostracized even from their own compatriots. It is the threat of formal social control that distinguishes crimes of dissent from other forms of civil disobedience. Placing oneself in legal jeopardy, or worse, for a righteous cause, is dubbed by Lovell as a "pure crime." He argues that such crimes are part of a larger movement strategy aimed at inciting a state response for tactical purposes.

> Crimes of dissent embody strategies through which political resistance can be manifested. Collectively, the crimes serve as open challenges to the laws and practices of the prevailing political climate. To that end, the acts are often staged to trigger a response from the justice system so that the people dissenting have access to a public forum where they can challenge the legitimacy of a law or social custom. And because the challenges are launched as a means of exposing existing injustices, those who engage in these behaviors defend their actions as "crime as virtue." (65)

It is through dissent that an official reaction is provoked. The intent of this aggravation of state power is to manifest a legitimation crisis and bring grievances and demands to the forefront.

Through the course of in-depth interviews, *Crimes of Dissent* profiles various activists and civil disobedients. Lovell acknowledges that criminology has been tepid toward a concept of crime that sees it as a transformative force in social change and proposes the concept of "cultural criminology" as a theoretical lens for understanding how dissent movements and social structure come together, interact, and create resolution or further tension. Cultural criminology argues that defining certain behaviors as criminal by statute ultimately gives rise to and confers a collective identity on subcultures within which moral and ideological codes emerge (Ferrell & Sanders, 1995). Focusing on the interplay between normative innovation and institutionalized social control, cultural criminologists examine the contexts in which ideas and actions are publicly contested (Ferrell, 1996).

Like several of the theoretical traditions referenced in this volume, cultural criminology occupies the maligned margins of criminological thought. It has rightly faced criticism as being morally relativist and having no systematic theoretical grounding. Therefore, while cultural criminology is one possible way to consider the viability of good trouble, other criminological approaches will be considered.

In the scholarship of civil disobedience, various popular and academic books investigate various aspects of dissent, social movements, and contentious action. While the literature cited for this volume consists mostly of articles and historical texts, books on the topic include historical works like *Dissent* (Young, 2015), and books on social movements such as *Black Movements* (Colbert, 2017). Again, while these are important historic analyses of specific social movements, my work will center on situating specific actions of heroic nonconformity within a clear criminological context. While it has a different perspective, the historical-biographical approach of *Americans in Dissent* (Piott, 2014) is a partial template for my approach. Lastly, general interest books such as *Dissent in America* (Young, 2005) give examples of criminals and deviants who have provoked social change, figures like those my book covers from a sociological perspective.

It would be impossible to document or adequately cover all types of dissent and all the social-movements that have embraced the tactic of good trouble as a means to realize the goal of progressive social change. Social-movement texts are more effective at detailing the theory and practice of dissent social movements. For instance, Tarrow's *Power in Movement* (2011) synthesizes social-movement literature to examine how contentious discourse is framed around social-movement opportunities, where social movement resources are mobilized around an opportunity structure that organizes means around chance openings. In this book, Tarrow argues that contentious actors (dissenters) may seize on movement opportunities by initiating a repertoire of illegal disruption (92–93). Tilly's (2004) historical appraisal of the origins of dissent over two-and-a-half centuries chronicles a wide breadth of various dissent movements in that time. More specifically, social-movement texts such as Piven and Cloward's *Poor People's Movements* (1977) give insight into the strategies used by the economically disenfranchised to achieve economic justice. The authors argue that forms of illegality such as wildcat strikes, direct action, collective refusal to pay bills, and sabotage have done much more to advance the interests of the lower classes than participation in legitimate processes like elections and lawsuits. Works like Epstein's *Political Protest and Cultural Revolution* (1991) note how illegality, in the form of civil disobedience, has nudged intramovement conflicts around issues of accommodation and reform toward more principled and politically effective stands.

The literature on social movements points to several key areas both in the United States and globally where social justice has been achieved through the use of illegal strategies. Lovell (2009) identifies five key areas where illegal dissent has overcome various systems of oppression. These areas include struggles for peace and against colonialism, the abolition of slavery, protections for workers and the economically exploited, women's suffrage, and civil rights. In each of these broad movements, illegal strategies helped raise awareness and advance the cause of social justice. Obviously many other movements and political opportunities exist where good trouble can be effectively exercised, including the environment; lesbian, gay, bisexual, and transgender (LGBT) rights; free speech; and nuclear disarmament. This book examines several of these areas: slavery and civil rights, labor and women's rights, war and colonialism, and free speech. However, before these areas can be considered, a thorough examination of both the sociological and criminological traditions for evidence of good trouble must be considered.

The next chapter will consider the plausibility of the notion of "good trouble" and the debate over the viability of positive deviant behavior and will situate the deviant hero in both classical and contemporary sociological theory.

Chapter Two

Good Trouble in the Sociological Tradition

Mario Savio was a key figure in the antiwar and free speech movements of the 1960s. His most famous speech, "Bodies upon the Gears," was a rallying cry for students to use direct action to contest the complacency of their universities in the war in Vietnam. Delivered in front of the administration building of the University of California, his address was a key moment in the early phase of the counterculture movement that defined dissent at that time.

> There's a time when the operation of the machine becomes so odious—makes you so sick at heart—that you can't take part. You can't even passively take part. And you've got to put your bodies upon the gears and upon the wheels, upon the levers, upon all the apparatus, and you've got to make it stop. And you've got to indicate to the people who run it, to the people who own it that unless you're free, the machine will be prevented from working at all. (Rosenfeld, 216–217)

The use of direct action, trespassing, and occupying tactics like those he proposed has its roots in classical Athens and has been refined and retooled by contemporary movements such as Occupy Wall Street and the resistance at Standing Rock, in North Dakota. Yet, in terms of how sociology typically considers deviant behavior, the actions Savio advocated are theoretically problematic: generally, social movements and criminology are considered separate subfields that rarely overlap. However, this book argues that deviant behavior is an important catalyst for the good trouble that provokes social change. How should sociology consider such behaviors? Are such deviant actions worthy of discussion in the context of crime and deviance, or should they remain confined academically to the realm of social movements and

political sociology? It will be shown that "good trouble" and "deviant heroism" may be incorporated into the major theoretical paradigms in the social
sciences. The classical traditions in sociology demonstrate that the initial
development of this discipline was not as constrained in its thinking about
crime and deviance as it is today. An important debate in the late 1980s and
early 1990s about positive deviance may help illumine how social theory can
reconsider crime and social change.

OXYMORON OR PARADIGM SHIFT? REVISITING THE POSITIVE DEVIANCE DEBATE

Despite the association of deviance with villainy and the tendency to nega-
tively stigmatize nonconforming behaviors, a handful of contemporary theorists have sought to expunge the exclusively negative association of the term
deviance. A number of renowned and routinely cited scholars, including
Clinard (1974, 15), Lemert (1951, 23–24), Wilkins (1965, 46), and Katz
(1975, 1384) have issued calls for research related to the subject of heroic or
positive deviance. Coser (1962b) saw deviance as creating a "normative
flexibility" in society, while Tittle and Paternoster (2000) mention how notions of deviance may be tied to social change. In the existing literature, the
concept of positive deviance or good norm breaking comes somewhat closer
to the conception of deviant heroism or good trouble.

Contemporary debates surrounding the possibility of good deviance center on a proposition sparked by David Dodge in the journal *Deviant Behavior*
(1985). Dodge argued that limiting the scope of deviance to overly negative
conceptualizations overlooks the totality of deviant behavior (1985). Describing positive deviance as actions departing from normality that bring
about positive sanctions, Dodge suggested guidelines for studying this concept and identified related conceptual and definitional issues that needed to
be reworked. Ben-Yehuda (1990) echoed Dodge's sentiments, adding that
incorporating the concept of positive deviance could spark innovation in the
field of deviance and result in a paradigmatic shift in thinking.

However, the proposal by Dodge and Ben-Yehuda for including positive
deviance in sociology was not well received among sociologists and was
dismissed by two important scholars (Sagarin, 1985; Goode, 1991) as an
implausible derivation of the concept and ultimately a contradiction. Sagarin
(1985) argued that entertaining the notion of a good form of deviance com-
plicates and obfuscates the cultural acceptance of deviance as bad behavior.
His central argument was that defining deviance from a social-reaction position implied negative action. The entire concept of positive deviance, he
asserted, was a contradiction in terms and, ultimately, an oxymoron. Goode
(1991) arrived at a similar conclusion, explaining that sociologists should not

accept the notion of positive deviance since it lacks the stigma normally associated with deviant behavior.

In the twenty-five years following Dodge's original proposition and the debates that ensued, there was never a "paradigmatic shift" in thinking among scholars of deviant behavior. This may be due, in part, to the paucity of research in this area, coupled with the lack of clear conceptualization of what good or positive deviance should represent. In an attempt to refashion the deviance archetype, Andrew and Druann Heckert (2002) have proposed a new typology of deviance based on integrating reactivist and normative understandings. Their typology allows for both negative and positive deviance based on normative approaches, but adds a reactive dimension as well, based on how the collectivity responds. In this typology, overly conformist behaviors can generate a negative social response, as in the case of "rate-busters" or people who exceed work quotas, and deviant behaviors may receive admiration, as in the case of mythical figures like Robin Hood, and other fictional characters who champion justice and fight for the underprivileged.

Heckert and Heckert's useful typology, detailed further in this section, gives much-needed attention to the one-sidedness of negative portrayals of deviance, but it still does not demonstrate how deviance may lead to positive social change. Limitations in the concept of positive deviance have confined the handful of studies of this phenomenon to behaviors that may generate an initial social response or are clearly a violation of norms but do not necessarily put the actor at risk in a heroic way. Studies using positive deviance have examined corporate responsibility (Spretizer and Sonenshein, 2004), bodybuilding (Ewald and Jiobu, 1985), and athletes (Scarpitti and McFarlane, 1975; Ewald and Jiobu, 1985), artists (Heckert, 1989), and movie stars (Lemert, 1951). The deviant actions of these groups may be positive but do not address social injustice while subjecting the actors to institutions of formal social control.

Organizational and decision sciences have also picked up the positive deviance debate. Vadera, Pratt, and Mishra (2013) argue that *constructive deviance* may be employed in hyper-conforming organizations. Defining constructive deviance as "more active behaviors that deviate from the norms of the reference group such that they benefit the reference group" (1223), they argue that deviant behaviors in leadership, creativity, and norm adjustment have prosocial consequences and result in positive outcomes by stimulating organizational change.

Social reactions to positive deviance may mirror the response to negative deviance. Certain types of nonconformity may be praised in one moment but stigmatized in another. For instance, gifted and talented students may be stigmatized as "nerds" or "teacher's pets" (Heckert and Heckert, 2002; Shoenberger, Heckert, and Heckert, 2012). Such positive deviants also experience labeling and internalization. In fact, a 2012 study found that high-achieving students are subject to the same neutralization techniques as those who are typically labeled negative deviants (Shoenberger, Heckert, and Heckert, 2012). In sum, scholars of crime and deviance do not universally accept the negative association of deviance, and some have found clear parallels between deviance, both good and bad.

While an important and valuable contribution, the current literature on positive deviance does not fully encapsulate the sociological dynamics underpinning deviance that is altruistic and aimed at changing oppressive social contexts. Not only has this debate on positive deviance been far from concluded, but the concept of the deviant hero as one who challenges unjust or oppressive norms has not been given full consideration. Although positive deviance may be a remedy for unjust normative contexts, the concept can and should be expanded to capture the actions of heroic individuals who selflessly break laws to change unjust conditions. Such heroic deviance can best be conceptualized as the antithesis of bad or villainous conformity. The deviant hero's societal role is qualitatively different from the positive deviant's, in that the deviant hero actively challenges and seeks to change unfair social norms, oppressive rules, and unjust laws, at personal risk to him or herself.

Moreover, those arguing the case for and against positive deviance have not adequately combed the classical theoretical perspectives that are predecessors to most contemporary theories about deviance and crime. Classical sociological theory, including the contributions of lesser-recognized scholars writing about the initial development of the sociological understanding of crime and justice, supports an expanded concept of deviance, thereby augmenting the consideration of the deviant and the possibility of good trouble in more contemporary contexts.

CRIME AND THE VALUE OF AGITATION: THE CLASSICAL ROOTS OF DEVIANT HEROISM

While the debates around the concept of positive deviance apparently ended in the journal *Deviant Behavior* in 1995 without resolution, it is useful to take the discussion further, and in a different direction. The concept of positive deviance represents an important first step in the consideration of the deviant hero, but it is an incomplete appraisal of how altruistic motivations may encounter systems of social control. Despite few contemporary studies probing the positive or heroic aspects of deviance, the premise of this book is based on some established literature in sociology and the larger public discourse. For example, West (2003) found references to the possibility of positive deviance in the classical works of Weber, Simmel, and Durkheim. Along these same lines, an examination of the classical traditions of sociology and its early analysis of society, norm-breaking, and social change yields insights into the heroic dimensions of positive deviance.

Durkheim, whose work was foundational to both the development of sociology and the establishment of the subfields that consider crime and deviance, presents a classic illustration of the deviant hero. Durkheim argued that crime serves the useful social function of defining what a society's values are and reinforcing social solidarity. In *Rules of the Sociological Method* (1966), he reasoned that crime can be a source of progressive social change, facilitating the redefinition of the norms and values of an entire society in a beneficial way. As an example, he uses the trial and execution of the ancient Greek philosopher Socrates:

> According to Athenian law, Socrates was a criminal . . . however, his crime, namely, the independence of his thought, rendered a service not only to humanity but to his country. It served to prepare a new morality and faith which the Athenians needed, since the traditions by which they had lived until then were no longer in harmony with the current conditions of life. . . . At the time . . . the violation was a crime . . . and yet this crime was useful as a prelude to reforms which daily became more necessary. (1966, 93)

Socrates never apologized for his crime, yet he accepted the punishment of death wholeheartedly. Had he apologized or pled for a lesser punishment, it would have diminished the effect of the "pure crime" he was committing. Ironically, Socrates's subversion and refusal to follow the rules of the court become a mainstay pedagogical device within law schools and a foundation for the practice of jurisprudence around the world (Lovell 2009, 66). While Socrates ultimately submitted to the will of the court, Socrates became a martyr for the truth, and his truths live on in teaching and the practice of law in democratic societies.

Using the example of Socrates, Durkheim reconceptualizes the role of the criminal (deviant) in society. For Durkheim and functionalist theory, the useful and positive function of crime (or deviance) is to bring about much-needed social change. Although he was deemed a criminal, his crime served to redefine justice and pave the way for much-needed legal and ethical reforms. History now regards him as a hero of democracy and academic freedom. Durkheim's insight reminds us that criminals can sometimes serve as moral prophets serving a greater good.

Other classical theorists also mention heroic deviance. Long-excluded founding sociologist W. E. B. Du Bois, in an essay titled "The Value of Agitation," states that "agitation is often unpleasant. It means that while you are peaceably and joyfully on your way, some half-mad persons insist upon saying things you do not like to hear" (85). The agitator sees that "this is a world where things are not right." Du Bois calls the agitator a "herald." The agitator "is the man who says to the world: 'There are evils which you do not know, but which I know, and you must listen to them'" (85). Du Bois reminds us that agitators (the deviant hero) may be stigmatized but they are a necessity for pointing out and challenging injustice.

Another foundational sociologist, Charlotte Perkins Gilman, also offers relevant words regarding the importance of deviance in bringing about needed social change. In her classic work of social theory, *Women and Economics* (1966), Gilman writes:

> In the course of social evolution there are developed individuals so constituted as not to fit existing conditions, but to be organically adapted to more advanced conditions. These advanced individuals respond in sharp and painful consciousness to existing conditions, and cry out against them according to their lights. The history of religion, of political and social reform, is full of familiar instances of this. The heretic, the reformer, the agitator, these feel what their compeers do not, and naturally say what they do not. The mass of the people are invariably displeased by the outcry of these uneasy spirits. In simple primitive periods they were promptly put to death . . . but this remarkable sociological law was manifested: that the strength of a current social force is increased by the sacrifice of individuals who are willing to die in the effort to promote it. . . . Our great anti-slavery agitation, the heroic efforts of women's rights supporters, are fresh and recent proofs of these plain facts. (41)

Gilman's point is that when it comes to social progression, "advanced individuals" defy unjust systems of norms, such as slavery and the oppressive systems of patriarchy, to champion a more humane system of norms and human progress. These "advanced individuals," like Du Bois's "agitator," subject themselves to risk in challenging systems of oppression.

SUPPORT IN OTHER THEORETICAL TRADITIONS

Besides the classical traditions, more contemporary sociological theories of deviant behavior can be updated using the concept of the deviant hero. For instance, at a very rudimentary level, statistical definitions of deviance readily operationalize both positive and negative deviance. Quantitative and statistical definitions of deviance generally assume a two-tailed bell curve, in which outliers more than two standard deviations at either ends of the curve are defined as deviant. For example, Wilkens (1965) explains that the majority of human behavior exists within the bell, while what he terms both saintly and sinful behavior exists at the opposite ends. For Wilkens, deviant behavior is simply behavior that is not considered normal. In the grade distributions of my introduction to criminology course, the two ends of the curve also represent outliers; at the furthest ends of these outliers, there were "anomalies" who managed to horribly fail (negative deviance) or manage to trudge through the alienation of a large and impersonal class to achieve perfection (positive deviance). Deviance may include failing class, murder, theft, or pedophilia, but it may also include perfect test scores, saintly behavior, and random acts of kindness. While a high test score is probably not heroic in most contexts, in a world filled with dehumanizing norms that call for getting ahead at the expense of others, simple acts of kindness may well qualify.

Labeling theorists have asserted that deviant acts are so named precisely because they are deemed negative or bad (Sagarin, 1985). Heckert (1989) has demonstrated just the opposite, demonstrating that since labels can vary over time and space, positive deviance may be labeled as negative in a different social and historical context. Heckert cites the example of French impressionist artists, once labeled negative deviants, only to be elevated later to a positive type of denotative nonconformity. These creative acts of nonconformity led to evolving new aesthetic standards.

Many of the other theoretical traditions used to explore deviant behavior are also well-suited for the study of heroic deviance. Conflict theories, which critique powerful relationships, may be utilized to examine how the status-quo social order functions to produce an environment in which deviant heroism challenges norms that result in inequalities and conflicts of interest. Conflict theories can be further extended to demonstrate how the deviance of social actors, acting on behalf of marginalized groups, have protested rules imposed on them by an oppressor. And interactionist approaches, such as the theory of differential association, may consider how deviant heroes learn their ideas and techniques of opposition.

HUMAN ACTION, TYPOLOGIES, AND DEVIANCE

Just as the concept of positive deviance challenges traditional assumptions that deviance is always a detrimental or antisocial behavior, deviant heroism similarly demonstrates that typical understandings of crime and deviance are due for a reconceptualization. Moreover, not only can norm violation represent a positive social force, but norm compliance or conformity can represent a negative social force when a collective follows and enforces unjust or evil social conditions. Therefore, conformity may be problematized. The possibility of good trouble requires reconceptualizing the phenomena of deviance in order to contrast positive deviance to other types of deviance and conformity. Building a new typology can aid in mapping this new analysis.

Typologies are widely used in the social sciences to clarify a social phenomenon under investigation. They are especially useful when trying to describe rather than explain a set of behaviors. Classical sociologist Max Weber (1946) preferred developing typologies of human behavior in his drive to establish an empathetic social science. For example, authority could be typified as traditional, charismatic, or rational-legal. Traditional types of authority are rooted in established traditions, family, and dynastic forms of rule. In contrast, rational-legal authority is legitimated through the law or formal rules. This is most typical in modern societies, and for Weber was most perfectly manifested in the bureaucratic state. Charismatic authorities are individuals who possess a gift to inspire others to follow their will on the subjects' own accord. Charismatic figures may inspire uprisings against traditional or rational-legal forms of authority. This type of authority structure was thought to be unstable. This last category, charismatic authority figures, may inspire horrible human acts, as was the case with Hitler. Charismatic leadership is also a characteristic of many deviant heroes, such as John Lewis or Gandhi.

Next, Weber developed several typologies of human behavior. Human action could be categorized as *rational-legal* (an efficiency-oriented, goal-directed strategy); *instrumental* (a value action, simply engaging in which was inherently worthwhile); *emotional*, which is driven purely by feelings and impulses that feel as if they are from the heart or gut; or *traditional*, which typifies behaviors that are carried out simply due to tradition as a cultural artifact. Since deviant behavior is a type of human action in defiance of authority, it can be subject to an analogous typology to deepen our conceptual understanding. Deviance and conformity may be typified as either good, bad, or neutral. For the purposes of this book, good trouble may be conceptualized as instrumental human action, but the charismatic deviant hero may have followers based on the emotion and the desire to have a more rational, goal-oriented outcome.

Perhaps the most famous typology in the field of crime and deviance originated from Merton's (1968) strain theory. Merton's adaptive typology, while originally developed and employed to explain street crime, can readily incorporate the deviant hero. For Merton, deviance was a function of the acceptance of the established goals of a society and the legitimate means to attain them. Table 2.1 illustrates the goals/means typology.

Those who accept both the goals and the means of a society are conformists. Innovators reject the accepted means but keep the goal. Ritualists embrace the means but reject the goal. Retreatists accept neither. Rebels reject the means and the goals and replace them with something else. Later in his career, Merton remarked how these labels may shift as new normative frameworks for a society are renegotiated, saying that "the rebel, revolutionary, nonconformist, individualist, heretic and renegade of an earlier time is often the culture hero of today" (1968, 237). In this scheme, the deviant hero is the rebel who challenges unjust goals and the accepted means of achieving them, and substitutes new ones, thus getting into "good trouble." For instance, Martin Luther King Jr. challenged the goal of a racially segregated society by

Table 2.1. Merton's Typology of Adaptations to Social Strain

Type of Adaptation	Cultural Goal	Institutionalized Means
1. Conformist	+	+
2. Innovator	+	–
3. Ritualist	–	+
4. Retreatist	–	–
5. Rebel	+/–	+/–

Adapted from Merton (1968).
Note: + indicates acceptance and – indicates rejection. +/– indicates the rejections of the goal or mean and the substitution of a new goal or mean.

using unorthodox means to achieve integration, providing a classic case of a rebel in Merton's typology.

TOWARD A NEW TYPOLOGY OF DEVIANCE

As this book has stressed so far, understanding the construction of deviance is fraught with pitfalls. What may be deviant in one context is not in another. The social construction of deviance and crime necessitates attention to context as well as normative appraisals of a given behavior. Given the complexities and nuances in defining and describing deviance, it may be more useful to develop a typology to illustrate the varieties of both deviant and conformist behavior. For example, Heckert and Heckert (2002) propose incorporating normative and reactive judgments into their typology of deviance; that is, social reactions may be positive or negative toward a deviant behavior. In addition, conformity is thought of as having the polar extremes of under- and overconformity. According to their derivation of deviance, nonconformity may be admired (in the case of some outlaws and bank robbers) while too much conformity could be scorned (in the case of a "teacher's pet" or overzealous insurance adjuster).

In the tradition of Max Weber and building on the work of scholars such as Heckert and Heckert, this chapter proposes a new derivation of deviance and conformity based on the social reaction and social consequence. Table 2.2 depicts an alternative vision of the standard deviance-conformity dialectic that incorporates norm compliance and violation with attention to the social consequence of the behavior. This typology is a reconsideration of deviance and conformity where either could be morally good, bad, or neutral. Therefore, there are six possible types of compliant or divergent behavior for consideration.

First, conformity or deviance may simply be a morally neutral behavior. Everyday acceptance of social norms and laws is necessary for the functioning of society. Morally neutral conformity is simply "adherence" and refers to the day-to-day activities "normal" people engage in, from getting dressed to not interrupting a conversation. This type of conformity is rarely if ever pathologized and not of much interest to scholars who study deviance. In contrast, morally neutral behaviors may generate a social reaction that deems a specific behavior deviant but neither "good" nor "bad." The examples of nudity or sexual orientation mentioned in chapter 1 exemplify this category of deviance, and such behaviors are relatively common topics in the sociology of deviance and some criminology (e.g., cannabis use).

Obviously, behaviors that are deemed "negative" receive much attention in the field of deviant behavior and criminology. Understanding conformity is vital to understanding its opposite—deviance. Horrible human atrocities like sanctioned massacres and genocide are regularly attributed to "just following orders." On a smaller scale, examples from everyday life like schoolyard bullying show how detrimental conformity can be. Such negative types of conformist behavior are termed "docility" and represent a type of passive complacency that deserves further analysis. Of course, negative deviant actions can also take the form of morally reprehensible behavior; entire categories of crime, like homicide, rape, and embezzlement, are given close attention in criminological literature. While a wide-ranging category, these negative deviant behaviors, representing "villainy," are not considered in this book except to juxtapose deviant villainous behavior with deviant heroic behavior.

Lastly, and more to the point of this book, both conformist and deviant behaviors can be highly positive activities. Deeds that represent a strict adherence to social norms for loving or altruistic behavior are generally considered positive, and people who engage in such behaviors will enjoy wide acceptance. On the other hand, certain people may violate unjust laws or break oppressive rules, making them clearly "deviant" in every sense of the word, but while they may be vilified at one time and celebrated at another,

Table 2.2. A New Typology of Deviance

Social Consequence	Conformity	Deviance
Neutral	Adherence "everyday acceptance"	Divergence "unusual"
Negative	Complacency "complicit conformity"	Villainy "evildoer"
Positive	Altruistic "harmonious acquiescence"	Deviant Heroism "good trouble"

their rule-breaking is ultimately a positive behavior that provokes much-needed social change. This is "good trouble," and those who seek it are deviant heroes, the focus of this book.

METHODOLOGICAL APPROACH

Based on other literatures, especially classical sociological theory, this chapter defined the deviant hero as one who altruistically violates unjust or oppressive rules in an effort to act as an agent for social change. These kinds of norm violation, which better the human condition or increase justice, deserve to be more thoroughly recognized and explored in sociological studies. Many classic cases in criminological research already cast deviance in a positive light. Sutherland's *White Collar Criminal* (1983), Becker's *Outsiders* (1963), and Anderson's *Streetwise* (1992) all allude to unjust normative environments in which a deviant hero could have existed, or may have, but was overlooked, fulfilling a desperately needed social role. Other literatures on social movements and change may also consider the role of the deviant hero throughout history and in modern society. Therefore, we should not neglect to investigate the ways in which other literatures have considered the role of the deviant hero throughout history. This can readily be incorporated into methodological approaches used in criminological research.

Several methods may be useful in demonstrating how deviant heroism and "good trouble" play a key role in changing the normative structures of a society. Case studies may demonstrate how rules are violated to bring about a new social order or new normative contexts. Interviews with individual people who have been in good trouble can also be a viable way to uncover the meanings and tactics of those who partake in contentious action. However, one approach seems particularly useful in considering the dynamic process of social change and individual agency (deviance), that of C. Wright Mills. The accounts of deviant heroism depicted in the following pages rely on the methodological approach Mills promulgated in his most famous book, *The Sociological Imagination* (1961). In this work, Mills criticized the sociology of the day, which promoted convoluted and unintelligible grand theories and scholarship that merely supported an administrative apparatus. Instead, Mills advocated for a sociology that aims to understand the interrelationship between the self and social structure. Proposing that sociology involve itself in the intersection of individual biography and history, he called for this discipline to understand how "personal troubles relate to public issues." In the final chapter, on "intellectual craftsmanship," Mills suggests ways to conceptualize questions and techniques for keeping research files on seemingly unrelated facts, which can then be revisited, organized, categorized, and pondered. Ultimately these files may be used to build a coherent framework that provides deeper understanding of complex social phenomena. This kind of intellectual craftsmanship, Mills believed, is a way of unbridling the sociological imagination.

Here, "personal troubles" are "good troubles," deviant acts that result in forces of social control coming down on an individual who is resisting an unjust normative context and, by implication, the social conditions or public issues that produced it. The individual biography of a deviant hero is shaped by and enmeshed in a specific historical epoch. History considers the social context of norm violation, while biography is mindful of how individuals' heroic norm violations affect positive social change. Consider the proposition of existentialist philosopher, Martin Buber (1966), as he explores the ramifications of Thoreau's *Civil Disobedience*:

> Thoreau did not put forth a general proposition as such; he described and established his attitude in a specific historical-biographic situation. He addressed his reader within the very sphere of this situation common to both of them in such a way that the reader not only discovered why Thoreau acted as he did at that time but also that the reader—assuming him of course to be honest and dispassionate—would have to act in just such a way whenever the proper occasion arose, provided he was seriously engaged in fulfilling his existence as a human person. . . . The question here is not just about one of the numerous individual cases in the struggle between a truth powerless to act and a power that has become the enemy of truth. It is really a question of the concrete demonstration of the point at which this struggle at any moment becomes man's duty as man. (19)

Buber reminds us that disobedience, though advocated by Thoreau in a specific context, may be required at any moment in a historical epoch. Humans are free to push back against the "enemy of truth" and realize their own existence as free-willed individuals. The kind of disobedience Thoreau advocated may change according to context and historical situation, but consideration of biography and history and their intersection remains a simple way to examine any change provoked by deviant heroes exercising their moral duty to violate unjust laws. Sociology has much to gain by interrogating deviant heroes' actions alongside their historical context.

Several of these figures, such as Martin Luther King Jr., Socrates, and Thoreau, are central to the thesis of this book and lived and acted in a historical context and normative environment where their actions were deemed deviant and criminal.

The Millsian proposition of asserting the sociological imagination at the juncture of biography and history properly underscores a longstanding interrelationship between the disciplines of sociology and history. In the words of John Seeley, "History without Sociology has no fruit, Sociology without History has no root" (Wells, 1920, 700). Keeping this in mind, Part II will consider individual accounts and discourses of deviance alongside the socio-historical context that made good trouble necessary trouble.

II

Good Trouble against Inequality

Chapter Three

Creative Maladjustment

The Words and Actions of Martin Luther King Jr.

This chapter examines the biographical-historical contexts of Martin Luther King Jr.'s ideas and words pertaining to acts of "creative maladjustment." As a derivative of good trouble, this concept was articulated in his 1963 book *The Strength to Love* where he declares that "the saving of our world . . . will come, not through the *complacent adjustment* of the conforming majority, but through the *creative maladjustment* of a nonconforming minority" (11, emphasis added). Insights into good trouble are especially derived from his well-known "Letter from a Birmingham Jail." King's principled stands for nonviolent resistance deserve special consideration as models of rule-breaking to advance the cause of humanitarian interests. Additionally, King's life and work show how the struggle against racism, for the cause of civil rights and human dignity, is a special case of the practice of what King called "disciplined nonconformity." This chapter is centered on the words and actions of King as an ideal case for the practice of good trouble, in addition, his words and writings serve to add greater insight into the development of good trouble as a viable concept in the social sciences.

The reasons for this chapter's singular focus on King are several. For one, King is among the most widely known and celebrated deviant heroes in American history. Schoolchildren learn about his principled stands and understand him as a champion of equality and justice for all. Some obfuscate the meaning and significance of his life and central message, and others reject him altogether, but for the most part he is renowned, respected, and admired. King is a hero who got into good trouble, effectively changing the collective morality of society.

Second, as a devoted activist, King was uniquely educated within the field of sociology and gave speeches and produced writings that are worthy of scholarly inquiry and are of textual significance to sociology. For instance, his concept of "creative maladjustment" provokes an interesting challenge to the preoccupation with the abnormal of sociology and psychology.

Thirdly, King's life and principled stands in his fight against racism and inequality, especially his letter, serve as an important textual artifact in elaborating on the process and virtue of deviant heroism. The letter contains a plethora of insight into the value and effect of the strategy of good trouble that can be readily adapted to teaching about the positive value of deviant behavior and crime. Once King's biography and writings are contextualized, they augment our understanding of the actions of others who got into good trouble for a variety of causes.

The method of C. W. Mills mentioned in the prior chapter instructs the possessor of the sociological imagination to appreciate how an individual biography intersects with history and social structure. As a starting point, the words, actions, and ideas of King in the historical-social context of the Jim Crow South serve as an ideal conduit for demonstrating the overall utility of the Millsian method and for considering how good trouble and deviant heroism may both be considered compelling topics in the sociological understanding of crime and deviance.

Of course, King's work as a civil rights leader and proponent of nonviolent direct action epitomizes nearly every aspect of the practice and value of good trouble. It is a textbook case not just for good trouble but for many other important lessons, from civics to philosophy to race and ethnic relations. Although many important texts have emerged from the civil rights movement, King's letter is a critical discursive artifact, one that facilitates the comprehensive understanding of the context and purpose of good trouble to students, activists, and observers alike. For these reasons, the text and social contexts of the letter are explored in some depth here.

THE PSYCHOLOGY OF ADJUSTMENT

Before delving into King's work, it is useful to understand how abnormality is conceived within another branch of the social sciences, psychology. Just as sociology looks at nonconformity through the lens of "deviant behavior," the field of psychology is similarly concerned with the categories of normal and abnormal behavior. The subfield of abnormal psychology is devoted to understanding maladaptive behaviors that may point to an underlying psychological "disorder" (Barlow and Durand, 2004).

Individuals employ adaptive behaviors to adjust to varying social situations and conditions within the "normal" spectrum. In contrast, maladaptive behaviors are regarded as pathological or dysfunctional, leading to detrimental consequences either to the individual or society. Just as sociologists have stigmatized deviant behavior, psychology regards maladjustment as almost exclusively detrimental and a cause for intervention. For example, studies in organizational psychology connect all maladaptive behaviors with either low emotional stability, detachment, disagreeableness, disinhibition, or psychoses (Dilchert, Ones, and Kruger, 2014).

Like the sociology of deviance, psychology has been criticized for its over-focus on detrimental and maladaptive behaviors, while overlooking deviant psychological traits and adaptations that may be positive (Haidt, 2012). In 1967, King was invited to give the keynote address to the annual meeting of the American Psychological Association. By that time, he had won a Nobel Prize, was head of the Southern Christian Leadership Conference, and was the most visible leader of the civil rights movement. In his address, given six months before he was assassinated, he implored social scientists to take an active role in advancing the cause of civil rights and outlined ways they could become involved in the struggle. He also argued that the field of social science should reconsider some of its central concepts and tenets:

> There are certain technical words in every academic discipline which soon become stereotypes and even clichés. Every academic discipline has its technical nomenclature. You who are in the field of psychology have given us a great word. It is the word maladjusted. This word is probably used more than any other word in psychology. It is a good word; certainly it is good that in dealing with what the word implies you are declaring that destructive maladjustment should be destroyed. You are saying that all must seek the well-adjusted life in order to avoid neurotic and schizophrenic personalities. (King, 1967)

King went on to point out, however, that there are conditions of life such as discrimination, bigotry, and segregation, to which no one should ever become adjusted. He argued that adjustment was driving the world to militarism and destruction. He closed his speech arguing that hope for the advancement of humanity rests in creative maladjustment.

> Men and women should be as maladjusted as the prophet Amos, who in the midst of the injustices of his day, could cry out in words that echo across the centuries, 'Let justice roll down like waters and righteousness like a mighty stream'; or as maladjusted as Abraham Lincoln, who in the midst of his vacillations finally came to see that this nation could not survive half slave and half free; or as maladjusted as Thomas Jefferson, who in the midst of an age amazingly adjusted to slavery, could scratch across the pages of history, words lifted to cosmic proportions, 'We hold these truths to be self-evident, that all men are created equal. That they are endowed by their creator with certain inalienable rights. And that among these are life, liberty, and the pursuit of happiness.' And through such creative maladjustment, we may be able to

emerge from the bleak and desolate midnight of man's inhumanity to man,
into the bright and glittering daybreak of freedom and justice. (King, 1967)

King's speech was probably delivered to a supportive and receptive audience. His speech was meant to provoke social scientists, in this case psychologists, to move out of the ivory tower of their academic pursuits and join the
cause for equality and justice. King's remarks point to an important critique
of what is regarded as normal or maladjusted and how these concepts are
applied.

The French philosopher Michel Foucault devoted much of his work to
understanding and criticizing the mechanisms used in the social sciences to
categorize people and behaviors into "normal" and "abnormal." His most
widely read books focus on different forms of abnormality—mental illness
(*Madness and Civilization*, 1965); physical illness (*The Birth of the Clinic*,
1963); criminality (*Discipline and Punish*, 1977); and sexual perversion (*The
History of Sexuality*, 1978). For Foucault, variations in the social construction of normality were in fact constituted through the definition of abnormality. The categorizing and defining of what is abnormal constituted a power
relationship through which a political entity could impose a totalizing hegemony upon a population. Foucault reasoned that defining and labeling people
as abnormal had more to do with excluding them from society than with any
objective concept such as madness or maladjustment.

Given Foucault's insight into how normality and abnormality are constructed via the pairing of administrative knowledge and the power of the
state apparatus, King's praise of maladjustment seems even more profound.
Through the valorization of certain types of deviance, King challenged the
law's function of maintaining dissymmetry between race, class, gender, and
other social strata. Despite the assumption by the social sciences that maladjustment is undesirable, creative and loving acts of deviance may be used to
overcome entrenched power relationships. From here, it is possible to consider the larger challenge King's letter poses to how normality is conceptualized
in the social sciences.

BIOGRAPHY, HISTORY, AND SOCIAL CONTEXT: "LETTER FROM A BIRMINGHAM JAIL"

Although scholarly discussions of crime and deviance do not often include
the historic struggle against racism and slavery, that struggle offers a multitude of examples of deviant behavior acting as a positive social force of
progress and change. King[1] himself, in his 1963 book *The Strength to Love,*
argues that the hope of the world rests with the "disciplined nonconformist,"
and asserts that "the trailblazers in human, academic, scientific, and religious
freedom have always been nonconformists" (1981, 26). He tells people to

look to the deviant as a model for how to challenge entrenched systems of injustice, declaring that "in any cause that concerns the progress of mankind, put your faith in the nonconformists!" (27).

The above text serves as an important prologue into embarking on a thorough consideration of deviant heroism and King's advocacy for creative maladjustment. King's letter serves as an important text that may be examined alongside general discussions on crime and how deviance may represent a positive social action. Before delving into the key tenets of the letter, some background is useful in discerning its context and overall significance; this context includes an understanding of the norms and laws of the Jim Crow South under segregation, and how the civil rights movement represented a bold new form of moral entrepreneurship in changing laws by breaking them.

In line with the sociologically imaginative methodology, King's biography intersecting with this specific social structure and historical era is quite significant. It notes King's role as one of the key figures in the struggle for equality in the United States, but it also notes his first training as an undergraduate sociology major at Morehouse College. Given this early education, it is likely that King encountered the writings of earlier black leaders such as Fredrick Douglass and W. E. B. Du Bois, and foundational sociologists such as Durkheim, Weber, and Marx. Along with these important details from King's background, it is useful to note the deep crisis and larger social context in which the letter was penned: April 1963, in a jail cell, after King had been arrested for demonstrating against segregation in Birmingham.

It is important to note the context that initially prompted the drafting of the letter, which was written in response to a group of local clergy representing a "moderate" coalition who argued that blacks in the South had it bad but condemned civil rights demonstrations and marches for creating a "crisis situation." The clergymen urged unity and implored Dr. King and his demonstrators to be "patient" and use the courts to gain civil rights. King's letter begins by addressing several of the clergy's central concerns, including the willingness of demonstrators to break laws, in effect earning them the label "criminal":

> You express a great deal of anxiety over our willingness to break laws. This is certainly a legitimate concern. Since we so diligently urge people to obey the Supreme Court's decision of 1954 outlawing segregation in the public schools, it is rather strange and paradoxical to find us consciously breaking laws. One may well ask, "How can you advocate breaking some laws and obeying others?" The answer is found in the fact that there are two types of laws: there are just laws, and there are unjust laws. (3)

In this early section of the letter, King opens by addressing his critics' charge that breaking laws and creating a crisis are depraved behavior, the exact problem students have noted in criminology textbooks. Legalistic conceptions of deviance and crime are very limiting. Those who prefer "law and order" were not very fond of King's tactics of direct action to achieve the goals of the civil rights movement. His detractors, such as the clergymen who provoked his letter, used an absolutist argument that asserts there is something in the essence of a crime that makes it morally reprehensible. Like legal absolutists, they tended to see crime, any crime, as bad in and of itself. However, criminology understands crimes such as King's as violations of what is known as *mala prohibita*—acts that are not bad in and of themselves, but only because a statute says they are unlawful. This perspective is mindful that moral codes do not fall out of the sky; mere mortals create laws. As such, unjust laws may reflect unjust social conditions, and it was King's belief that one has a moral duty to violate an unjust law.

Next, King outlines his objectives, explaining that the goal of direct action is to address an immediate injustice and crisis. The immediate and direct action required was to pressure the Birmingham, Alabama, government. Here he describes the reasoning behind this pressure:

> I must confess that I am not afraid of the word "tension." I have earnestly worked and preached against violent tension, but there is a type of constructive nonviolent tension that is necessary for growth. Just as Socrates felt that it was necessary to create a tension in the mind so that individuals could rise from the bondage of myths and half-truths to the unfettered realm of creative analysis and objective appraisal, we must see the need of having nonviolent gadflies to create the kind of tension in society that will help men to rise from the dark depths of prejudice and racism to the majestic heights of understanding and brotherhood. (2)

Deviant heroism is not unique to the civil rights movement or this moment in history. Just as there are many contemporary deviant heroes, many came before, fighting for an array of needed changes. King notes in his letter the long history of principled civil disobedience in Western civilization, referencing as partial inspiration for his actions the Boston Tea Party and the willingness of American patriots to challenge repressive laws of the British Crown. He describes a list of others who have broken the law to effectively challenge injustice or change history:

> Of course, there is nothing new about this kind of civil disobedience. It was seen sublimely in the refusal of Shadrach, Meshach, and Abednego to obey the laws of Nebuchadnezzar because a higher moral law was involved. It was practiced superbly by the early Christians, who were willing to face hungry lions and the excruciating pain of chopping blocks before submitting to certain unjust laws of the Roman Empire. To a degree, academic freedom is a reality today because Socrates practiced civil disobedience. (3)

King, in the letter, is situating the struggle for civil rights in its historical antecedents, defending rule violation as an important catalyst in the progression of humanity. He includes in this context the more recent problem of totalitarian rulers in the earlier part of the twentieth century:

> We can never forget that everything Hitler did in Germany was "legal," and everything the Hungarian freedom fighters did in Hungary was "illegal." It was "illegal" to aid and comfort a Jew in Hitler's Germany. I hope that if I had lived in Germany during that time, I would have aided and comforted my Jewish brothers and sisters, even though it was illegal. I would also like to think that if I lived in a Communist country today, where certain principles dear to the Christian faith are suppressed, I would openly advocate disobeying these anti-religious laws (3).

King's letter provides an opportunity and context to reconsider the problems of authority, conformity, and human freedom. The letter reminds us that conformity can be as transgressive as the violation of norms and include brutal acts where norms and laws may compel conformists to act as agents of injustice. King, in referencing some of the other injustices of the day, notes the courage and heroism it takes to stand up to unjust systems cemented by conformity.

As conformity can be downright brutal, passive acquiescence can be toxic as well. King's harshest criticism is leveled against the "white moderate," whom he condemns as being more devoted to "order than to justice" (4). That critique is leveled against a citizenry who cringe in fear at the chaos and disorder that ensue when other people struggle for basic rights and human dignity:

> I must confess that over the last few years I have been gravely disappointed with the white moderate. I have almost reached the regrettable conclusion that the Negro's great stumbling block in the stride toward freedom is not the White Citizens Counciler [sic] or the Ku Klux Klanner but the white moderate who is more devoted to order than to justice. (3)

This passage underscores King's critique of the moderate who acknowledged that blacks had it bad but urged them to wait and use the courts or otherwise acquiesce. This passage serves as a teachable moment to demonstrate the pervasive brutality of conformity and how following established rules and laws can often be as bad as the cruelest form of deviance. Too often, acquiescence represents not only an impediment to progress but an unjust social force in itself.

The final item of significance in the letter is its description of how social control is used to maintain unjust laws. This represents an important application of the distinction between formal and informal social control. Informal social control took place in the form of his fellow clergymen ostracizing and condemning him. In addition, the moderate who was turned off by his tactics, as well as various types of exclusion by society, can be a type of informal control. Formal social control in the letter is represented by the official violence and repression King and his fellow marchers faced. In addition, the criminal-legal charges leveled against him and his compatriots, ultimately depriving him of his liberty, are a type of formal social control. The police and the staunch racist Bull Connor represented important roles that King mentions near the closing of the letter. In this passage, he admonishes both the police and those who praised them as "restrained" and "orderly":

> You warmly commended the Birmingham police force for keeping "order" and "preventing violence." I don't believe you would have so warmly commended the police force if you had seen its angry violent dogs literally biting six unarmed, nonviolent Negroes. I don't believe you would so quickly commend the policemen if you would observe their ugly and inhuman treatment of Negroes here in the city jail; if you would watch them push and curse old Negro women and young Negro girls; if you would see them slap and kick old Negro men and young boys; if you would observe them, as they did on two occasions, refusing to give us food because we wanted to sing our grace together. I'm sorry that I can't join you in your praise for the police department. (5)

Besides condemning the overall conduct of the police, King questions the role that they served in the segregated South: "It is true that they have been rather disciplined in their public handling of the demonstrators. In this sense, they have been publicly 'nonviolent.' But for what purpose? To preserve the evil system of segregation" (6). This passage offers an opportunity to discuss the concept of social control and how various institutions may prop up the status quo through both formal and informal sanctioning systems. Expressing a radical theorization of punishment and control, the passage illuminates how a demand for conformity that fails to ensure the consent of the people results in social control mechanisms being used to individually or collectively punish people for violations of unjust norms. These formal systems of social control then serve as an oppressive and reactionary force. While King does not harshly criticize the police the way he does the white moderate, he invites us to consider how police have supported and acted on behalf of unjust systems of social control.

PRACTICING GOOD TROUBLE

To illuminate the significance of King's words and actions to the conceptualization of good trouble, it is useful to examine how the letter can inform a specific praxis. As a critical textual artifact of U.S. history, King's letter is widely read and known among both activists and academics. Some of my students mention that they read it as far back as middle school in rural Idaho school districts. In the college classroom setting, the letter gives neophyte sociology students a distinct opening to use their sociological imaginations to understand crime, deviance, and conformity. A central sociological insight of the letter is not only that society enables us (socialization) and constrains us (social control) but that we also act back on our society (human agency). Socialization represents the power of society over the individual, but deviance represents the power of individuals over their society. The letter provides a chance to specifically consider the important sociological role of the deviant hero and to understand the plausibility of good trouble as a remedy for injustice. King's letter, which engages several arguments against the essentializing of crime as always bad, serves as a critical vehicle to investigate the emancipatory potential for deviance in pursuit of social change. This letter is also illustrative of several sociological concepts including the Millsian method of understanding biography and history in a specific context.

The sociological application of the insights surrounding the letter is twofold. The first involves the identification of specific deviant heroes or acts of deviant heroism (individual or collective). The second determines how a sociological imagination is useful in examining these specific acts or actors in light of the specific context or historical situation in which they occurred.

The first step involves simple identification and description. When one considers people who made a difference, who impacted history, or changed the world for the better, one often finds that these individuals were acting deviant in their specific social context. Probing history, well known individuals, ranging from Thomas Paine to Nelson Mandela, people who are widely admired to this day, were considered deviant in their time and place. Scholars of social movements may be quick to note the parallel between various outcomes sought by social movements and the deviant heroism described in King's letter. Leaders of the labor, women's, and LGBT movements can fall into this category. Figures in current events may also exemplify the deviant hero. Several recent Nobel Prize winners, such as female education activist Malala Yousafzai of Pakistan and Yemini journalist Tawakkol Karman of the "Jasmine Revolution," are superb examples of deviant heroes. In the United States, as of the writing of this book, "enemy-of-the-state" Edward Snowden is a useful example in the debate over what constitutes a hero or villain. Is he a traitor to his country or a protector of individual liberty? Questions such as this are addressed in subsequent chapters. For example, trailblazers in sports and popular culture, Michael Sam and Mo'ne Davis, are clear examples of contemporary deviant heroes. Nonscholars may invoke religious figures, heroes of the republic, or even family members as exemplary of the principles articulated in King's letter. The point here is to establish that key movers and shakers throughout history may have been both altruistic and deviant when seen against the specific context of their actions.

The second, more analytical step involving a sociological approach to good trouble is one that integrates the themes contained in King's "Letter" while understanding how unjust social conditions are interconnected to individual acts of deviance. Engaging the Millsian assertion that sociology be involved at the intersection of biography and history, and Mills's postulate to look for "how personal troubles relate to public issues" (1961, 8), King's letter illuminates acts of altruistic deviance in the furtherance of justice. Utilizing this method, the individual deviant, or defiant act, is seen as being enmeshed in a specific historical epoch. In this analytical framework, identifying a contemporary or historical figure who made a difference or made the world a better place, may yield insight into how deviance provokes social change. King's letter, with the attention to how various examples of "extremism" and "lawbreaking" actually advanced the cause of justice in human history, provides a starting template to consider how good trouble is a key aspect of needed social change.

This involves a consideration of the specific context or epoch in which that individual's actions took place, and why they might be considered deviant. In King's case, he points to how the specific social conditions in segregated Alabama represent an injustice perpetuated in the unequal application of the law. Explaining that

> a law is unjust if it is inflicted on a minority that, as a result of being denied the right to vote, had no part in enacting or devising the law. Who can say that the legislature of Alabama which set up that state's segregation laws was democratically elected? Throughout Alabama all sorts of devious methods are used to prevent Negroes from becoming registered voters, and there are some counties in which, even though Negroes constitute a majority of the population, not a single Negro is registered. Can any law enacted under such circumstances be considered democratically structured? (4–5)

King's letter is an important textual artifact of a much larger movement against injustice. It can be an important tool in bridging commonsense understandings of norm violation among neophytes who consider the causes and consequences of crime and the application of justice in society. King's words and ideas also contain fundamental questions about the problem of associating norm violation with morality. The passages highlighted here demonstrate how nonconformity is an important tool in overcoming oppressive laws. His letter references the need for lawbreaking to transform society. This was just one aspect of a much larger movement, but it proved critical in advancing the cause for racial equality in the United States.

Lastly, King's letter points to how deviance may be a remedy to racial inequality and injustice. Chapter 4 looks at other heroes in the fight against slavery and racial oppression—those heroes who advanced the civil rights movement and the disciplined nonconformity that encompasses the struggle against formal and informal racist norms.

NOTE

1. Although Dr. Martin Luther King Jr. is best known for his work in civil rights and secondly as a minister, his first training was as a sociologist, earning a degree in sociology from Morehouse College in 1948.

Chapter Four

Disciplined Nonconformists

The Struggle against Racism

W. E. B. Du Bois famously declared in his 1903 book *Souls of Black Folks* that the "problem of the twentieth century was the problem of the color line" (1). That pronouncement rang resoundingly true as the century saw the rise of fascist regimes in Europe, the entrenchment of segregation in the US, and apartheid in colonized Africa. The end of slavery in the US was marked by the institutionalized reassertion of racist principles through legal means such as Jim Crow. However, these laws were challenged in open acts of deviance in an attempt to change the fabric of a society organized by racial oppression. This project remains incomplete. The twentieth century ended with stubborn relics of a racist past in housing, policing, public life, and elsewhere. This chapter looks at deviant acts committed against the legal and normative codes enmeshed in racist society. It is argued here that deviant heroism is an important remedy to the "problem of the color line" Du Bois identified. Such deviant behaviors also represent the disciplined nonconformity that Martin Luther King Jr. instructed those who want to advance the cause of civil rights to engage in.

Good trouble is an attempt to renegotiate norms and laws through the process of active resistance against unjust rules and those who brought them into place. From the establishment and perfection of slavery in the New World to the Black Lives Matter movement, racism, and the legal structures it gives rise to, demonstrate the unjust context in which laws and norms are sometimes constructed. Racist institutions represent a social structure rife with both oppression and contradiction (Brennan, 2017). Legal institutions may be impacted or directly support this structural arrangement. These conditions inevitably give rise to deviant heroes and the good trouble they bring.

Those who have fought against racist institutions, including the heroes of the civil rights movement, represent some of the most critical deviant heroes in history. While racism persists, especially the kind entrenched in our social institutions, acts of good trouble on the part of deviant heroes have moved societies away from slavery, segregation, and apartheid toward greater inclusion and justice.

It is impossible to capture in a single book, let alone a single chapter, the amount of suffering and injustice committed as a result of racism and arch crimes like slavery; what follows is not a comprehensive or systematic documentation of the struggle against racism and the civil rights movement. Instead, this chapter simply aims to underscore how lawbreaking against a morally repugnant social system may undermine and ultimately change that system. To illustrate this, acts of good trouble and individual deviant heroes are profiled for three distinct eras of state-supported racial injustice. This includes slavery and the resistance of the Underground Railroad; next is an examination of the civil rights movement against legalized segregation; lastly forms of good trouble in countering stubborn vestiges of racism that manifest in our current period, especially in the criminal justice system, are considered. Specific instances of deviant heroism are briefly described, and their extensive and broader historical context is acknowledged.

CRIMES AGAINST SLAVERY

Slavery, as an economic mode of production, required a normative structure to justify the existence of human chattel. For example, the moral and ethical framework that allowed slavery to exist was reliant on racism and the ideology that suspended it. Slavery was also dependent on a complex legal system, supported by the state, to regulate and subjugate the black Americans who were deprived of liberty. While the American Civil War sealed the abolition of the practice of slavery, lawbreaking, by both free and slave, undermined and hastened the eventual overthrow of this violent system of exploitation. Several examples of this kind of good trouble are considered here.

The Turner Rebellion

Within one hundred years following the establishment of slavery in the American colonies, organized slave rebellions and uprisings, though rare, were a constant source of fear among slave owners (Zinn, 2005, 176). Historians have documented at least three dozen of these, and there were surely more (Gates and Yacovone, 2013). The most famous of these was Nat Turner's 1831 rebellion, which resulted in the killing of some fifty to sixty whites after religious visions instructed him to do so. In his confession to Thomas

Gray (1831) before his trial and execution, Turner explained the events in his biography that brought him to the moment of murdering dozens.

> I was not addicted to stealing in my youth, nor have ever been—Yet such was the confidence of the negroes in the neighborhood, even at this early period of my life, in my superior judgment, that they would often carry me with them when they were going on any roguery, to plan for them. Growing up among them, with this confidence in my superior judgment, and when this, in their opinions, was perfected by Divine inspiration, from the circumstances already alluded to in my infancy, and which belief was ever afterwards zealously inculcated by the austerity of my life and manners, which became the subject of remark by white and black (8–9)

The facts of the Turner Rebellion are obscured by historical erasure of marginalized voices and a subsequent veneration of his story in historical fiction, such as the controversial *The Confessions of Nat Turner* (Styron, 1967). This novel depicts Turner and his rebels as undisciplined louts who get drunk and rape defenseless white women. Other depictions of Turner, like that in the 2016 film *Birth of a Nation*, gave a more positive portrayal of Turner as a leader who sowed the seeds for the resistance of enslaved blacks in a nation founded on doggedly racist principles (Cunningham, 2016).

What is clear from the historical accounts is the legal response to the Turner Rebellion. For a brief time in 1832, the legislature of the Virginia Commonwealth considered the "gradual" abolition of slavery (Brophy, 2013). However, slavery prevailed, and harsher treatments and more brutality were legally sanctioned by the states. Slave rebellions like Turner's and the ennoblement of both the enslaved and abolitionists led to the establishment of heightened social controls through the sheriff posse system and harsh criminal penalties for people who assisted the opponents of slavery (Campbell, 1970). The Fugitive Slave Act of 1850 strengthened existing criminal laws against assisting fugitive slaves; it was a law that abolitionists broke with increasing audaciousness and enthusiasm (Basinger, 2003). The fugitive slave laws produced a generation of deviant heroes who actively sought to break and undermine them. Indeed, the Underground Railroad to the northern United States and Canada was a direct affront to the Fugitive Slave Act.

While slavery is intrinsically a violent institution that was ultimately remedied through a violent response—the Civil War—not all those who challenged slavery engaged in violent behavior. Slavery was also undermined through subversion and other forms of illegality that challenged the basic principle on which it was founded, that humans could be sold as property. The institution of slavery and the laws spawned to maintain it produced opportunities for deviant heroism to thrive. The motives and actions of this good trouble are contained in the autobiographical accounts of prominent abolitionists and former slaves such as Frederick Douglass and Harriet Tubman. Both are superb examples of deviant heroes.

Frederick Douglass

Born into slavery, Frederick Douglass was twenty years old when he escaped and went on to become a prominent abolitionist and critic of segregation and lynchings. His three autobiographies, *Narrative of the Life of Frederick Douglass, an American Slave* (1845), *My Bondage and My Freedom* (1855), and *The Life and Times of Frederick Douglass* (1882), weave an intricate narrative of personal feelings and experience along with unfulfilled dreams of freedom of those who did not escape and suffered under slavery and the subsequent horrors of Jim Crow. Douglass's biography, like King's, reflects a life of continued agitation and resistance against laws enforcing slavery and discrimination.

In *Narrative,* Douglass documents the wretched conditions of living as a slave and indicts the system of morals and laws of the master-slave mode of production. Describing slavery as "brutalism," Douglass documents the beatings and abuse he and other slaves endured, making special mention of how the law effectively absolved slave owners of any legal or moral responsibility for the mistreatment of slaves. All three of his autobiographies recollect his journey from slavery, beatings, and imprisonment to freedom. In his *Life and Times*, he recounts:

> Men who live by robbing their fellow men of their labor and liberty have forfeited their right to know anything of the thoughts, feelings, or purposes of those whom they rob and plunder. They have by the single act of slaveholding voluntarily placed themselves beyond the laws of justice and honor, and have become only fitted for companionship with thieves and pirates—the common enemies of God and of all mankind. (37)

From slavery to freedom, from the margins to the center of political and intellectual life, as an abolitionist and a masterful author and orator, Douglass exemplifies the power of disciplined nonconformity to challenge unjust social conditions.

Other former slaves have written accounts of slavery and escape similar to Douglass's. Consider J. W. Loguen, who escaped slavery on his master's horse. In the North, he joined the black resistance to slavery and denounced the Fugitive Slave Act, working to undermine it on several fronts. In a meeting in Syracuse, New York, he declared of the act:

> I don't respect this law—I don't fear it—I won't obey it. . . . I will not live as a slave, and if force is employed to re-enslave me, I shall make preparations to meet the crisis as becomes a man. (quoted in Zinn, 2005, 183).

As slave revolts and uprisings exposed the contradictions and injustices from within, abolitionists worked to illegally undermine the institution of slavery from the outside, most famously through the Underground Railroad. With courts ruling that runaway slaves were property that had to be returned to their owners, operators of this network assisted fugitive slaves in finding shelter as they made their way to the northern US and Canada. The Underground Railroad was an extraordinary association between whites and free blacks to systematically undermine the material foundations of slavery. With the courage of their conviction, conductors placed themselves in great legal jeopardy.

The Underground Railroad offers an important case study in the criminological theory of differential association. This theory asserts that criminal behavior is an interactive process in which values, techniques, language, and motives are learned through association with others (Inderbitzin, Bates, & Gainey, 2016). At the heart of interactionist approaches to crime is the observation that deviants learn from each other. They study each other's methods; they see what works and what doesn't. This is true of deviant heroes as well. To some extent, contemporary examples of deviant heroism are indebted to the good trouble that has happened before.

For the purposes of orienting the understanding of the Underground Railroad in the context of this book—crime is a tool for social change—it is useful to link some aspects of the Underground Railroad to criminological theory. For example, the theory of differential association is used in criminology to note how social networks may act as a nexus where deviant attitudes and ideas are communicated and acted upon. Differential associations between like-minded people serve as an interactive process of learning and communication, where both techniques of committing deviant acts are learned. In addition, the motives, rationalizations, and meanings associated with crime are affirmed through these differential networks. With the Underground Railroad and subversion of the Fugitive Slave Act, it is apparent how differential associations facilitated acts of good trouble. The informal network consisted of a well-organized collection of free and enslaved blacks, abolitionists, and other activists, such as Quakers. Like any illegal organization, the Underground Railroad adopted specialized railroad metaphors and euphemisms to describe their activities. Slaves got a "ticket," hiding places were "stations," and "agents" helped slaves find the railroad.

Harriet Tubman

One of the conductors on the Underground Railroad was Harriet Tubman. Born a slave herself, poorly treated and beaten, her family was broken up and sold off to various slaveholders in Maryland (Larson, 2004). She herself escaped using the Underground Railroad, where she developed several contacts and learned the routes and methods to best help slaves reach freedom (Clinton, 2004). Putting herself in great peril, working in the winter and at night, she ingeniously avoided detection as she helped scores of slaves escape their plantations. Nicknamed "Moses," it is estimated that she guided three hundred slaves to freedom. Her actions were not just an affront to the Fugitive Slave Act but a blow to an entire social structure that relied on slavery.

Though honored today, the workers on the Underground Railroad were effectively criminals who risked serious legal consequences if caught. The social organization of the Underground Railroad contained many of the same features as other deviant subcultures. As criminologist Edwin Sutherland astutely observed, criminal behavior affirms social ties and networks that enable the further commission of crimes (Sutherland, 1939). This is absolutely true for good trouble as well. Tubman's biography, recounted to Fredrick Douglass, mentions dozens of connections, informal ties, and networks of trust affirmed during her nineteen journeys to liberate slaves from the South (Douglass, 1882; 266). The Underground Railroad relied on an informal network based on trust, language, and a solidarity forged by the common commitment to end a legal but barbaric practice.

John Brown

One compatriot Tubman came into association with was the militant abolitionist John Brown. Active in the Underground Railroad, he discerned that slavery could be overturned only through the use of force. Only an armed rebellion or war could defeat such an entrenched system (Zinn, 2005; 172). Born into privilege as a white, Brown was an outsider even among abolitionists and Underground Railroad workers. His commitment to violence was solidified in Kansas as antislavery settlers were attacked by Missouri militias. The militancy of proslavery forces in spreading slavery in the western frontier affected him deeply.

Du Bois offers much admiration for Brown in his biography *John Brown* (1909). Du Bois, prolific in his description of life in America, offers stunning, often firsthand insight into the "color line" he described in the *Souls of Black Folk* (1903). Opening Brown's biography, he states that "the mystic spell of Africa is and ever was over all America." This harkens back to his indictment of racism in *Souls*, which simultaneously affirmed that Africa and the United States were forever joined though the "archcrime of slavery." Entering the controversy surrounding Brown's life and times, Du Bois weaves a thoughtful narrative about how national events changed Brown's perceptions and life course. He argues through Brown's biography that though slavery was a legal and an accepted practice among white Americans, it is always costly. The system of slavery was maintained, through official violence, posses, militias, and other institutional responses, at vast public expense. The inhumanity of the practice also generated militant opposition, such as Brown's, that would eventually not be contained. Brown's most seditious act came in the form of a raid on a national armory in Harpers Ferry in 1859. Aiming to provoke a rebellion and hasten the end of slavery in the US, Brown and eighteen men attempted to seize the armory (Oates, 1970). Ultimately, the raid was thwarted by a militia and a company of soldiers led by Robert E. Lee. Brown was arrested, found guilty of treason, and executed.

> "I. John Brown am now quite certain that the crimes of this guilty land will never be purged away but with blood. I had, as I now think vainly, flattered myself that without very much bloodshed it might be done." These were the last written words of John Brown, set down the day he died—the culminating of that wonderful message of his forty days in prison, which all in all made the mightiest Abolition document that America has known. Uttered in chains and solemnity, spoken in the very shadow of death, its dramatic intensity after that wild and puzzling raid, its deep earnestness as embodied in the character of the man, did more to shake the foundations of slavery than any single thing that ever happened in America. (Du Bois, 1909: 365–66)

While the raid was unsuccessful, historians consider the actions of Brown and his men to be a symbolic precursor to the American Civil War. Brown's raid was an act of treason that helped set the groundwork for the abolition of slavery and the passage of the Fourteenth Amendment. Du Bois wrote in the biography that the cost of ending slavery could have been much less had Brown been successful, arguing that "the price of liberty is less than the price of repression, even though that cost could be in blood" (383). This calculation is mired in historical debate; it is not the small-scale violence of Brown that is remembered as ending slavery, but the large-scale violence ordered by Abraham Lincoln. Nevertheless, Brown's sedition and acts of treason against the South deserve to be remembered as extreme versions of good trouble. As with several other deviant heroes, Brown's status as a deviant hero is enmeshed in controversy and open to debate.

CRIMES AGAINST SEGREGATION

Of course, the Emancipation Proclamation and the passage of constitutional amendments guaranteeing rights to all people did not mean an end to official subjugation of blacks in the United States. The establishment of Jim Crow at the end of Reconstruction is a particularly cruel legal framework that enforced dual systems of justice. Supreme Court decisions such as *Plessy v. Ferguson* affirmed this legal apartheid, effectively sanctioning segregation. Although there was plenty of resistance to segregation from its inception, it was not until the mid-twentieth century that a political opportunity opened for the greatest generation of deviant heroes, those who stoked the civil rights movement.

It would be myopic to see the evolution of the civil rights movement as a mere collection of individual acts of disobedience. The narrative of the struggle against racism and segregation is necessarily constructed through the biographical narratives of heroes and villains. However, individual acts of deviance that change history have their own long history. The young students who sat in at a Woolworth's lunch counter in Greensboro in 1960 were connected to a much larger movement that had been simmering for five hundred years. These students were arrested for trespassing, but they inspired others to follow. Within a decade, legalized segregation had disappeared. Individual acts of good trouble galvanized a constituency and exposed the injustice of discrimination, but it is important to understand that it was the broad social context and collective movement that sowed deviant heroism.

Doug McAdam's classic sociological analysis of black insurgency in the mid-twentieth century, *Political Process and the Development of Black Insurgency,* traces the emergence of the civil rights movement. Arguing that the collective role of black churches, black colleges, and movement organizations, in particular the National Association for the Advancement of Colored People (NAACP), produced the unique character of the American civil rights movement (McAdam, 1999). While the focus of McAdam's insight is the formation and subsequent decline of black insurgency, he argues that effective movements capture political opportunities while effectively mobilizing resources. Given McAdam's thesis, the coordinated breaking of laws may help stoke and then seize the political opportunities that give rise to social movements. Thus, good trouble was a fundamental catalyst for the contentious action that shaped the civil rights movement.

Through slavery, Reconstruction, and legally codified segregation, the oppression of racism and the yearning for freedom and equality manifested as a widespread attempt to upend and redefine the underlying structure of American society. While a multitude of processes galvanized the movement for civil rights, some of the most transformational were the direct action and civil disobedience that drew a response from both formal and informal forces of social control. This direct action took the form of unpermitted marches, sit-ins, and other violations of the bundle of laws known as Jim Crow. In the spirit of Martin Luther King Jr. and using the method suggested by C. Wright Mills, it is worth considering several of the actions, both famous and forgotten, that defined the "creative maladjustment" that aimed to change the racist political and legal system in the United States.

John Lewis

John Lewis did more than coin the phrase "good trouble"—he has also practiced it his entire life. In the 1960s, he was president of the Student Nonviolent Coordinating Committee and the youngest of the "Big Six" civil rights leaders[1] of that era. During his lifetime, he has been arrested over forty-five times (Blakemore, 2016). Most of these arrests happened during the campaign for civil rights across the Jim Crow South in the 1960s. In Nashville, he was arrested for "resisting the peace." In Mississippi, he was arrested and jailed for using a "whites-only restroom." In the famous march for voting rights in Selma, Alabama, state troopers fractured his skull as he and other marchers tried to cross the Edmund Pettus Bridge (Zinn, 2005). *March* (2013, coauthored by Aydin) is Lewis's unique historical memoir, in the form of a graphic novel. Lewis describes the actions of freedom marchers and the civil rights movement as "necessary trouble." Now a member of Congress, Lewis is regarded as a national treasure by most people, even his opponents. Sixty years after the signing of the Voting Rights Act, he hasn't wavered in his commitment to principled resistance. In 2013, he was arrested at an immigration rally, and in 2016, he led a sit-in on the floor of the House of Representatives to demand a hearing on gun-control legislation.

In 2012, I accompanied five Latina students who followed in Lewis's footsteps by marching across the Edmund Pettus Bridge. Alabama was proposing HB 56, which prohibited undocumented immigrants from receiving any public benefits and prohibited employers from hiring the undocumented and landlords from renting to them. HB 56 also empowered local police to determine the legal status of anyone that they thought was undocumented. The law was clearly aimed at the small but growing Hispanic population in the state. The students came from Idaho, to cross the bridge and complete the subsequent fifty-four-mile journey from Selma to Montgomery in protest of the discriminatory intent behind HB 56.

The Selma march was a lesson in sociology in action and a memorializing of the power of good trouble. Besides King and Lewis, hundreds of marchers were brutally beaten by police. Yet, two days later, they marched again, this time going all the way to the Alabama Statehouse. As my students retraced these steps, they were able to stand on the corner of Montgomery and Molton Streets, the very place that Rosa Parks boarded the bus she refused to move to the back of.

Rosa Parks and Claudette Colvin

Some deviant heroes are lionized and studied in public schools, while others are seemingly forgotten, only to be discovered later. Consider the provocateurs of the Montgomery Bus Boycott. Rosa Parks is an obvious deviant hero whose arrest for defying the laws of segregation provoked a boycott that spurred further actions across the Jim Crow South (Theoharis, 2015). The image of her being fingerprinted and booked into a local jail is an iconic representation of good trouble in its most pure form—a deviant hero, *par excellence*.

Parks's bravery in committing her crime is rightly celebrated. Yet the willingness of thousands of others to engage in good trouble at the risk of beatings, jail, and even death must be acknowledged. In addition, this civil rights movement happened through the efforts of others who were erased or forgotten for their heroism in provoking the coordinated civil disobedience of the civil rights movement. For instance, fifteen-year-old Claudette Colvin was arrested for refusing to move to the back of a Montgomery bus nine months before Rosa Parks was famously arrested for the same crime. Colvin's act of good trouble has been depicted in a biographical account intended for young adult readers:

> One of them said to the driver in a very angry tone, "Who is it?" The motorman pointed at me. I heard him say, "That's nothing new. . . . I've had trouble with that 'thing' before." He called me a "thing." They came to me and stood over me and one said, "Aren't you going to get up?" I said, "No, sir." He shouted "Get up" again. I started crying, but I felt even more defiant. I kept saying over and over, in my high-pitched voice, "It's my constitutional right to sit here as much as that lady. I paid my fare, it's my constitutional right!" I knew I was talking back to a white policeman, but I had had enough. (Hoose, 2010, 34)

Effectively paving the way for Parks and the Montgomery Bus Boycott, Colvin was one of several women who refused to give up their seats on the bus system. Typically, women were quietly removed from the bus and fined, and not much else was heard about it (Hoose, 2010). Colvin was among the first to openly and brazenly challenge the law. Refusing to remove herself from the bus, she was forcibly arrested and jailed and went on to become one of four plaintiffs in *Browder v. Gayle*, the district court case that overturned the bus segregation laws in Montgomery. Colvin later recounted her feelings and her adult response to her good trouble:

> But worried or not, I felt proud. I had stood up for our rights. I had done something a lot of adults hadn't done. On the ride home from jail, coming over the viaduct, Reverend Johnson had said something to me I'll never forget. He was an adult who everyone respected, and his opinion meant a lot to me. "Claudette," he said, "I'm so proud of you. Everyone prays for freedom. We've all been praying and praying. But you're different—you want your answer the next morning. And I think you just brought the revolution to Montgomery" (Hoose, 2010, 36).

The erasure of Colvin from the annals of the civil rights movement is remarkable and deserving of more investigation than a mere historical footnote. According to Colvin's biography, Parks was selected by the NAACP to be the face of resistance to segregated transportation because she was seen as a respectable woman who would resonate more with whites and a broader constituency (Hoose, 2010). The NAACP thought a teenager would not be a reliable representation of the movement for equality. In addition, Colvin's skin was thought to be too dark, whereas Parks, it was believed, had the dress, hair, and demeanor that would draw an aura of respectability (Hoose, 2010). The fact that Colvin became pregnant a few months after her arrest reinforced the unease of the NAACP.

There were much deeper tensions with the civil rights movement than who would be memorialized as its heroes. While King sought to enlist the sympathies of a white majority to achieve the goal of racial integration, others rejected the message of unity as conciliatory and opted for black nationalism. By definition, all deviant heroes are valorized as part of the controversy they create; this is especially evident in the biographies of more militant and radical provocateurs in the struggle over civil rights.

Malcolm X

The black power movement disagreed with the goal of integration and King's pacifist methods. Most notably, Malcolm X, one of that movement's most prominent leaders, advocated for more forceful methods of confrontation. His autobiography, as recounted to Alex Haley, describes his various identities, from child to hustler to prisoner to Muslim and human rights activist and his evolving views about race, white society, and the plight of blacks (X, 1973). His biographical journey includes several periods of introspection where he casts away his given identity and conversion to Islam. These views are deeply personal and mark a series of personal transformations. For example, after his Hajj to Mecca, Malcolm recognizes that whites may be an ally in successfully overcoming racial struggles. Each waypoint in the complexities of his personal narrative was linked, in some way, to the nuanced and changing structural relationships between whites and blacks.

Malcolm X is controversial for his contrast to Martin Luther King and his insistence on black self-defense "by any means necessary." He is also a complex figure for his embracing of black nationalist movements. For a time, he came under the sway of black nationalism and embraced the divisive ideas of the Nation of Islam. Malcolm not only clashed with the values of white society and the tactics advanced by more mainstream elements in the civil rights community, but he ultimately came to reject the Nation of Islam as extreme. Like several deviants profiled in this book, it is difficult to parse where his good trouble became just trouble (or even bad trouble). Yet, his ideas were popularized in his autobiography, which became the intellectual underpinnings for the Black Power movement that emerged after his assassination in 1965.

Huey Newton and the Black Panthers

Also divergent from King and the Southern Christian Leadership Conference, the Black Panthers, under the direction of Huey Newton, asserted the right to defend themselves with violence when necessary and openly carried firearms in public spaces. Decried as a criminal organization (as opposed to a political one) members clashed with police and, on several occasions, found themselves in violent confrontations with authorities in cities such as Oakland and Chicago.

The actions of the Black Panthers and the acceptance by militant black nationalists of violence as a tactic or for use in self-defense obfuscate the identification of their heroes as individuals in good trouble. On one hand, the actions of black nationalist movements may be heroic (and clearly, they sought trouble), but on the other, the means utilized may not fit the operational definition of "deviant heroism." In order to practice good trouble, one should not participate in or advocate the harming of others. Panthers earned a reputation as a violent organization, despite only advocating violence as a form of self-defense (Austin, 2008). Instead, Panthers tried to emphasize social issues, and constitutional rights, which included the right to arm themselves (Seale, 2016). Yet, famous Panthers were regularly arrested for violent offenses (undoubtedly trumped up in some cases) where others, such as Huey Newton, died in violent circumstances. Panther Bobby Seale was imprisoned for inciting riots at the 1968 Democratic National Convention in Chicago. Upon his release, Seale renounced violence as a tactic of contention (Seale and Shames, 2016). He tried to reorganize the Panthers into a more mainstream political force, running for mayor of Oakland, California. Ultimately, the Panthers became defunct, along with a decline in the viability of black nationalist movements. The causes for this decline were many, but the violent death of several members of the Black Panther Party, along with social and structural changes, contributed to the decline of militant civil rights movements.

It should also be acknowledged that mechanisms of social control exacted a massive cost on the heroes who devoted their life to challenging racism. Not only did those who participated in the good trouble of the civil rights movement face official violence, harassment, and detention, but they were also chastised, spat on, beaten, and sometimes murdered by a white citizenry. Many of these heroes and movements were subjected to unconstitutional surveillance and sabotage through programs such as the FBI's COINTELPRO (Church Committee, 1975). Too many of those who participated in the civil rights movement were killed. Malcolm X was shot by rivals, Fred Hampton was murdered by police, and Martin Luther King was assassinated, allegedly by a white racist.

From the Montgomery Bus Boycott to the emergence of black radicalism, the deviant heroes who challenged racial discrimination were successful in several of their stated goals. This is evident in the passage of laws that prohibited overt discrimination. It also introduced a new normative context that asserted blatant racism is unacceptable in public and semi-public environments, such as politics or business. However, the overarching goal of ending racism and rooting out discrimination at an institutional level remains elusive. From housing to labor markets to life expectancy, the color line remains one of the deepest fissures in American society. Thus, the possibility of good trouble as a remedy for racial divisiveness has remained a viable course of action in addressing contemporary racial issues.

Black Lives Matter: Disciplined Nonconformity for the Current Era

Despite the victories of good trouble in overturning the racist laws of segregation, vestiges of a racist past remain entrenched within the institutional framework of American society. Institutional racism and the inertia of historical injustice continue to haunt the delivery of justice in the US. The repeated and persistent killings of unarmed blacks by police officers are a constant feature on the news. According to the U.S. Bureau of Justice Statistics, 234 unarmed people were killed by police in 2015. Those killed are disproportionately African Americans (Fryer and Roland, 2016; Mapping Police Violence, 2015). While civil rights legislation has effectively scrubbed legalized discrimination from the official books, racism remains one of the biggest fissures both in perception and in its relation to the criminal justice system. For instance, while a plurality of all racial groups supports their local police, blacks are significantly more likely to doubt their efficacy and accountability (De Angelis and Wolf, 2016). Blacks have long reported increased scrutiny and double standards in the application of laws. Attention to their disparate treatment by the criminal justice system has brought renewed calls for the kind of good trouble perfected during the struggle against legalized segregation.

Institutional racism has a way of getting people in trouble even when they are not seeking it out. As Michelle Alexander explains in her best-selling book, *The New Jim Crow* (2011), criminal justice in the United States functions as a system of racialized control that simultaneously relegates blacks to impoverished conditions while targeting minority youth for heightened surveillance and incarceration. The structural inequalities embedded both inside and outside the criminal justice system continue the same divisions along the color line that Du Bois described more than a hundred years ago (Du Bois,

1899). The "color of justice" is highly racialized, with blacks singled out for unequal scrutiny by the state. This manifests in a high disparity of young black males being incarcerated and under supervision through probation and parole. In addition, blacks are singled out for increased scrutiny under programs such as stop and frisk and "routine" pullovers.

There is no question that unequal justice has impacted blacks disproportionately, especially black male youth. These social patterns manifest in several different ways. For instance, blacks are more likely to be detained, arrested, and imprisoned for drug offenses despite having use rates similar to those of whites (Walker, Spohn, & DeLone, 2016). Other studies have found systemic disparities in justice from minor interactions with police to capital punishment. This includes that blacks are more likely to be pulled over, and twice as likely to be given the death penalty, than a white for a similar crime (Alexander, 2011). The most chilling of these stories is the attention brought by the emergent Black Lives Matter movement to the killing of blacks based on little more than a hunch or suspicion.

In recent years, several high-profile instances of vigilantes and police officers shooting unarmed blacks have entered the public discourse. In 1999, four New York City Police Department (NYPD) officers fired forty-one shots at an unarmed Amado Diallo. The fatal shooting of Timothy Thomas, the fifteenth African American shot by police in five years, sparked riots in Cincinnati in 2001. An unarmed seventeen-year-old Trayvon Martin was killed by a citizen vigilante under the equivocation of a "stand your ground" law. His killer's acquittal prompted the Twitter hashtag "BlackLivesMatter." Such incidents, despite the court acquittals of officers involved, have raised questions of systemic brutality and doubts about the legitimacy of the use of violence by police. With the officer-involved killings of Michael Brown and Eric Garner in New York City, Black Lives Matter (BLM) became recognized as a viable (and polarizing) movement to protest the killing of unarmed blacks by police.

While the extrajudicial killing of blacks has been going on since the days of slavery, public outrage was catalyzed by what Keeanga-Yamahtta Taylor (2016) describes as a coalescence of structural inequalities like mass incarceration and a generational awareness of new tactics for addressing racism. It also addressed the deep inequalities that remained entrenched in the criminal justice system and society as a whole. BLM diverged from the civil rights movement in that it addressed police violence explicitly while mobilizing members through social media without a visible leadership structure (Cobb, 2016). These new forms of mobilization represent a kind of good trouble that directly confronts how social control is conducted in the United States. The open conflict with police by BLM is more reminiscent of the Black Panthers than any other movement or organization to come out of the civil rights era.

Besides direct confrontation with law enforcement, other instances of deviance emerged as a result of BLM. As of this writing, a controversy has swelled in the National Football League over players kneeling during the national anthem before the start of the game. Most of those who kneel are black. The movement began with a lone act of defiance by football player Colin Kaepernick, who first sat and then took a knee during the anthem in protest of police brutality and racial inequality (Levin, 2017). By 2017, dozens of players were kneeling. This prompted President Trump to enter into the fray, suggesting that the players should be fired. Individual threats to private workers' jobs by the White House was an unprecedented form of social control for a nonviolent act of defiance. Despite being a talented athlete, Kaepernick has not secured employment in the league, and many believe he has been blacklisted for his actions (Moore, 2017).

The controversy over the anthem protests in the National Football League (NFL) is indicative of how protests evolve, and heroes and villains are constructed in the public sphere. Kaepernick and people who kneel during the anthem are seen as "unpatriotic millionaires" protesting the flag, a judgment that distracts from the original intent of their nonconformity. Similarly, some saw Rosa Parks's deviance as merely the act of a tired woman who did not want to give up her seat. The movement she belonged to had to fight against the perception that her act of defiance was about a seat on the bus (Gilmore, 2018). In reality, it was about Jim Crow. Whites at the time saw the original lunch counter protests as an act of hooliganism, a counterproductive side show, or worse. The overall point is that any consideration of individual acts of deviant heroism must take place with an awareness of the overall social context in which they occur and the broader social movement that makes the recognition of deviance as heroism possible.

The social construction of heroes and villains is a dramaturgy of social actions and discursive claims that resonate with a particular constituency. Deviants become heroic when their actions are recognized as selfless, are done in service to a community, involve some kind of personal risk, and are ultimately successful in mobilizing to their cause a broader movement of dissent. As with the social response to crime, heroes are socially constructed as a reflection of larger values in the community. Abolitionists and leaders of the civil rights movement may be generally regarded today as heroes; however, the next generation of people who seek good trouble as a way to raise awareness and remedy continued injustice may be met with hostility, threats, and outright social control.

It remains to be seen how successful BLM will be as an antidote to continued racism and inequality in the criminal justice system. Regardless of its success, it demonstrates a contemporary application of good trouble to bring awareness to clear disparities in the application of justice.

This chapter has considered the propensity for good trouble during three epochs of racial injustice. Runaway slaves and the Underground Railroad served as a seditious challenge to the institution of slavery. During the civil rights era, good trouble was perfected and refined as deviant heroes became symbolic icons in a much larger struggle to overcome the racist beliefs that upheld segregation. Today, stubborn relics of a racist past remain entrenched in criminal justice and other social institutions. Good trouble continues to be an antidote to this continued discrimination and will continue to be necessary trouble until inequality is finally rooted out of society and the legal and normative structures that reflect racism.

The next two chapters will examine how the ethos of good trouble and the deviant heroes that engage in it have been at the forefront in the cause of women and workers in the United States.

NOTE

1. Martin Luther King Jr., James Farmer, John Lewis, A. Philip Randolph, Roy Wilkins, and Whitney Young

Chapter Five

Heretics

Women in Good Trouble

This chapter is premised on the now famous quip by Laurel Thatcher Ulrich that "well-behaved women seldom make history" (2007). Women who do make history often do so in the context of good trouble. The next two chapters are devoted to outsiders, agitators, heretics, and troublemakers who force an otherwise content mainstream to reexamine norms that it takes for granted. Here, the heroines of women's liberation are conceptualized as heretics. In the classic sense, heretics are those who violate orthodox, deeply held beliefs or central tenets of a set of practices, especially those pontificated by religion. The term is used here in a broader sense to describe those who question the orthodoxy of patriarchal laws and norms. Like the disciplined nonconformists in the struggle against racism, the heroes of the women's rights movement profiled here are effectively heretics, defying the accepted doctrine that men are "naturally" better inclined for positions of power and authority. Unlike the truth-tellers and peacemakers portrayed in subsequent chapters, these heretics instigate change as provocateurs or iconoclasts. Their actions stir reactions from people who are otherwise content to conform. At the same time, agitation may provoke important social changes. Looking into both the women's movement (this chapter) and the labor movement (the next) in the twentieth century, one can readily find many instances, both individual and collective, of agitation in the spirit of good trouble that advanced the rights of women and workers.

During the 2016 presidential election, a favorite rallying cry at campaign events for supporters of the eventual winner was to chant "Lock Her Up!" in reference to his opponent, Hillary Clinton. Clinton's candidacy was historic in that she was the first female major-party nominee for president of the

United States. It would be inaccurate to call Clinton an outsider, nor could she easily be labeled a deviant. She was clearly an establishment candidate with the backing of Wall Street and much of the rest of the power elite. Yet her historic rise was marked by her own refusal to conform to gender norms, both symbolic and substantive. When her husband was running for governor of Arkansas, she declined to take his last name, a decision that drew responses ranging from ostracism to outright ire. As First Lady, she tossed aside the traditional roles of the office—refusing, metaphorically, to "bake cookies" in the White House or to limit her job to simply "standing by her man." Like her opponent in the presidential election, feelings toward her established which side of a largely fabricated culture war one was on.

While Clinton opponents ostensibly claimed that the chant "Lock Her Up" was a valid allusion to unsubstantiated crimes that she and her husband allegedly committed, the phrase evoked a well-established misogyny and the will to criminalize women who seek power and authority equal to men. Flaws and shortcomings of the failed candidate aside, criminal law has long been used to keep women in subordinate roles and to stymie women who are ambitious or seek influence. For instance, in the United States, owning property or exercising constitutional rights afforded to men, such as voting, were not guaranteed to women until the 1920s. Laws governing contraception and reproductive choices point to clear gender inequities manifested in the criminal justice system (Morash, 2006, 44–52).

Even more insidious are laws aimed at women who are economically vulnerable and do not have the means to fight back. As of this writing, women and girls who come to the United States fleeing danger are being separated and detained indefinitely. Several states are seeking to criminalize women's reproductive choices by introducing a dizzying array of laws aimed at stemming their medical options. While rich women will be able to travel to circumvent some of these laws, the overt intent is control of women's bodies and their choices through criminalization. Women who lack power and influence, who speak out against sexual harassment and assault, are threatened with litigation and lawsuits.

It is fitting that many of the individuals described in this chapter on "the heretics" are women who defied convention to advance the cause of reproductive rights, assert the role of women in religion, and bring awareness to a variety of other issues that affect women and children. The thousands-year-old marginalization of half the human species has created tensions and crises in response to which heroic deviance is a necessary imperative. Feminism emerged in academic disciplines, in part, to explain the repressive social conditions that women live in under patriarchy. Feminism also informed the movement to overcome sexist oppression.

Like other norms, expectations about behaving based around gender norms are bound to a cultural process in which individuals (family, friends, coworkers) and institutions (media, education, government) create and fortify beliefs surrounding the construct of gender and reinforce norm expectations about what constitutes appropriate gender behavior. At the same time, these institutions and individuals apply pressure to conform to those roles. Informal sanctions for a woman violating a gender norm, who is not acting "feminine enough," might involve ostracism or name-calling. Institutional sanctions are more far-reaching and can result in the deprivation of the liberty of those who violate such norms. Here it is worth considering how ill-behaved women have placed themselves in jeopardy to advance the cause of women both in the United State and elsewhere.

This chapter delves into several examples of individual and collective action that represent just a few of the deviants who acted on behalf of the rights of women. Laurel Thatcher Ulrich's book with the same title as this chapter's epigraph, *Well-Behaved Women Seldom Make History* (2007), is a tribute to the unsung feminist hero whose silent actions have helped challenge oppressive and unjust systems.[1] As the words imply, rule-breaking has always been a key driver for advancing the cause of progress. This is especially true for women. Ulrich's research details the vital role of silent and often unknown women who have resisted not just patriarchy but other unjust conditions in a variety of social contexts.

Ulrich's chronicle of women who made history combines historical biography and textual analysis of three women and their historic texts: Christine de Pizan's *Book of the City of Ladies*, written in 1405; Elizabeth Cady Stanton's *Eighty Years and More*, published in 1898; and *A Room of One's Own*, based on two lectures Virginia Woolf gave in 1928. These women were not heretics per se, nor were they even iconoclastic; however, their words and ideas challenged the doctrine that men were in charge and women were subordinate. Ulrich uses the narratives of these three women as anchors to explore other women who made history. She writes:

> Each used history to argue against narrow definitions of womanhood. They did so by reading against the grain of existing narratives and by writing new ones of their own. All three breached the equality/difference divide. Pizan invited women warriors into a city dedicated to the Virgin Mary. Stanton turned grandmothers' tales into a political argument. Woolf allowed an androgynous mind to comprehend a women's culture. All three demonstrated that women were both like and unlike men, and they argued that stories told from the female perspective changed presumably universal notions of human behavior. (37–38)

While this is a work of history, it shows how the (slow) progress of women has been accomplished through various forms of deviance. For example, Pizan pushed the boundaries of what was accepted for women by reorienting the notion of womanhood. Stanton questioned a legal system that gives husbands and fathers rights over wives and daughters. Meanwhile, Woolf utilized a feminist historical narrative at a time when it was presumed that women did not make history.

MORALS, MANNERS, AND FEMINISM

In addition to the exclusion of women from other aspects of society, women were also long prohibited from the academy. Until the women's movement of the 1970s, it was assumed that this exclusion meant that there were few women founders involved in the establishment of the social sciences. However, the "discovery" of scholarly writings of women such as Jane Addams, Charlotte Perkins Gilman, Julia Cooper, and Ida B. Wells clearly demonstrates that, besides being important early advocates of feminism, these and other women made distinctive contributions to the development of the discipline (Lengermann & Niebrugge-Brantley, 1998). This work is just now being recognized.

One pioneering feminist and early founder of sociology, Harriet Martineau, made several important contributions in terms of the understanding of how society enforces normative orders. In her autobiography, Martineau reflects on her early life of relative comfort in England, a period that quickly ended when the family business failed and her father died (Martineau, 1879). She was expected to be a seamstress to support her family, but she started writing instead, and went on to become a prolific author. Several of her books are regarded as foundational to the development of the social sciences. Martineau was not just a scholar and writer; she was also politically engaged at a time when women were expected to stay out of matters that were regarded as men's troubles. In the 1830s, she took a two-year-long trip to the United States. Famous from her writings, she was able to visit twenty states, meet with governors, senators, and congressmen, and even dine with President Andrew Jackson. Along the way, she was committed to interviewing Americans from all walks of life, including women and slaves.

Martineau's inclusive sociology extended its reach to marginalized groups. In America, her heresy was to speak out against slavery. In Boston, she found good trouble when she spoke at an abolitionist rally. After that, she received death threats and was barred from reentering the southern United States (Logan, 2002). Her otherwise long trip (by today's standards) to America was cut short, and she returned to England.

However, Martineau's time in America proved to be pivotal for her intellectual development and establishment of sociology as a recognized discipline. In 1836, she published *How to Observe Morals and Manners* based on her experiences as an outsider in the United States. Occupying an intellectual niche somewhere between De Tocqueville and Durkheim (both chronologically and intellectually), she argued that "morals and manners" should be the primary subject of sociology. Morals were the collective ideas prescribed by a society and manners were the way of acting on them. This insight is astonishingly similar to the values (morals) and norms (manners) that Durkheim articulated as "social facts," which are the object of sociological analysis in his *Rules of the Sociological Method*. Martineau argued that differences between stated morals and actual manners were of particular interest to social scientists as important contradictions, who can derive useful sociological insight from such anomalies and contradictions. In her observations of the United States, she noted that despite the imperatives of independence, self-determination, and freedom that are the cornerstones of the American identity, clearly stated in the founding documents of the republic, the country nevertheless enslaved a significant amount of the population and denied full independence, self-determination, and freedom to women. In other words, she derived a contradiction between the morals of the United States (freedom) and the manners that are in practice (slavery, sexism). Martineau argued that the resulting social malaise would ultimately prove disruptive, until the morals and manners of a society were brought into alignment with one another. Again, this concept is remarkably similar to Durkheim's "anomie," according to which a breakdown of individuals' moral direction was thought to cause societal malaise and fragmented social identities.

Martineau advocated a women-centered approach to sociology that asked a basic question—perhaps the most critical of feminist questions: "Where are the women?" (quoted in Lengermann & Niebrugge-Brantley, 1998, 43). In *Morals and Manners,* her postulate for the methodological approach to sociological insight into women is "Are women present and under what law of liberty?" (ibid. 42–43). The invisibility of women in a country whose founding document espouses universality and inclusion was astounding to Martineau. She writes that the anomaly had to be reconciled, as acquiescence to this system was degrading. However, she notes that "this acquiescence is only partial; I for one, do not acquiesce . . . I know that there are women in America who agree with me on this. The plea of acquiescence is invalidated by us" (quoted in Lengermann & Niebrugge-Brantley, 1998, 42–43). In other words, women should work to violate the "manners" that ask for their subjugation, effectively seeking good trouble.

Martineau deserves to be recognized not just for her advocacy for women as an early feminist; her writings make for good sociology in its own right. As Ritzer and Stepnisky explain, Martineau may be not only the founding mother of sociology, but the founder of the discipline (2016, ch. 10). *Morals and Manners* provided a blueprint for the further development of key sociological concepts. It demonstrated how norms and values are reproduced and enforced, along with an understanding of their violation. As traced in this chapter, many women found actionable good trouble in the furtherance of the cause of women, but Martineau, in considering the morals and manners of gendered expectations, also revealed how they might be broken.

Feminism as Good Trouble

As the social sciences were established, feminism emerged in several waves to bring women's narratives out from the margins of history and counter sexist ideologies that maintain the oppression of women. In addition, feminism has challenged taken-for-granted gender norms and expectations. Precise definitions of feminism are likely to provoke much debate, at least in academic circles. Although often maligned outside of the academy, feminism generally means equality between the sexes (Mitchell, Oakley, & Cott, 1986). However, even in the most simplistic and seemingly consensus definitions, feminism is necessarily deviant, as it challenges established sexist norms. Borrowing from bell hooks's operational definition, feminism is conceptualized here as a deviant movement against sexist oppression (2000:12) and thus a struggle that counters normative frameworks that have traditionally held women in a subordinate role. Challenging this normative framework is a form of good trouble.

In terms of legal and moral codes, longstanding gender double standards have been well documented going back to chauvinistic conceptions of law and property articulated in ancient Greek and Roman customs (Posner, 2009). In the Abrahamic religious traditions, the subjugation of women has been part of unquestioned doctrine for thousands of years. Women who acted up or spoke out were seen as not just violating norms and codes but defying the deity and, in effect, committing a heresy.

In criminology, the theorization of women and crime has constituted a complex dilemma. On one hand, women make up fewer than 15 percent of arrestees and are even less represented in the prison inmate population. At the same time, women's voices, as victims, professionals, and scholars, have been poorly represented in academic literature on matters of crime and justice (Morash, 2006). While women tend to receive lighter sentences than men for violent crimes, their sexuality or femininity may themselves be cause for suspicion, in addition to whatever wrong they may have committed. Some have noted that when women do commit crimes, they are subject to a dual prosecution—one for their crime and one for their gender (see Hart, 2005; Hasian & Flores, 2000). For instance, popularized media accounts of women who kill or teachers who sleep with their male students are often sensationalized, and may descend into prurient or cruel public exposé of the woman offender. In the United States, this phenomenon dates as far back as the Puritans and the Salem witch trials.

In Erikson's *Wayward Puritans* (1966), a landmark historical account of the sociology of deviance, Erikson argues that deviance plays an important role in defining shared moral frameworks and maintaining a social order. In Massachusetts Bay Colony, in the late seventeenth century, the trying and execution of witches served to reinforce a collective sense of morality and identity. Erikson links the public declaration of deviants—heretics deemed a threat to the Puritan way of life, to three crises including a schism in the Puritan Faith (Antinomian Controversy), the perception of threats from a rival religious group (Quakers) and their subsequent persecution, and finally the external threat that was represented by the heresy of witchcraft. For Erikson, the exclusion of townspeople and the excommunication of church members served to define symbolic spaces about what was and was not acceptable. In particular, mass hysteria surrounding the practice of witchcraft served to cement into place a judicial system whose relics can be found in contemporary legal practices. For instance, moral panics over drugs, immigrants, teenage pregnancy all contain vestiges of the practices of the Puritans of Plymouth Bay.

Erikson notes that there was a notable over-representation of women who were accused and tried as witches, but his book offers no systemic insight or analysis of gender or power in that period. However, several other accounts of the Salem witch trials adopt feminist frameworks to theorize the role of gender, power, and the marginalization of women. For instance, Federici (2004) links the declaration of women as witches and their trials as heretics with the genesis of capitalist accumulation that aimed to deprive women of economic autonomy through the limitation of access to common property. Other feminist accounts argue that, in the transition to modernity, the trials were meant to reinforce long-existent patriarchy (Karlsen, 1987; Reis, 1997). Such historical accounts point to the ways that the law and judicial process have reinforced the subordination of women.

As the case of Salem shows, women and girls have not fared very well in thousands of years under Western legal traditions. Laws have enforced differential treatment based on customs that derive from patriarchal power structures. Until only very recently, women have been legally regarded as the chattel or possessions of their fathers and husbands, and they were long barred from entering business or holding property without the consent of a male guardian. This has been the case since the establishment of the first nation-state, effectively making women the original "second-class" citizen (Posner, 2009). Given the level of entrenched patriarchy in the legal traditions of Western societies and the legal subjugation of women, only through the breaking of laws—through good trouble—could a movement for gender equity hope to succeed.

Before moving on to specific instances of good trouble in the advancement of women's rights, it is useful to consider how the criminal justice system and the field of criminology have treated women and girls. Until recently, questions of women and gender have not been that important to criminology. The assumption was that since men made up the vast majority of offenders and it was "unthinkable" that women would want to work in most aspects of the criminal justice system, the entire field of criminology was devoid of any systematic appraisal of women and crime. At the same time, the female offender has long been a source of some speculation in criminological literature, although typically as a side note or anomalous oddity. Up until the 1970s, rigorous scholarship exploring issues of women, crime, and deviance was almost nonexistent, and in explaining crime (Morash, 2006) the question of gender has generally been excluded. The portrayals of women in crime literature were paternal at best and more often than not sexist and misogynist (Belknap, 2014). The nineteenth-century Italian criminologist Cesare Lombroso considered women to be lesser evolved than men, especially women who got into trouble. Women who committed crimes did so, he assumed, because of an atavistic evolutionary "throwback," expressed in physical traits such as crooked teeth, hairy arms, or some other phenotype (Lombroso et al., 2004).

In general, when criminology did look at women, it treated male offending as "normal," while women were regarded as a generalized "other" (Pollock, 2014). For instance, female prostitutes were thought to be oversexed nymphomaniacs (Davis, 1971) or women who were working out an Electra complex. It was not until the feminist movement of the 1970s that serious consideration of gender was brought inside the margins of criminological discourse. In this movement's defiance of sexist norms and patriarchal power relationships, one can identify the essence of good trouble.

What follows is a consideration of several women who were regarded as normative nonconformists, heretics, or agitators and outsiders who questioned what many feminists regard as the original inequality human beings have constructed. The women who advanced the causes of women's rights, reproductive rights, and workers' rights did so by breaking norms about gender roles and, in some cases, broke laws that ensured their second-class status.

Suffragettes

The "first wave" of feminism was generally part of a global struggle in advanced capitalist democracies to foster legal changes in how women are considered under the law. This movement understood that the elevation of the legal status of women in society began and ended with the right to vote. Nowadays, it is taken for granted that women vote, but historically, it was a hard-wrought process, one that relied on relentless determination and a little bit of good trouble. The most famous of the suffragists in the United States were Susan B. Anthony and her compatriot, Elizabeth Cady Stanton, along with rivals in the same cause such as Lucy Stone and Julia Ward Howe.

While black men technically had the right to vote with the passage of the Fifteenth Amendment in 1870, it would take another fifty years for women to secure that right with the passage of the Nineteenth Amendment.[2] During that time, suffragists deployed good trouble to gain access to the ballot box and political process.

Ulrich's inclusion of Elizabeth Cady Stanton in her trinity of ill-behaved heroines makes the point well. Stanton was a militant abolitionist who was thought to be the intellectual founder of the women's rights movement. The daughter of a wealthy slave owner and politician, her early ideas were squarely at odds with those of her family. Prohibited from attending college because she was a woman, she went to a seminary instead. The discrimination, as well as the threats of damnation, led her to avoid religion the rest of her life. In 1895, she published the *Women's Bible*, which questions the subservience of women in Christian doctrine. The controversy isolated her further from the mainstream and even more radical members of the women's movement who felt religious heresies might alienate potential supporters and confirm accusations from the pulpit and elsewhere that suffragettes were working on behalf of the devil (Faulkner, 2011). A clear heresy, Stanton's book was condemned as inspired by Satan by both clergy and fellow suffragists, clouding her critical contributions to the plight of women in the United States.

Stanton's contributions to the suffrage movement included the Declaration of Sentiments adopted by many of the attendees at the Seneca Falls Convention. The declaration, modeled on the Declaration of Independence, asserted, among other things, that women had the right to property, fair wages, and equal treatment under the law. The work is regarded as the intellectual underpinning of the women's rights movement and guided the cause of suffrage through the passage of the Nineteenth Amendment.

While Stanton was the theory behind the early women's rights movement in the United States, Susan B. Anthony was the action. Like Stanton and several other suffragists, she was also a committed abolitionist and social activist against slavery. Not only did Anthony petition against slavery; she assisted Harriet Tubman in the underground railroad (Harper, 1899). She was also active on behalf of the cause of teachers and education, arguing, among other things, that blacks should be admitted to public schools (Harper 1899, 221). In addition, Anthony challenged the widely held beliefs that women were less intelligent than men and should receive less pay for the same work. Her staunch opposition to these beliefs was clearly heretical in the mid-nineteenth century.

Anthony is best known, however, for her work in the suffrage movement and has been widely celebrated as a hero of women's rights, becoming the first woman to grace the front of official US currency in 1979. In her own time, though, her efforts attracted legal trouble. In 1872, along with eight others, Anthony illegally cast a ballot for president. She was later arrested and tried for violation of the Enforcement Act of 1870, which criminalized voting of "unqualified persons" under state law. The trial was a national phenomenon and received widespread coverage in the press. At her conviction, Stanton defied the judge's orders to be silent, questioning the rendering of law by saying:

> Yes, but laws made by men, under a government of men, interpreted by men and for the benefit of men. The only chance women have for justice in this country is to violate the law, as I have done, and as I shall *continue* to do. . . . Does your honor suppose that we obeyed the infamous fugitive slave law which forbade to give a cup of cold water to a slave fleeing from his master? I tell you we did not obey it; we fed him and clothed him, and sent him on his way to Canada. *So shall we trample all unjust laws* under foot. I do not ask the clemency of the court. I came into it to get justice, having failed in this, I demand the full rigors of the law (quoted in Gordon, 2012, 613).

Anthony was convicted of violating the Enforcement Act, but refused to pay the fine and asked for jail time. The fine was not enforced, thus depriving her of the opportunity to appeal up to the Supreme Court. It would be another fifty years before women had universal suffrage in the United States, but Stanton and Anthony both continued to push the cause for equality through the close of the nineteenth century.

Besides the Stanton-Anthony duo, there were many other suffragists who utilized the principles of good trouble, acting as deviant heroes for the cause of political equality. For instance, there was Lucy Stone, who was also involved in the abolition movement and was an early advocate of access to the ballot box. During her time at Oberlin College, she earned a reputation as an agitator for her efforts and was expelled from her church (Million, 2003). There were international counterparts such as Alice Paul, a key heroine of the suffragette movement in England, who then came to the United States, where she was arrested for her activities on behalf of women's rights. She protested with a hunger strike and endured being forced fed (Zahniser & Fry, 2014). Countless others defied conventions and risked arrest and punishment so they could prevail in the establishment of gender equity in the United States and elsewhere.

As the biography and actions of suffragists demonstrate, good trouble was necessary in the struggle of women for political autonomy. However, vast gender inequalities remain entrenched in the United States and elsewhere despite near universal suffrage around the world. The subjugation of women did not end with the passage of the Nineteenth Amendment. Yet, the deviant heroines of the suffrage movement, using good trouble, effectively paved the way to gender equality, including women's autonomy over their own bodies, economic equality, and full access to military, educational, and religious, and other social institutions.

Family Planning as Crime

Feminist criminology demonstrates the extent to which criminal justice has been a decisively male-oriented enterprise. In the reinforcement of gender norms that tend toward the exclusion of women from the protective or beneficial aspects of the criminal justice system, that same system may also apply excess scrutiny to women who violate gender-specific norms and laws. Nowadays, one of the most tangible and perhaps pervasive ways the criminal justice system asserts formal control over women is through the control of reproductive choice. As Jeanne Flavin explains in *Our Bodies, Our Crimes* (Flavin, 2009), among the many informal social-control functions of the criminal justice system is its policing of gender performance and expectations. Although this has an effect on the actions of both men and women, it is especially pronounced for women, as their bodies are objects of legal inquiry and control.

> By restricting some women's access to abortion and obstetric and gynecological care, by telling some women not to procreate and pressuring them to be sterilized, by prosecuting some women who use drugs and become pregnant, and by failing to support the efforts of incarcerated women and battered women to rear their children, the law and the criminal justice system establish what a "good woman" or "fit mother" should look like and how conception, pregnancy, birth and child care and socialization are regulated. (Flavin, 2009, 4; found in Barak, 2015, 54).

For Flavin, the control of women's reproduction and the criminalization of women's bodies is part of larger efforts at the subjugation of women. Through the regulation of biological functions of women, the law presents a substantial obstacle for the full autonomy Martinau envisaged. The legal regulation of women's bodies also provides opportunity for good trouble.

Anecdotes regarding the legal regulation of sex and the body are found in many court cases. In *Jacobellis v. Ohio*, the Supreme Court justices were debating where to draw the line between art and obscenity when Justice Potter Stewart uttered his now famous quip: though he couldn't define obscenity, he said, "I know it when I see it" (Gewirtz, 1996, 1023). The is a useful anecdote in discussions of crime as a socially constructed phenomena. Like obscenity, crime is a socially defined phenomenon. As Lowney and Best (1995:33) observe, the reality of deviant behavior (and of social problems) emerges through the agitation of individuals and groups. The reality of crime is negotiated in the public square through an iterative process of introducing claims, gauging reaction, and modifying the overall message. Constructionists tend to focus on the social and political activities of individuals and groups, termed *claimsmakers,* who compete within a "social problems marketplace" (Best, 1995). Social constructionists look to see how dominant groups maintain status-quo normative structures, while marginalized groups seek to convince an audience that continued stigmatization of an act or activity is unjustified (Loseke, 1999). Considered here is the trouble of two women, Margret Sanger and Emma Goldman, who got into good trouble by challenging dominant ideas about sex and sexuality—in particular, birth control.

Women's sexuality and women's bodies have long been subject to control by the state apparatus. Michel Foucault (1978) noted how limits imposed on even the discourse about sex and sexuality were a product of larger power relationships involving gender. Sex and sexuality are, after all, completely natural but highly regulated aspects of human behavior (Kempadoo and Doezama, 1998). Even societies that are considered permissive have a lot of norms and rules about sex, including where, when, and with whom sex can happen and how individuals must talk about it. These normative controls can have varying social consequences. How a society regulates and controls sexuality, especially women's sexuality, is in fact very telling about other aspects of that society.

Obscenity laws themselves have been a longstanding source of tension between the state and agents of social change (other than pornography dealers). Only since the 1970s has it become impossible to ignore the ways that social inequality and notions of gender are embedded in the formation and enforcement of laws governing what constitutes decency. Moreover, the formal responses to infractions of these norms are typically harsher to women than men. The violation of obscenity laws has thus been a form of good trouble that has nudged social progress forward.

The Comstock Laws were drafted during the 1870s to prohibit the use of the postal service for trade and transport of materials deemed obscene. These laws targeted pornography, sex toys, and other erotic materials but also included a prohibition on the production and distribution of materials relating to contraception or abortion. In opposing this set of laws, deviant heroes Margret Sanger and Emma Goldman found good trouble.

Margaret Sanger

Sanger grew up with ten brothers and sisters, and her mother lost several children due to miscarriages and stillbirths (1970). These pregnancies took a toll on her mother's health, and she died at the age of forty. Trained as a nurse, Sanger worked among the poor and immigrant communities of New York City. During this time, she treated several women who had been injured, some fatally, from unhygienic, illegal abortions. In 1911, she wrote a pamphlet titled *What Every Girl Should Know* about women's reproduction and how to prevent pregnancy. This was followed by another publication three years later called *The Rebel Woman*, which openly advocated birth control, putting her in violation of the Comstock Act. Threatened with a five-year jail sentence, she fled to England.

However, Sanger, a pragmatist, saw the single issue of birth control and abortion as her life's work (Chelsea, 1993) and returned to the United States. In 1915, she established the Brownsville Clinic in Brooklyn, New York, which was devoted exclusively to giving women advice about contraception, and popularized the term *birth control*. The police raided the clinic, and once again invoking the Comstock Laws, had Sanger arrested. She was brought before Judge John Freschi. Holding a cervical cap from the bench, the judge asserted that a woman does not have "the right to copulate with a feeling of security that there will be no resulting conception," adding that "if a woman isn't willing to die in childbirth, she shouldn't have sex" (Lepore, 2014). Sanger responded:

> With me it is not a question of personal imprisonment or personal disadvantage. I am today and have always been more concerned with changing the law and the sweeping away of the law, regardless of what I have to undergo to have it done (Katz, 2000).

Given the chance of leniency if she agreed not to break the law, Sanger said that "I cannot respect the law as it exists today" and was found guilty and sentenced to thirty days in jail (Katz, 2000, ibid.). Sanger later went on to establish a new birth control clinic and founded an organization that eventually became known as Planned Parenthood. Birth control devices such as the diaphragm and other barrier methods were legalized two years later in 1917.

Like Socrates two millennia earlier, Sanger was distributing knowledge that empowered her pupils but threatened the established social order. And like Socrates, Sanger got into good trouble. The knowledge she distributed was about women's body parts and how they worked, but by implication, she was also disseminating knowledge about how women could assert their independence, an act that was fundamentally political as well.

Emma Goldman

Another deviant hero who crossed the Comstock Laws to find good trouble was Emma Goldman. Like Sanger, Goldman was an agitator, a labor organizer who worked among the poor and immigrant populations of New York. Unlike Sanger, Goldman linked birth control to more systemic issues of oppression. According to her autobiography, *Living My Life* (1931), she became an anarchist the day she emigrated to the United States at the age of twenty. This two-volume memoir details a life of rebellion, agitation, and good and bad trouble. Goldman expresses her admiration for other deviant heroes, such as Thoreau, whom she applauded as revolutionary for asserting the primacy of individual conscience over the hegemony of authority. She also noted her admiration for the actions of John Brown in leading a slave insurrection at Harpers Ferry, writing, "If not for the direct action of John Brown and his comrades, America would still trade in the flesh of the black man" (330).

As an immigrant, Goldman thought the key to revolutionary change in the United States was to infuse the revolutionary spirit of her home country with the unique cultural characteristics of Americans. Her autobiography gives critical insight into the thinking of radicalized immigrants at the turn of the century. Goldman's anarchist beliefs, at direct odds with values held dear by many Americans, are condemned to this day as naïve and treasonous. Her political views and associations with rabble-rousers made her an outsider even among former compatriots.

> I want freedom, the right to self-expression, everybody's right to beautiful, radiant things. Anarchism meant that to me, and I would live it in spite of the whole world—prisons, persecution, everything. Yes, even in spite of the condemnation of my own closest comrades I would live my beautiful ideal. (Goldman 1931, 56)

Despite the marginalization of Goldman by her adopted country and confederates, her views on sexuality and birth control were clearly at the leading edge of a new moral framework. In 1915, she was arrested under the Comstock Act for handing out advice on contraception to immigrants. At her trial she declared, concerning the distribution of birth control information,

> [T]owards the betterment of the human race, towards a finer quality, children who should have a joyous and glorious childhood, and women who shall have a healthy motherhood, if that is a crime, your Honor, I am glad and proud to be a Criminal. (Goldman, 1916, 503).

Goldman was found guilty and given the option of a fine or fifteen days in jail. Goldman took the time. In the process of her trial and conviction, she managed to turn her tangles with the legal system into a national debate on the topic of birth control. There is no doubt the publicity surrounding her trial served as a conduit for the normalization of this topic, empowering women and couples—many of whom had never heard of family planning—to talk openly about birth control for the first time.

Despite *Roe v. Wade* effectively legalizing reproduction and abortion services nationwide, working in women's clinics and providing reproductive health services remain a widely denounced and dangerous occupation. Abortion workers report being highly stigmatized due to the toxic cultural and political discourse, which affects their relationships with family, friends, and patients (Harris, Debbink, and Hassinger, 2011). To this day, those advocating for and performing reproductive services are in a contentious and sometimes life-threatening situation. In July 1994, Paul Hill, a domestic terrorist, shot and killed Dr. John Bayard Britton and a clinic volunteer, James H. Barrett, outside a women's health center in Pensacola, Florida (Stack, 2015). Similar acts of violence and intimidation have become routine across the country. Another doctor, George Tiller, was murdered in 2009 in Wichita, Kansas, after having been shot sixteen years earlier. Three clinic workers were murdered in Colorado Springs, Colorado, in 2015, and threats and acts of violence against other clinics have become commonplace.[3]

Although Sanger and Goldman were harassed by the authorities, put on trial, placed in jail, and subjected to multiple threats and other forms of harassment, their nonconformity made discussions of family planning a mainstream, socially acceptable topic. Not only did their defiance challenge the injustice of an antiquated law, but it represented an affront to a chauvinistic social and legal system that saw women as passive subjects rather than active agents in their own lives. Although we have looked at the so-called crimes of these two women, thousands of others were part of the long campaign to decriminalize contraception. Many of the Comstock Laws remained intact and enforced until the 1980s, when the Supreme Court struck them down after more than a hundred years as violations of the protections of the First Amendment (Gurstein, 1996).

PLAYING IT FORWARD: HERETICS OF THE TWENTY-FIRST CENTURY

The dual fights for women's access to the ballot box and control over their reproductive choices are two important examples of how good trouble has been used by deviant heroines to advance women's rights. As has been noted, the woman heretic is one who has questioned traditional, commonsensical, or taken-for-granted gender norms. Deviance, that is to say, good trouble, has shown itself to be an effective tool for raising awareness and changing normative frameworks; contemporary heretics continue to use good trouble to violate doctrines that are unfair or unjust. This section considers a few contemporary examples, including women who have been jailed for the outrageous—like performing nude in an orthodox church, or for something as seemingly mundane as driving to a shopping mall.

Although norm-breaking must be understood in a specific social context, deviance is a universal cultural phenomenon, and deviant heroes are found in a variety of cross-cultural contexts. Comparative criminology, an oft-overlooked perspective in criminology (Beirne and Hill, 1991), studies crime and the response to crime across two or more cultures yielding enhanced depth of perception regarding how matters of crime and justice are treated. Good trouble may be similarly viewed comparatively. The deviant actions of suffragettes in other countries, for example, can serve as an important reference point in comparing the various first-wave women's movements for the vote in evolving democracies. By giving an outsider view, the comparative perspective can make deviant heroism more apparent.

Manal al-Sharif

A case that perfectly demonstrates the contemporary application of feminist good trouble and the comparative perspective is that of women seeking the right to drive in Saudi Arabia. Although the ban on women driving was reversed in the summer of 2018, this was achieved only after emboldened women began openly defying its enforcement by the repressive Committee for the Promotion of Virtue and Prevention of Vice (CPVPV). Although not the first woman to protest the ban on driving, Manal al-Sharif was one of the boldest in her defiance. In 2011, she began posting films of herself driving on social media both to protest the ban and bring awareness of the legal status of women in Saudi Arabia. She was promptly arrested after her first video post, but persisted.

In al-Sharif's autobiography *Daring to Drive* (2017), she recounts a childhood and coming of age in Saudi Arabia shaped by the spread of religious fundamentalism in the Kingdom. She fully internalized religious radicalism, even turning her own family members into the CPVPV (22–23). But she also had the privilege of an education, and in her twenties went to work for a firm in cybersecurity. During that time, she describes an awakening to the reality that the rules she had always accepted were an irreconcilable contradiction. At work, she was called a "slut" for talking to men. Al-Sharif recounts her realization that the double standards for men and women in her home country were incompatible not only with the imperatives of self-determination but also Islamic concepts of justice. Restrictions on women driving represented not only clear differential restriction on women but also limited their societal mobility in a society heavily dependent on their ability to travel to meet their economic needs.

The plight of al-Sharif and her deliberate deviance brought worldwide attention to the Saudi government's strict policies restricting the movement of women and the treatment of women overall. The attention has led to incremental changes in the Kingdom's laws and decrees concerning women. In 2017, women were allowed for the first time to attend sporting events, and in 2018, the restriction on women driving was finally lifted. Such changes would likely never have occurred if women such as al-Sharif were not willing to risk imprisonment or at least severe ostracism. Her insistence on driving represents how seemingly small acts of deviance may provoke much wider changes in a society.

Pussy Riot

One can also see women in good trouble throughout other parts of the world. Women have also found trouble, and international solidarity, through acts of defiance expressed through creative expression. In Russia, the musical group Pussy Riot found good trouble by performing guerrilla punk rock performances in public spaces. The music of Pussy Riot railed against Putin and the Russian Orthodox Church, drawing attention to the repression of civil liberties, the subjugation of LGBT people, and the marginalization of women in modern Russia.

The group gained international notoriety in 2012 when they held an unauthorized performance, a "punk prayer," in Moscow's Cathedral of Christ the Savior. The intent of the performance was to protest the collusion of the Russian Orthodox Church and the Putin government. Three members of Pussy Riot, Nadezhda Tolokonnikova, Maria Alyokhina, and Yekaterina Samutsevich, were subsequently arrested and put on trial for hooliganism and "religious hatred." Their trial brought worldwide attention, and they quickly became lionized around the world, if not at home. The three members were imprisoned, which served to advance their grievances against the Russian government.

> When we were jailed, Pussy Riot immediately became very popular and widely known, and it turned from just a group to essentially an international movement. Anybody can be Pussy Riot, you just need to put on a mask and stage an active protest of something in your particular country, wherever that may be, that you consider unjust. And we're not here as the leaders of Pussy Riot or determining what Pussy Riot is and what it does or what it says. We are just two individuals that spent two years in jail for taking part in a Pussy Riot protest action. (Kedmey, 2014).

To be clear, few Russians would describe Pussy Riot as heroes. In fact, many figures in Russia's opposition movement have dismissed the group's actions as pranks and attention-seeking antics. One opposition leader dismissed them as "silly girls" who should be granted mercy for no other reason than that they need to be with their children (Mackey & Kates, 2012). Prior to their trial, an oligarch who is currently in jail for his own opposition to the Russian government, referred to Pussy Riot's protests as ineffective "mistakes of youthful radicalism" (Khodorkovsky, 2012b).

The imprisoned women were released in 2013 ahead of the Olympics in Sochi, perhaps as a show of clemency before an international spotlight. Pussy Riot staged a protest during those games, where they were attacked by

Cossack militias as police passively looked on (Walker, 2014). While Pussy Riot is probably much more popular abroad than in their home country, their actions have brought awareness to the condition of women in Russia and raised to prominence questions about the treatment of LGBT citizens. While it is yet to be seen if Pussy Riot is on the edge of any permanent or lasting change in Russia, they offer a blueprint of a modern heresy in a comparative perspective. Whether Pussy Riot is constructed as a deviant creative movement or a major political force, they serve as another example of how women are challenging patriarchal norms.

Mormon Women in the Priesthood

The final example of contemporary women in good trouble is closer to my home state of Idaho, where close to a quarter of the population identify as Latter Day Saints (LDS). Those who subscribe to the Mormon religion understand it as not just a belief but a way of life. However, a uniquely modern heresy is brewing in that church: a small but growing movement of feminists are advocating that women be allowed into the priesthood. Kate Kelly, a Mormon feminist, founded the organization Ordain Women in 2013. The aim of the group is to promote "equality in faith" and to the right of women to serve the community as LDS priests.

Kelly's biography traces a path similar to that of the most devout Latter Day Saints, including a year and a half of missionary work and a degree from Brigham Young University. Yet she eschewed norms typical among Utah Mormons that encourage women to settle down and raise children (Dehlin, n.d.). Instead, she elected to become a human rights attorney, and she identifies as "childless by choice." Kelly adhered to her Mormon beliefs while identifying as a feminist—yet those two were unable to be reconciled. A modern-day heretic in every sense of the word, Kelly was reprimanded for her activism and asked to disaffiliate from Ordain Women. When she refused, the Mormon church excommunicated her in 2014 (Goodstein, 2017). Religion and feminism are clashing in other denominations that deny women access to the pulpit, including Roman Catholicism, and Kelly has continued her activism on behalf of women by claiming an unsanctioned ordination in the Catholic priesthood.

Equality and Good Trouble

Both abolitionism and the civil rights movement a century later provided a template and analogue for women's emancipation from suffrage through economic parity. As Kristof and WuDunn detail in their book *Half the Sky* (2009), slavery remains very much alive in the twenty-first century. The subjugation of women is especially evident across much of the developing world where women and girls are sold into sexual slavery, or indentured as domestic servants. Kristof and WuDunn note that the time is now ripe for a new, global emancipation movement for women and girls that incorporates elements of the civil rights and environmental movements (233–246). Ultimately, this revived movement could exert democratic pressures on countries where no such traditions exist.

Positively, Kristof and WuDunn praise the democratization of democratic movements. Where the civil rights and antiwar protests of prior generations were overwhelmingly male, women have now taken a lead role in civil sector initiatives. While still lagging in corporate and governmental sectors, women are leaders in NGOs and wide-ranging social movement organizations (both pro- and antifeminist). In essence, good trouble has undergone a gender equitization. The incorporation of women into other movements against oppression has made them, in effect, twice as powerful.

This chapter examined several cases of ill-behaved women making history, heretics who dared to question the taken-for-granted truth that women were inferior and should be held subordinate under the law. While women have long been marginalized from history and excluded from the intellectual classes, so many women, through good trouble, have assisted in altering the arch of history. Feminism, in the broadest sense, challenges the patriarchal practices that permeate all aspects of society including the family, economy, politics, and religion. Feminists and women founders of the social sciences demonstrate important insight into how normative and legal practices continue to subjugate women in the United States and elsewhere. Feminist sociology and criminology offer something of a blueprint for how good trouble can augment norms and laws that essentialize gender and deprive half the world's population of autonomy. The example of women's suffrage shows how prominent women, heroes of the women's movement, were heretics in their own day. The same may be said for women who practiced disobedience to assert the right of women to control their own bodies and decide when and with whom to have children. The deviant heroism practiced by these women can be found today in other causes for gender justice around the world. From here, we can see how women, along with other men, have been involved in subsequent causes for economic justice, peace, and the search for truth.

NOTES

1. The quote originally appeared in a 1976 scholarly paper by Ulrich about Puritan funeral services. The quote has since taken on a life of its own.

2. As was clearly demonstrated in chapters 3 and 4, the right of black men and women was systematically denied until the mid-1960s, despite the Fifteenth Amendment.

3. Despite the odium with which abortion providers are regarded by some, Dr. Willie Parker, the last abortion provider in Mississippi, says he is motivated to continue because of the compassion and love dictated by his strong Christian faith (Richardson, 2014). Such views

mark him as a heretic and outsider in an area where evangelism and Southern Baptist traditions dictate otherwise.

Chapter Six

The Agitators

Labor Trouble

From the early sit-down strikes of the 1930s to syndicalism—aimed at worker appropriation of the means of production—major movements to advance the rights of the poor, the wage laborer, and the unemployed have been accompanied by widespread and often collective deviance. In response to radical labor actions and unionization, government and business have often responded with virulence (and sometimes violence) while using legal means to slow the progress and reverse any gains that the poor and working classes may have won (Kimeldorf, 1999). This chapter considers the deviant agitation that found a choke point on capital to advance the interests of the wage laborer and the poor. These outsiders and agitators questioned the tough, sometimes inhuman working conditions of those who toil in fields, factories, and offices for a living; they worked for the betterment of those who have little more to sell than their labor and creative energies. Pursuing these goals by making good trouble brought social control down upon them—arrests, trials, occasionally violence, even death.

In the shared efforts to improve the plight of the poor and working people, many deviant heroes have been women or members of racial and ethnic minorities; when these and other oppressed groups join the struggle, the longstanding fight for dignity and economic security is catalyzed. In fact, when Martin Luther King was assassinated in Memphis, he was advocating for sanitation workers, who were on strike there for fair pay and safer working conditions (Honey, 2007). Many feminist heroes, such as Mother Jones and Emma Goldman, are deviant heroes of the labor movement as well. Legal structures and normative codes create overlapping and interreliant systems of disadvantage based on gender and class—a phenomenon described by the concept of *intersectionality*,[1] which enables deeper discernment of the dynamic social processes that underlie good trouble.

To fully consider the outsiders who agitated on behalf of the cause of labor, it is useful to look at how laws and social control have typically been used to intervene on behalf of monied interests. Thus, a Marxian analysis of matters of crime and justice will first help to frame the concept that good trouble advances the cause of the worker. Second, labor trouble will be conceptualized as a form of agitation that challenges economic injustices entrenched in a normative and legal system in mid- and late-stage capitalist societies. Finally, this chapter will profile several labor heroes, showing how their "crimes" and positive deviance facilitated the gains of workers in the early and mid-twentieth century.

WAGES, LABOR, CAPITAL . . . AND TROUBLE

The labor rights movement used many of the same tools that the deviant heroes of the civil rights movement used to counter the racist laws of the Jim Crow era—protest, confrontation, organizing, and deviant action. It relied on the same process of agitation Du Bois described in several essays in the journal *Crisis* (Du Bois, 1959). In one of these essays Du Bois states that "Agitation is a necessary evil to tell of the ills of the Suffering" (73). He calls on disruption to be a necessary outcome in the face of inequality and injustice. In a second essay, "The Value of Agitation," Du Bois analogizes it to pain. "Pain is not good but Pain is necessary. Pain does not aggravate disease—Disease causes Pain." Concluding that, "Agitation does not mean Aggravation—Aggravation calls for Agitation in order that Remedy may be found" (ibid.). From Du Bois's perspective, agitation is a useful tool in instigating much-needed reforms or even revolution. "If we remember all of the great reform movements, we remember that they have been preceded by agitation." From the perspective of Du Bois, good trouble is an act of agitation that brings attention to urgent issues. The deviant hero embraces the ethos of agitation by challenging unjust rules, disquieting those who may be inclined to passively accept a status quo.

The agitator may also be a type of outsider. Howard Becker (1963), in his seminal book *Outsiders: Studies in the Sociology of Deviance*, describes the role of the deviant as well as the role of those involved in the production and enforcement of normative codes. Sociologists define roles as a way of describing social positioning or status without mentioning specific individuals. To use a theatrical metaphor, just as different actors may play the same character, roles are key social occupations that remain relatively stable regardless of the personality in that position. For Becker, *outsiders* are those who do not accept the rules that they are being judged by; they may also doubt the competency or legitimacy of those in the role of judging. In contrast, *rule enforcers* impose the rules the collective has established. Rule enforcers do not typically care about the content of these rules or in making sure there is no rule violation at all. Instead, they are more concerned with establishing their legitimacy and having their authority respected by the public. The last role is fulfilled by *moral entrepreneurs* who are involved in a public and iterative process of finding problems and proposing solutions through changing the rules. Moral entrepreneurs stoke widespread movements and typically are thought the instigators of moral panics, which aim to stoke a mass movement in reaction to a perceived threat or interest (Goode, 2015). While moral entrepreneurs are thought of as those who instigate or profit from moral panics, in direct antithesis to the deviant hero, anyone involved in the active process of maintaining or changing norms may be considered a moral entrepreneur.

Given Becker's description of these roles, the "deviant hero" may be an astute addendum to his timeless portrayal of crime and deviance in society. Like moral entrepreneurs, deviant heroes may pursue the removal or establishment of a norm, but unlike moral entrepreneurs, deviant heroes agitate by working as *outsiders* to this system. As such, deviant heroism does not rely on generating moral panics that moral entrepreneurship is reliant on; rather good trouble seeks to establish a new moral framework through actively defying and questioning existing laws and norms. Good trouble is an attempt to renegotiate social conventions that are no longer in lockstep with changing social realities.

Live Nude Girls United

For years in my social deviance class, I showed a documentary film entitled *Live Nude Girls United* (Funari & Query, 2000) to illustrate deviance, work, and intersectionality. I stopped showing feature-length films in my classes long ago as they made for better optional "homework" in a flipped classroom environment, but I kept this one out of retirement because it was provocative and generated lively discussion (despite occasional complaints about nudity). The documentary chronicled the efforts of women at a San Francisco peep show to form a union. Sex workers stripped inside of a mirrored room while clients pumped quarters into a slot to keep a panel open. The maximum pay for doing this was about $20 an hour. The women organized and petitioned for union recognition. At issue were wages, hours, and working conditions but also the peep-show workers' objections to the scheduling of work shifts based on race and body type. At its core, the film was about a labor struggle among wage earners who are often not thought of as workers at all. It also engaged in the feminist debate surrounding sex work and the treatment of women. In short, the film highlights the intersectionality of women, sexuality, work, and an occupation deemed deviant.

The filmmaker, Julia Query, a graduate-school dropout, also worked as a dominatrix. The daughter of a nationally known physician and public health advocate, Query placed herself at the center of the story of how she and her coworkers, in seeking a labor contract, had to contend with a management hostile to organizing and a public sentiment that saw their work as both illegitimate and immoral. To achieve their goals, the Exotic Dancers Union engaged in picketing and staged a walkout. In response, their employer locked workers out of the peep show and fired one agitator.

Despite the perceived salaciousness of the workers' occupation, the contentious struggle between workers and management was a classic labor dispute. Sex work is best understood when removed from moralizing and understood as what it is—work.

Crime and Good Trouble in the Marxian Perspective

The working classes have long been an object of suspicion by powerful interests. Bottom-up social movements among the poor and working classes are typically met, at least initially, with a suppressive government response (for example, see Lukas, 1997). This seems especially true for the disenfranchised. Piven and Cloward (1977) note that poor people's movements are initially met with official resistance, followed by negotiation and resolution, and (often) a later backlash. Minimum wage, overtime, occupational safety, the right to organize, healthcare, unemployment insurance, and programs for the elderly and needy all sound like policy problems for a Washington insider. However, many of the laws that protect wage laborers were the result of radical agitation, of behaviors that were considered deviant, if not criminal.

Among these deviants are intellectuals who question the accepted ways that power is concentrated and resources are distributed. Intellectuals propose new and often controversial ideas that may be dismissed by critics and chided by peers; they are declared heretics by clergy and, in some cases, are arrested by authorities. Karl Marx is one such intellectual. Marx offered a scathing assessment of capitalism, which to his followers exposed the theft inherent in a system based on exploitation and effectively lifted the veil on the means the ruling class used to preserve its ill-begotten wealth. To Marx's critics, and there are many, both in and out of the academy, his ideas are foolish at best and seditious at worst (Fischer & Marek, 1996). To his followers, Marx's ideas were prescient.

Marx's main concerns were the capitalist economic system and the revolutionary potential of the working class. He did not directly study matters of crime and deviance beyond looking at those mechanisms used to ensure the control by the political and economic system of the laboring classes. Nevertheless, his analysis can lend crucial insight into matters of crime and justice and provides another lens through which to evaluate good trouble.

Indeed, in the academy, Marxian analysis serves as a regular standby critique of how law-breaking is regarded among the economically disadvantaged in a capitalist society. From a Marxian perspective, criminal laws unduly target the least powerful classes, while programs of incarceration are maintained at public expense to house a reserve army of labor—workers left idle by a wage-labor system dependent on unemployment—as a check on rising wages (Reiman and Leighton 2015, 134–36). Criminal justice serves a dual purpose from this perspective, servicing a system reliant on exploitation as well as maintaining inequality.

According to Marxian analysis, criminal laws defend the property and status of the capitalist class. At the same time, legal institutions assert direct control over the working classes through the threat of state sanction (Norrie, 1982). Criminal justice also serves an ideological function by defining what is and is not acceptable from the point of view of the ruling class (Reiman and Leighton 2015, 155–57). For example, under a pure capitalist system, the law may allow industrial hazards and environmental risks, while prohibiting strikes and direct actions by workers to remedy these risks. Similarly, public-order laws against vagrancy, homelessness, theft, and trespassing are singularly directed at the poor, while the well-off are free to do as they please so long as they do not impede other capitalists. Thus, the ideology of the dominant class effectively defines criminals as those who occupy the lower strata of society.

For Marx, capitalism exists within a system of exploitation and forced labor (Marx, 1889). Individualism and choice are mere illusions, manufactured by a social reality that above all promotes the needs of capital. The economic base of any society determines its social relationships and the nature of all its other institutions. The emergence of capitalism produces social relationships of exploitation—the exploitation of workers by the bourgeoisie (Tucker, 1989). Capitalism, in effect, transforms the worker into a mere commodity, something to be bought and sold for its use value, the worker's labor power. Because owners are free to maximize their wealth with minimal investment in workers, capitalism fosters innovation, but the relationships fostered under the capitalist mode of production result in alienation for the proletariat. This occurs because the workers do not own the commodities they are producing, have no say in the production process, and are forced into competition with other workers to work for the lowest subsistence wage (in Tucker, 1989; 70–75). This exploitive and alienating economic relationship forms what Marx called the superstructure of society; within this superstructure, other social institutions spring up to reflect the ideals of the dominant classes and service the needs of capital.

From this point of view, laws and the criminal justice system serve the capitalist class at public expense by focusing the social control apparatus entirely on the working classes. Anyone who challenges this arrangement through deviant agitation may be subject to social control. Suppression of deviant heroes reinforces a hegemony in which laws are fixed and "natural" and challenging them criminal.

Paul Leighton and Jeffery Reiman, in their mainstay text of critical criminology, *The Rich Get Richer and the Poor Get Prison* (2015), explain that, in a capitalist system, criminal justice functions not as a system of security but as an instrument of reinforcing the prevailing ideology. The construction of crime obscures both how people think of crime and who people think of as criminal. The criminal justice system, in effect, minimizes dangers posed by the capitalist class and exaggerates the threats posed by lower classes.

> Criminal justice plays an ideological role in support of capitalism because people do not recognize that the principles governing criminal justice are reflections of capitalism. The principles of criminal justice appear instead to be the result of pure reason, and thus a system that supports capitalism is (mistakenly) seen as an expression of rationality itself! (2015, 219)

Crime is accepted as an objective reality, and the treatment and processing of those deemed criminal seem rational. Under the Marxian perspective, the law represents an *idealized* norm that affirms the material requirements of an economic mode of production (Reiman & Leighton, 2015, 228). The law gives the capitalist the right to own factories and exploit labor, it grants corporations personhood, and it intervenes on behalf of property, which, for a Marxist, was stolen in the first place. As Quinney (1970). demonstrated in his classical work on crime and class relations in capitalist society, crime is defined by the power structure. This is what Quinney called the "social reality of crime." The label of "crime" is used not to label the actions that cause the most serious damage and have the most negative consequences but is reserved primarily for the actions of the poor and racial minorities.

However, despite its "natural" and "rational" appearance, for a Marxist the law under a capitalist mode of production is not static. The agency of the working class may pose a cycle of successive challenges to this system. Marx saw this happening in the form of mass movements initiated by the oppressed and, ironically, united by the socializing process of the mode of production.

> Along with the constantly diminishing number of the magnates of capital, who usurp and monopolize all advantages of this process of transformation, grows the mass of misery, oppression, slavery, degradation, exploitation; but with this too grows the revolt of the working class, a class always increasing in numbers, and disciplined, united, organized by the very mechanism of the process of capitalist production itself. The monopoly of capital becomes a

fetter upon the mode of production, which has sprung up and flourished along with, and under it. Centralization of the means of production and socialization of labour at last reach a point where they become incompatible with their capitalist integument. This integument is burst asunder. The knell of capitalist private property sounds. The expropriators are expropriated. (in Tucker, 1989, 438).

Marxists saw that through the agency of the working classes, there could arise a transformational challenge to the status quo (McCarthy & Zald, 1977). The collective efforts of the working class, united by the very relations of production that oppress them, could reorganize those relations and bring about social change. It follows that deviance, or crime, in the form of good trouble could foster this transformation by challenging the normative dimensions in which the social relations are embedded under capitalism. This form of deviant heroism would be a direct affront to an economic arrangement in which the law affirms the right of a small number of people to monopolize the production of a society's wealth.

HEROES OF THE LABOR MOVEMENT

Given the Marxian perspective on law and social change, it is now possible to understand how both groups and individuals have challenged the normative framework created under a division of labor based on exploitation. Just as the "deviant" movement for civil rights in the United States required challenging racist normative contexts, other movements have been stoked by individuals in good trouble who act as agitators to challenge normative contexts and change history. The struggle of workers and the economically disadvantaged is another venue that demonstrates the transformational power of deviant heroism. Working-class movements, especially the radicalized wing of the labor movement of the early to mid-twentieth century, produced especially compelling (and controversial) deviant heroes and a defiant rank and file who challenged both their bosses and their unions. The movement for a shorter working day, safer working conditions, a minimum wage, and fair treatment by employers has typically been met with hostility from capital (Kimeldorf, 1999). From the Industrial Revolution to the present, private armies, militias, Pinkertons,[2] police, prosecutors, and judges have been deployed to thwart concerted efforts to challenge the dominance of bosses in the factory and fields.

Many of those who found trouble to advance the interests of labor have been subjected to formal social control under the auspices of trumped-up or flimsy charges. Since the beginning of mass labor mobilizations, workers and labor leaders have been subject to official harassment from both employers and police. This was first apparent during the Haymarket Square rally that started in Chicago on May 1, 1886. A mass mobilization of workers who demanded an eight-hour workday (Foner, 1986) turned into a strike that lasted four days, drawing a large police response. On the fourth day, an unknown person threw a bomb into the middle of a skirmish, killing both police and strikers. This led to the police firing on the crowd, effectively sealing a violent end to the demonstration. Eight anarchists were convicted on what historians regard as flimsy evidence of conspiracy related to the bombing (Messer-Kruse, 2011). Many believe Pinkertons were the ones to blame (Messer-Kruse, 2011). The incident, which underscored the tension between the incessant agitation of the labor movement and the suppressive conformity of capital, is remembered by many as the birth of the labor movement in the United States. Some of the heroes of this movement are considered next.

Eugene Debs

An important outsider and agitator on behalf of the American labor movement, Eugene Debs was a socialist, pacifist, and five-time presidential candidate who aimed to bring social democracy into the mainstream (Zinn, 2005, 340). Debs was an advocate of better wages, equality among all workers, and social justice. He was jailed several times for his labor activism and later incarcerated for ten years for his opposition to World War I and the draft. In fact, he ran one of his presidential campaigns on the socialist party ticket from prison (Ginger, 1949).

There were no obvious signs of good trouble in Debs's early life. His father was from a well-off family, and Debs went to work after dropping out of school, mostly on the railroads. His early views were that labor and management could exist in harmony as long as mutual respect was assured (Ginger, 1949). However, his views started to change when he began to feel that trade unions were not fighting in the interests of the working class. He participated in successive strikes in the 1880s and 1890s. During the Pullman railroad strikes of 1894, he was arrested for violating a court injunction. The railroads carried U.S. mail, and disrupting that service was a federal offense. Debs spent six months in jail, where he encountered the writings of Karl Marx. After a succession of life experiences that intersected with key moments in labor history and exposure to ideas of radical unionism, Debs became a socialist, wanting to instigate far-reaching change in the social structure of the United States.

Considered a radical, Debs and outlaw unions such as the Industrial Workers of the World (IWW) laid the groundwork for rights and protections for workers, such as a minimum wage, overtime pay, better working conditions, social security, and the right to organize. The good trouble sought by Debs and others gave wage laborers a share of the American Dream. However, over time, working people began to think of these protections as normal, or as generous gifts from management, until many of them were removed or weakened in the twenty-first century.

Besides his labor activism, Debs was a staunch critic of the way the criminal justice system treats the condemned. He linked the plight of convicts to the overall treatment of the working classes by capital. Echoing a Marxian analysis of the wage-labor-capital system, Debs argued that low wages caused business panics, since workers were not paid enough to buy back the goods they produced. In turn, these panics and resulting unemployment caused crime, as men were driven to it to support their families. At the same time, the poverty of the working classes benefited capital by depressing wages and keeping a ready supply of exploitable labor. Arguing that "industry has not been impoverished by prison labor, but prison labor is the result of impoverished industry," Debs asserted that the exploitation of labor and treatment of the impoverished were crimes against humanity (in Ginger, 1949, 197).

Debs's book *Walls and Bars* (1927), part memoir and part social critique, contains a collection of reflective essays and columns criticizing the prison system. Much of the book reads like a timely assessment of the current practices of criminal justice in the United States. In an early section recounting his own experiences as an inmate, Debs contends that prisons are "incubators of crime," advancing an analysis strikingly similar to the theory of differential association. He asks readers to consider a boy convicted of a first offense and taken to prison. From his own vantage point as an inmate, he ponders what it must be like for the boy to go from being convicted of a petty crime and thrown in with hardened criminals. Debs describes the "degenerating process" that scars the prison neophyte, tearing down his humanity (Debs, 1927, 38–39), writing that "he is schooled in nameless forms of perversion of body, mind, and soul that cause human beings to sink to abysmal depths of depravity which the lower animals do not know" (Debs, 1927, 51). From there, the convict develops a new mental orientation and language, one that rationalizes and neutralizes his position. Differentially associating with others in the prison solidifies that mind-set. He is then returned to society, hardened and perfected as a labeled criminal. He reoffends. Though not as sophisticated as contemporary criminological critiques of the modern prison system, this insight aligns with current research identifying prisons as being, by design, criminogenic.

Like many heroes of the labor movement, Debs's sacrifices for and contributions to the labor movement are scrubbed from most history texts given to children. Few know about his opposition to war and his status as a political prisoner. Though his status as a hero has never been officially acknowledged (confirming the adage that history is written by the victors), his contributions are impossible to ignore. Comparing Debs to other deviant heroes, Ginger writes:

> Like his own personal hero John Brown of Harper's Ferry, Debs' life and purpose fit awkwardly into respectable historical pantheons or narratives of national progress. Yet Debs, the ghost of that other, radical America, refuses to go away. Whether as the leader of the Pullman strikers in 1894, as a founder of the Industrial Workers of the World in 1905, as the Socialist presidential candidate in 1912, or as Woodrow Wilson's most famous political prisoner in 1920, he loomed too large in contemporary history to be easily expunged by the condescension of an ignorant or hostile posterity (Ginger, 1949, xi).

Debs remained true to the principles of deviant heroism enshrined by those who came before him. At his trial for violating the Sedition Act in speaking out against the draft and World War I, he exclaimed to the court that "while there is a lower class, I am in it, and while there is a criminal element, I am of it, and while there is a soul in prison, I am not free" (1918). Through the indictment of unequal justice and the social divisions reflective in the court system, Debs inspired others to question the taken-for-granted character of law and justice.

Albert and Lucy Parsons

The militancy of the IWW generated the most good trouble of any other wing of the American Labor Movement. The philosophy of the IWW was to shun the conservatism present in craft unionism while promoting the class-based concept of "one big union" to prevent scabbing, strike breaks, and employer tactics used to buy off dissent. To advance this cause, the IWW used tactics that were outside the law, including sit-down strikes, general strikes, free speech programs, and other forms of direct action. In some cases, members openly advocated sabotage. The movement was quickly dubbed un-American and drew surveillance and interference from both the state and employers.

Despite being marginalized and vilified, the IWW also produced the most memorable heroes and leaders of that era. In that era, newspapers held enormous power and regularly stirred up popular fears through stories about militant immigrants (Green, 2006). One of those convicted and hung (also on scant evidence) for the alleged Haymarket bombing plot was a southerner and former Confederate soldier named Albert Parsons, who found much trouble during his short life (Green, 2006; Parsons & Parsons, 1889). The husband of Lucy Parsons, a founder of the IWW, Albert was publisher and editor of socialist and anarchist periodicals. Lucy Parsons deserves special consideration for her activism in the labor movement and her status as a woman of color agitating in a movement dominated by white men. The IWW heavily promoted the use of direct action, like sit-down strikes, to advance the interests of wage laborers. Lucy Parsons was routinely arrested by the Chicago police for distributing flyers and pamphlets promoting the cause of the nascent labor movement and her anarcho-syndicalist ideas. Her revolutionary viewpoints stoked agitation and led the Chicago police to call her "more dangerous than a thousand rioters" (Parsons & Parsons, 1889). After Albert's sentencing, she began a nationwide appeal for his clemency, though she was regularly confronted and barred entry into meeting halls by local police (IWW, n.d.).

After Albert's execution, she lived in poverty, devoting herself to the anarchist cause and to organizing and securing amnesty for workers. Lucy was unrelenting in her opposition to capital, and led poor women to confront it. She was more than simply an agitator for radical unionism. She was also a steadfast advocate of free speech and challenged racism in the court system.

The daughter of a slave who married a Civil War veteran, she identified herself as an anarchist, communist, and socialist at different times in her life. Although she is remembered as a founder of the labor movement, her biography intersects with other social issues in important ways: she was organizing at a time when women did not have the right to vote. Biracial, she was married to a white person when miscegenation laws were fully enforced. And she consistently voiced viewpoints that were considered subversive and un-American. As with many deviant heroes, it is difficult to categorize someone like Lucy Parsons.

Elizabeth Gurly Flynn

The model of direct action favored by militant unionism necessarily brought forces of social control on those involved in syndicalist labor actions. This was especially apparent in the labor struggles in the western United States, where groups like the Western Federation of Miners combined with the spirit of the lawless West to create a unique kind of confrontational unionism. This ethos is personified in the biographies of Wobblies (as IWW members were called) like Elizabeth Gurly Flynn, who clashed with both police and her union. Arrested at least ten times, with no convictions, Flynn's contributions to the advancement of workers' rights and free speech and the advancement of the status of women at the turn of the twentieth century personifies the multiple fronts good trouble can affect. Like Lucy Parsons, Flynn agitated on behalf of labor but found good trouble in the fight for civil liberties and free speech.

Flynn came to prominence during the Spokane free speech fights of 1909, as the IWW mounted a display of civil disobedience in defiance of a city ordinance banning speaking on the streets (Camp, 1995). The ordinance was aimed specifically at IWW organizing. At issue was employers' use of job brokers to provide workers for mines, logging camps, and construction crews. Brokers charged workers for each job referral, and the employer would dismiss the worker after a day or two. This led to a mass of laid-off workers in Spokane, who began protesting about brokers as well as wages and working conditions. Aggravated workers, speaking from a soapbox, would arouse the rest of the unemployed. The soapboxing issue became such a problem that the job brokers persuaded the Spokane City Council to pass the speech ordinance prohibiting speaking in public.

In response to the ordinance in November 1909, Wobblies put up a soapbox and workers began to stand and speak. One by one, each speaker was arrested and put in jail. By one account, it got to the point where someone would stand up and say, "Fellow workers . . ." and then wonder where the cop was if they were not arrested (Flynn, 1955). By the end of the day, 103 people were arrested and over 500 by the end of the month. The jail was overfilled. The War Department became involved in assisting in the enforcement of the ordinance against free speech. Flynn's biography recounts impassioned speeches about abuses of power and the mistreatment of workers. Speaking in defiance of the speech ordinance, she was able to delay her arrest by chaining herself to a lamppost. The direct-action problem became so bad, the city eventually relented and allowed public speaking, a victory for the Wobblies of the IWW.

The Flint Sit-Down Strike

Three decades later, the firebrand ethos of the Spokane free speech fight was evident in other collective acts of good trouble in the labor movement. Perhaps the most remembered and effective of these was the Flint, Michigan, sit-down strike. During the height of the Great Depression, autoworkers physically occupied a General Motors plant, demanding recognition of the United Auto Workers. Opposed to a conventional picket line, workers favored the tactic of occupation because it prevented strikebreakers from taking over production. However, it was also illegal and drew an armed response by police and a string of court injunctions (Fine, 1969). But the autoworkers persisted, and the strike was resolved with recognition of the union. The sit-down strike also led to legislation that protected the right to associate and organize into a union and to greater protections for workers.

The Flint strike was a prelude to other conflicts over free speech and became a model of direct action during free speech struggles like those in Berkeley, California in the 1960s. In these strikes—Spokane, Flint, and Berkeley—each action broke the law and drew forces of social control. The organizers all faced scorn and ridicule, but each case helped to change the collective moral framework, moving it toward the understanding that free speech and association are fundamental rights and freedoms. Like any other rights, the boundaries are regularly tested and oscillate over time. These early agitators of the labor movement are either forgotten or still vilified, but they made a lasting impact on preserving and expanding our civil liberties.

Joe Hill

Besides Debs, Parsons, and Flynn, other activists in the labor movement reached folk-hero status with the rank and file. For example, Big Bill Haywood, a labor leader and advocate of industrial unionism, was hounded by prosecutors during most of his time as a union leader. His trial and acquittal were superbly told in John Anthony Lukas's *Big Trouble* (1997), which superbly documents the western labor and mine wars that surrounded the assassination of Idaho governor Sternberg. Haywood was tried and ultimately acquitted of the murder. The book links dozens of other agitators organizing on behalf of the immigrants and working classes who were shaping the West. For instance, Joe Hill was an immigrant from Sweden who spent most of his hard life as an errant laborer doing odd jobs in New York and out West. According to his biography, *The Man Who Never Died* (Adler, 2012), Hill had a harsh life, like many immigrants, who were treated as mere appendages of the factory machine. Like other proletarianized immigrants, he became involved in a brutal and violent class war. In the United States, Hill became a union agitator, was blacklisted from working in many shops, and was arrested for being "too active" in a San Pedro, California, dockworkers strike (AFL-CIO, n.d.-a). Hill wrote songs that bit at the elite, the wealthy, and the church and extolled the virtue of the good trouble sought by agitators and the rank and file of the labor movement (Zinn 2005, 334). His song "Rebel Girl" was a tribute to Flynn and the women who struck at the textile mills in Lawrence.

Hill was charged with murdering a storekeeper in Salt Lake City. Despite sloppy evidence, the prosecutor cited Hill's membership in the IWW as putative evidence to confirm his guilt. He was convicted and sentenced to death, sparking cries for amnesty. The governor of Utah refused a commutation, and he was executed by firing squad on November 19, 1915. In a final message to IWW General Secretary Bill Haywood, Hill urged, "Don't waste any time in mourning—organize." A testament to the injustice of the death penalty and the perpetual struggle against inequality, Hill was immortalized in poetry and fiction, and in this now-famous song about him written by British-born writer and poet Alfred Hayes: "The Copper Bosses killed you Joe, / They shot you Joe" says I. / "Takes more than guns to kill a man" / Says Joe "I didn't die" (Hays, 1936, first verse). Despite a biography, *The Man Who Never Died,* by William Adler, much of Hill's life remains obscure and undocumented; one thing is certain—in death, he became more famous than he was in life. His folk songs appeared in IWW publications and are still sung by members of the AFL-CIO. His work inspired artists such as Woody Guthrie, Johnny Cash, and Bruce Springsteen, all of whom produced "outlaw" songs about the hardships of working as a wage laborer.

Mother Jones

Perhaps the most virtuous of the deviant heroes of the labor movement was Mother Jones. She was also controversial, and was dubbed the most "dangerous woman in America." Born Mary Harris Jones in Dublin, Ireland, she emigrated to the United States, where she endured a personal life of tragedy and suffering. After she lost her husband and four children to the 1867 yellow-fever epidemic in Memphis, she moved to Chicago to work as a dressmaker, where her interest in the union movement was stoked and seeing the contrast between the wealthy and working poor radicalized her (AFL-CIO, n.d.-b). After losing everything in the Great Chicago Fire, she began to travel the country to agitate for the cause of working people.

Jones's biography intersects with the rapid transformation of the United States into an industrial economy. A powerful orator who addressed workers in union halls and coal fields, Jones was adored by those for whom she advocated. She called the miners of all ages her "boys," and they called her "Mother." The name stuck. She traveled the country, going anywhere workers were striking—steelworkers in Pittsburgh, child laborers in Philadelphia, coal miners in West Virginia. Mother Jones was at Ludlow, Colorado, when striking miners were massacred by national guardsmen. Folk singer Utah Phillips recounts the story:

> Mother Jones wasn't an organizer; she was an agitator. Which meant often enough she was hated as much by the organizers as by the bosses. One time Mother Jones was out in Colorado at the great Ludlow strike. Now that was a strike to enforce the eight-hour day, which the state of Colorado had made a law; but they couldn't enforce it, cause Rockefeller owned the militia. Now, the governor promised not to send the militia into the coal fields, but he lied, and he did. Mother Jones was in the union hall down there at Ludlow and word came that the militia had entered the coal fields. Well, she leapt up and she screamed, "Let's go get the sons of bitches!" and she stormed out. She didn't look to see if anybody was following her." (in Woot, 2011)

The slaughter of workers and their families undoubtedly stoked her already fierce and feisty attitude. She also attracted Pinkertons, police, and prosecutors. Mother Jones was denounced on the floor of the House of Representatives. According to legend, a U.S. attorney named her the "most dangerous woman in America" (Gorn, 2015). That is some kind of good trouble.

Jones's autobiography recounts her multiple run-ins with the law and other agents of social control. In 1902, she was meeting with miners about the possibility of a strike in Clarksburg, West Virginia. An injunction was filed in federal courts against her and any miners speaking out against the company. A marshal came to the meeting to tell her about the injunction gag. Jones spoke anyway, addressing her "boys." Looking at the marshal she said,

> Goodbye, boys; I'm under arrest. I may have to go to jail. I may not see you for a long time. Keep up the fight! Don't surrender! Pay no attention to the injunction machine at Parkersburg. The Federal judge is a scab anyhow. While you starve he plays golf. While you serve humanity, he serves injunctions for the money powers. (in Shetterly, 2009:18)

Jones was promptly arrested. Before the judge, the prosecutor reiterated her status as the "most dangerous woman in America." According to Jones's biography, the judge was appointed, at the behest of the mining companies, to take the seat that his father had (Jones, 1925). In her testimony, she confirmed to the judge that she had called him a "scab" because he had taken his father's appointment to a federal bench (Woot, 2011). She said she was only talking about the constitutional rights to "life and liberty." According to Jones, she and several of her compatriots were released without further inquiry. Jones continued to find good trouble for three more decades, where she endured other criminal and civil court proceedings, including a slander and libel case brought against her by a major publisher.

César Chavez

While radical unionism won some protections for workers in mining and manufacturing, those who toiled in the fields were exempted from the hard-wrought gains of the labor movement. Migrant farm workers, especially from Mexico, faced deplorable working conditions that included long hours, wage theft, and workplace and environmental hazards. Racism also played a role in impeding the progress of the migrant farm worker. César Chavez, the founder of the United Farm Workers (UFW) union, emerged as one of the principal heroes of the cause of the migrant farmworker. The UFW addressed the working conditions of migrant laborers in the fields of the western United States. His heroic activism won victories for farm workers that included worker protections and the right to organize. In the 1980s he began to champion bans on pesticides that exposed farm workers to unknown hazards.

Today, streets and schools are named after Chavez. Chavez has been on postage stamps, his birthday is a state holiday in Colorado, California, and Texas, and he was posthumously awarded the Presidential Medal of Freedom in 1994. His rallying cry *"Si, se puede,"* first coined by UFW cofounder and longtime organizer Delores Huerte, evoking the spirit of mass mobilization for justice, was adopted by Barack Obama during his 2008 presidential campaign. Huerte explained in an NPR interview, "They had passed a law in

Arizona that if you said, 'boycott,' you could go to prison for six months. And if you said 'strike,' you could go to prison. So we were trying to organize against that law" (Godoy, 2017). Both Huerte and Chavez faced violent opposition for their work on behalf of farmworkers, but Huerte was "double deviant" because she was organizing as a woman in a world of machismo. Today both are recognized as a hero, but Huerte is overshadowed by Chavez.

Both were heroes and they were also deviant, and while persistence and dedication secured recognition of farmworkers, it was deviance that forced their hard-won gains. Like many activists of the sixties and seventies, Chavez was under FBI surveillance for a "possibly subversive background" (FBI 1996, 8). His biography features run-ins with growers, courts, and rival unions like the Teamsters, who opposed his movement and tactics (Levy & Chavez, 1975). In 1970, Chavez spent twenty days in jail for leading pickets against a major grower in California. Martin Luther King's widow, Coretta Scott King, visited Chavez in jail and declared that he was in prison because his organization of the working poor threatened the well-off. Coretta declared in her public remarks, "Social progress has always come when the people on the bottom, who in organized strength and from the foundation shook the whole structure."[3] The State Supreme Court ordered Chavez's release on Christmas Eve.

Chavez was born on a homestead that his family later lost during the Great Depression. Beginning at age ten, he worked as a migrant farm worker through the southwestern United States. Like King, Chavez embraced the principles of nonviolence in bringing to attention the plight of migrant farm workers in the Southwest. He was first arrested in 1946 for sitting in the "whites only" section of a movie theater. He recounts that he was politicized through personal experiences as a Mexican American farm worker and through writings and speeches that okayed the use of deviance to advance the cause of justice. According to his autobiography, Chavez's beliefs were forged through the blending of two seemingly divergent philosophies: radical labor organizing, grounded in the philosophy of the IWW, and a spiritual ethos rooted in Catholicism that paired with elements of the liberation theology embraced from the margins of Catholic clergy in Latin America (Levy & Chavez, 1975, 56–91). In the 1950s he came under the tutelage of Saul Alinsky, who had organized the Community Service Organization to facilitate engagement between citizens and government. In addition to Alinsky, Chavez absorbed the teachings of Gandhi and taking firm cues from Martin Luther King, fashioned the farmworkers movement in the spirit of the civil rights movement.

Agitation in the Post-Industrial Era

This chapter explored the working-class heroes of the American labor movement. Like the deviant heroes of the civil rights movement, a great degree of social control was exerted on those who contested the laws that sanctioned exploitation and enabled capital accumulation. The Marxian analysis of crime and the role of capital in defining criminality provides another lens through which to view the taken-for-granted character of the law. Marxism itself, as a nonconformist theoretical orientation, has been subject to much critique and even ridicule (Fischer & Marek, 1996). While Marxism remains a cogent critique into the interworkings of capitalist societies, classical Marxian analysis does not throw much light on the inner workings of criminal justice systems. While Marxism may not provide a detailed picture of the criminogenic aspects of a social system, it does provide grounds to interrogate normative frameworks and is therefore able to sow seeds of change in existing social orders. Indeed, important social changes in the fabric of Western democracies have originated with the activism of marginalized, impoverished people from the lower rungs of the social stratum—Marx's proletariat.

Many individual deviants, early heroes of the American labor movement, were labeled as criminals and provoked harsh mechanisms of social control, including even execution. However, their efforts resulted in programs for the poor, worker protections, and important changes to the legal system. Joe Hill, Mother Jones, and Eugene V. Debs all achieved (deviant) folk-hero status in the American labor movement, but as they would be the first to tell, it was the willingness and sacrifice of the rank and file that achieved the hard-won gains. The Flint sit-down strike was a raucous example of collective good trouble in the labor movement. The Spokane free speech fight demonstrated the power of collective noncompliance As labor scholar Howard Kimmeldorf (1999) notes, it was the willingness to resist, often in the face of violent incursions by law enforcement and private militias, that led to the most significant gains. The deviant tactics of these actions were perfected by subsequent movements for civil rights and women's equality.

Echoes of the agitative trouble of the labor movement can be found today. In March 2018, teachers in West Virginia, the state where Mother Jones gave her rousing speeches to miners, went on strike for eight days over low wages. Like many strikes in the past, this one was declared unlawful by the state attorney general, who asserted that public employees had no right to strike against the government. Despite threats of dismissal, the teachers persisted, closed down every public school in the state, and won all their demands. Similar teacher strikes followed in in Kentucky and Oklahoma, the home state of Woody Guthrie. His songs lament the legal inequities under a system of private property. For instance, in his famous "This is Your Land" he said "As I went walking, I saw a sign there / And on the sign it said 'No Trespassing.' / But on the other side it didn't say nothing." He also praised the good trouble of the rank and file who were intimidated by the law and hired security. "There once was a union maid, she never was afraid / Of goons and ginks and company finks and the deputy sheriffs who made the raid. . . . She always stood her ground" (Guthrie, 1940).

This chapter examined the various agitators who challenged the economic inequalities fostered under exploitive economic systems. This also delved into intellectuals and leaders who questioned a legal system suspended under a capitalist mode of production. From here, we can look at those who got into good trouble by exposing truths like Marx or lampooning them through creative expression, as Woody Guthrie did. With an understanding of how good trouble exposes and remedies inequalities on the basis of race, gender, and now class, the book moves from agitators to truth-tellers.

NOTES

1. Intersectionality is a sociological framework that investigates the ways that class, race, sexual orientation, age, disability, gender, and other forms of stratification that most affect the marginalized are interwoven.

2. Pinkertons were a private detective agency who were regularly hired by employers to infiltrate and undermine labor unions.

3. The full speech was published in *El Malcriado*, a newsletter of the United Farm Workers' Organizing Committee, on January 15, 1971.

Chapter Seven

Truth-Tellers

The previous four chapters showed how good trouble confronts social inequalities as they relate to areas such as race, gender, and class. This chapter examines deviant heroes who have catalyzed the progress of humanity by telling the truth.

On the surface, telling the truth seems like an everyday act of conformity. Most parents raise children to tell the truth and own up to trouble they may have gotten into. "Bearing false witness" is condemned by religious texts, and perjury in the criminal justice system is a crime with severe punishments. Integrity about the truth is a quality found in most heroes. Folklore about the first president and founding hero of the republic noted as evidence of his character that, even as a young man, "he could not tell a lie." Clearly, honesty is widely recognized as a trait of conformists, whether they are heroes or not. But we live in strange times. In a variety of contexts, truth-telling may actually be seen as a form of deviance, with serious consequences to the truth-teller. This is especially true when facts are inconvenient or embarrassing to vested interests.

In 2005, during the premiere of his satirical program, *The Colbert Report*, comedian Stephen Colbert coined the word *truthiness* to describe the quality something may have of seeming to be true even if it is not (Zimmer, 2006). The word exemplified the divisive emotional appeals made by politicians and other claimsmakers who rely on facts only when it suits their purpose. By 2016, something extraordinary had manifested in the American political discourse as matters of fact became contested knowledge. Sharp partisan divides morphed clearly into divides about what constitutes truth. Americans were openly presented with "alternative facts," as elected officials openly disputed matters of fact (McIntyre, 2018). It is not that lying by people in power is a new thing—precursors to this phenomenon had been festering for years—but the passive acceptance of deceit by the public as a new normal was disconcerting to those whose profession was to find the truth, especially scholars and journalists. "Post-truth" politics has been noted as a new era in which arguments appeal to emotions rather than facts (Madison, 2018; McIntyre, 2018).

In a variety of contexts, "telling the truth and nothing but the truth" may be an act of heroic defiance, as when a scientist must convey information that the public does not want to hear, or when a deviant employee blows the whistle on unethical corporate conduct. At other times, truth-telling may simply be creative expression that pushes new boundaries or expresses a narrative that is deemed subversive or even obscene.

In our post-truth epoch, the days when truth-tellers such as scientists were thought of as heroes and factual reporting was regarded as the illuminator of democracy seem long forgotten. When reporting facts is fake news, scientific evidence for climate change is a hoax, and legal birth certificates are branded as forgeries, it's easy to see how truth-telling can get someone into good trouble. It would be far more convenient for the status quo if truth-telling that exposes power relations and corrupt practices and causes good trouble, was left unexposed.

Inspiration for several of the people profiled in this chapter was drawn from *Americans Who Tell the Truth* (Shetterly, 2009), a book and its companion website by author and artist Robert Shetterly. Shetterly identifies fifty champions of truth, justice, and democracy, including politicians, writers, environmentalists, academics, and activists who have moved to challenge the status quo in the United States. They include Frederick Douglass, Rachel Carson, Abraham Lincoln, Helen Keller, Howard Zinn, Rosa Parks, César Chavez, James Baldwin, Woody Guthrie, and many others. The book includes pithy and inspiring quotations from these heroes. For example, Thoreau's entry is "the law will never make men free; it's men who have got to make the law free" (5). Mark Twain's entry, aptly, is "there is no distinctly native American criminal class except Congress" (6). And among contemporaries, he quotes journalist Amy Goodman's comment that "our mission is to make dissent commonplace in America" (34).

Since the publication of the original illustrated book, Shetterly has gone on to paint dozens more portraits of Americans who have spoken up against injustice and continues to profile them on his website.

Americans Who Tell the Truth is designed to be accessible to a middle-school student, but the short narratives are an exercise in the basic Millsian method of viewing the biographies of these individuals in the context of social structures that acted back on them. Almost all those profiled in the book have been condemned or characterized as unpatriotic at one time or another. In the prologue, Shetterly explains:

Often it takes great courage to stand up to people in the government or press the demand for the truth. All of us must ask ourselves what it means to be patriotic. Does it mean obeying people in powerful positions and doing whatever they ask us to do? Or does it mean discovering for ourselves what truly serves the common good, the hope for justice and the real ideals of America? We must remember that in a democracy the people have rights, not government. (2009, 1)

Truth-tellers are deviant heroes who bravely stepped forward out of an otherwise comfortable job or position. Often, they are employed in an organization where entrenched practices encourage acquiescence or passive acceptance. Truth-tellers get into good trouble shining light on corrupt and dishonest practices that would otherwise fester in the dark. Many are scientists who have professional obligations to speak the truth but may have their funding cut by doing so; others are whistleblowers who may lose their jobs or even be charged as criminals for speaking out, and still others are artists or entertainers who use creativity or satire to lampoon or push the limits of artistic expression.

In this post-truth era, Americans have come to expect dishonesty as normal. It says a lot about public life in contemporary American society that truth-telling is an act of both heroism and deviance. Though the actions of the individuals profiled in this chapter are seemingly divergent, they represent a process of norm violation that enlightens society and expands the human prospect.

SCIENTISTS IN GOOD TROUBLE

In 2007, climate scientist James Hansen alleged that administrators with NASA had attempted to manipulate the results of his work on climate change and atmospheric science (Hansen, 2009). Hansen spent most of his thirty-plus-year career as a climate scientist at NASA's Goddard Institute. In the 1980s, his work was among the first to document and predict the effects of greenhouse gasses on the climate. By the 1990s and early 2000s, his research was showing rapid and alarming changes in atmospheric and meteorological conditions. In his work as a scientist, he took NASA's mission to "protect the planet" to heart and fulfilled his duty as a scientist to present facts about the well-being of the Earth. However, his research contradicted the political discourse of an administration that took the position that anthropogenic climate change was just a theory, unconfirmed by science. In fact, public relations officials were "filtering" Hansen's research, which was showing the alarming effects of greenhouse gas emissions (Hansen, 2009). Although Hansen was told that he was jeopardizing his position at the institute, he spoke out anyway. Several fellow scientists even condemned him for entering the fray of politics and policy debates. Hansen's quest to publicize the scientific findings of his research got him into good trouble.

Since the days of Socrates, the state and reason have long clashed. The distortion, manipulation, and denial of scientific knowledge can be traced to the beginnings of the scientific revolution, when facts contradicted the prevailing ideology of the time. Today, the science of climate change replicates this tension with politics in the pursuit of knowledge. Nowadays, the politicization and official regulation of scientific fact have led normally reserved and cloistered scientists to enter the public foray of popular discourse.

The publishing of scientific truth has brought many scientists tribulation. Some have been labeled odd or eccentric, others dismissed as nerds, still others have faced legal jeopardy or been deemed heretics. One study of Nobel laureates found that anti-traditionalist attitudes, along with marginalization, are two key aspects of innovators. Thus, Jews, who historically have been marginalized, are overrepresented among Nobel Prize winners. Similarly, dissatisfaction with established ways of doing things drives innovation (Zuckerman, 1997). Innovators who publish unpopular scientific truths often violate norms and may thus be called deviants.

Popular fictional depictions of scientists, from Dr. Frankenstein to Dr. Strangelove, often present a vilified character. In movies such as *E.T.*, *Jurassic Park*, and *Terminator*, the scientist is portrayed as a force for evil. As Andrew Pollack wrote in the 1990s, "from the grave robbers of yesteryear to the cloners of today, scientists in movies are almost invariably mad, evil, antisocial, clumsy, or eccentric. And science and technology themselves are usually seen as forces of destruction rather than good" (Pollack, 1998). The chemist Walter White, in the series *Breaking Bad*, personifies a special type of malice.

Despite such representations, scientists are also depicted as pioneers in medicine or space exploration. Films such as *Hidden Figures* depict the struggle of the African American women mathematicians and scientists working out of sight who contributed to great advances during the early days of NASA. The film portrays the heroism and hope for the future of these scientists, who were faced with the double burden of being black and female.

One of the few textbooks on deviant behavior that mentions the possibility of positive deviance as a possible source of social change is Humphrey and Palmer's *Deviant Behavior* (2013). They discuss the function of positive deviance in provoking positive change and establishing the legitimacy of what was formerly socially constructed as negative deviant behavior (Humphrey & Palmer, 2013). Humphrey and Palmer also discuss how individuals who innovate and make important discoveries are deviant individuals. For instance, Albert Einstein was a deviant in the sense that by rejecting the orthodoxy of Newtonian physics that dominated that field, he radically changed the way physicists viewed the world. Such scientist truth-tellers may clash with authorities as well as their own colleagues in the process of forging their insights.

The classic example of the tension between scientific advancement and the status quo is Galileo, who demonstrated mathematically that our solar system is heliocentric—that is, the planets revolve around the sun (Kuhn, 2012). This finding of fact refuted the old geocentric view promoted by the Church, based on its interpretation of scripture. Amid the controversy this stoked, Galileo continued his work, arguing that biblical text supported his findings as well. Despite Galileo's attempt to stay above controversy, he was brought before the Roman Inquisition, where he was tried, found guilty of heresy, and spent the rest of his life under house arrest.

Khun, in *Structure of Scientific Revolutions*, proposed that scientific knowledge is a result of advances that occur in fits and starts rather than as a cumulative developmental progression (Kuhn, 1970). For Khun, science may be either "normal" or "revolutionary." Normal science exists within the boundaries of accepted scientific inquiry, using standard methods and drawing conclusions that do not challenge conventional understanding. In contrast, revolutionary science redefines knowledge and results in paradigm shifts that may dramatically alter worldviews and accompany broader changes in the world order.

> The transition from a paradigm in crisis to a new one from which a new tradition of normal science can emerge is far from a cumulative process, one achieved by an articulation or extension of the old paradigm. Rather it is a reconstruction of the field from new fundamentals, a reconstruction that changes some of the field's most elementary theoretical generalizations as well as many of its paradigm methods and applications. During the transition period there will be a large but never complete overlap between the problems that can be solved by the old and by the new paradigm. But there will also be a decisive difference in the modes of solution. When the transition is complete, the profession will have changed its view of the field, its methods, and its goals. (1970, 84–85)

Khun's book documents the underlying material and mental factors that produce shifts in knowledge and understanding in science. While the book is focused on the scientific community, he also points to parallel revolutions in the political sphere that are met with resistance by the established order. The discoveries of Copernicus, Galileo, Newton, Darwin, and Curie not only precipitated revolutionary change in science, but jolted the way humanity sees itself. It is not an accident that, while regarded as pioneering heroes today, these scientists were seen as subversives and heretics in their own time. Darwin's findings about evolution, though long established, still draw the dismissive ire of political and religious authorities.

Darwin, in fact, proposed that anomalies or "deviations" were natural and the source of the adaptive traits that accounted for the biological diversity of species as they undergo evolution (Levins, 1985). Through natural selection, species with the most favorable biological traits for survival pass those traits on to the next generation. Darwin's discovery that evolution explained the origin of species was a heresy that deprived religion of its last claim of explaining the universe.

Evolution has had many days in court. One of the better known cases was the Scopes Monkey Trial of 1925, in which a high-school teacher, John Scopes, was put on trial for teaching evolution in class. Scopes was charged with violating the Butler Act, which affirmed the biblical account of the origin of humans and prohibited the teaching of anything to the contrary. The trial was largely a show, drawing a three-time populist presidential candidate William Jennings Bryan for the prosecution and famed attorney Clarence Darrow for the defense (Johnson, 2007). While Scopes was not sure he had even taught the offending material, he went forward in a very public trial. Just as the Athenian elders said of the teachings of Socrates, Bryan and the religious leaders warned that teaching evolution would corrupt youth and bring about the downfall of society. Scopes was convicted of a misdemeanor, but Darrow outmaneuvered Bryan in court, humiliating the prosecution (Kersten, 2011). Although the Butler Act was declared unconstitutional in 1968, some school boards have continued to conflate science and religion by mandating that creationism, and more recently "intelligent design," be taught in schools. In some school districts and private schools, teachers who refuse to incorporate theology-as-fact materials in courses risk alienating themselves or losing their jobs.

As in the biological sciences, scientists who delved into the science of human sexuality were initially met with opposition and moral condemnation. The Kinsey studies on human sexually, though methodologically flawed, represented a genuine attempt to transcend myths and half-truths in favor of scientific understanding. These studies, credited, in part, with changing the public's attitudes about sex and homosexuality, were described by one biographer as one of the most controversial publications since Darwin's *On the Origin of Species* (Robinson, 1972). Like Darwin's work, the Kinsey studies were criticized on both scientific and moralistic grounds. Scientists found methodological flaws with his sampling and statistical procedures. But scientists and intellectuals also found moral issues with the studies, with some disapproving the scientific study of sex removed from the emotional context of the sexual experience (Dunn, 2004).

The Kinsey study paved the way for Masters and Johnson's studies on the human sexual response. These studies chronicled the human physiological response to sexual pleasure. Deemed perverse and obscene, Masters was pushed out of his professorship at Washington University and continued his research with Johnson on the human sexual response in St. Louis (Maier, 2013). Their research subjects often used prostitutes and unmarried persons, even though it was against the law in Missouri for unmarried people to have sex until the 1970s. Like the Kinsey studies, Masters and Johnson's reports generated moral outrage and condemnation. While flawed, these investigations opened the door to a more mature and analytic understanding of human sexuality. At the very least, they found plenty of good trouble.

Since 2017, there have been official attempts to block access to knowledge, about sex, violence, and history. For example, laws such as the Dickey Amendment in the United States currently prevent most scientific studies of gun violence (Frankel, 2017). Poland has recently passed a law that makes it a crime to investigate any facts concerning any assistance of Pols to Nazis during the occupation and Holocaust (Santora & Berendt, 2018). Similarly, Turkey prohibits scholarship that looks into the Armenian genocide (Lauer, 2015). In the United States, a movement has emerged to present a sanitized version of pre-Civil War history that scrubs the brutal aspects of slavery and the slaughter of indigenous populations (E. Brown, 2015). Such laws, aimed at the airing of the dirty laundry of a society, effectively make truth-telling an act of defiance.

Other academics across disciplines may agitate some kind of good trouble. As mentioned in Chapter 6, Karl Marx's calls for philosophers to reject a mere interpretation of the world in favor of changing it attracted the attention of not just intellectual critics, but police and spies from countries all over Europe. Looking at C. Wright Mills's own biography, who is known mostly for his iconoclastic sociology and a methodological approach that inspired this book, his brief life and career were punctuated with conflict. Of course, as was noted in Chapter 5, feminist authors and writers have generated much trouble through the critique of patriarchy and challenge to sexist norms.

ORGANIZATIONAL DISSIDENCE: WHISTLEBLOWERS AND LAMPLIGHTERS

Whistleblowing can be another form of truth-telling that breaks with norms and social conventions. Whistleblowers are typically insiders, many of whom have privileged information. They are expected to toe the line and follow norms and expectations that include protecting the organization they work for. Caught between organizational pressures to conform and the more difficult but righteous path of following what their conscience tells them, they may thus get into good trouble by exposing wrongdoing and corruption from within an organization or institution. Whistleblowing in this sense is an act of truth-telling that defies norms or expectations of silence the individual has

pledged to act in accordance with, no matter how egregious or felonious the
activities being exposed.

As a result of their actions, whistleblowers often face threats of reprisal
and retaliation. From Watergate to Wikileaks, this nuanced kind of truth-
telling presents an added dilemma for criminology. On one hand, the unsanctioned release of information is a valuable tool for exposing fraud, illegality,
deceit, abuses of power, and perversions of justice by those in powerful
positions. For instance, consumer activist Ralph Nader (who got into good
trouble with General Motors) describes the whistleblower as someone who
believes "that the public interest overrides the interest of the organization he
serves, blows the whistle that the organization is involved in corrupt, illegal,
fraudulent or harmful activity" (Nader, 1972, vii). In this sense, the term is
used to connote bravery, an honorable defiance that progresses a society
through lies, deceit, and darkness.

On the other hand, whistleblowing may be deemed unethical, illegal, or
even traitorous, at least by those who are being exposed. Corporate employees may be fired or even prosecuted for telling "trade secrets," government
workers may lose security clearances or be placed in rubber rooms for the
remainder of their careers, and people who work in law enforcement will be
marginalized for speaking out about any wrongdoing. Therefore, given the
social context of whistleblowing, in which taciturnity is expected, it is easily
classified as a deviant behavior.

To understand the social construction of a whistleblower, it is useful to
understand the origins of the term. The act of whistleblowing once referred to
the use of whistles by British bobbies (police officers) to get the public's
attention.[1] In a more modern context, it evokes the whistle of the referee at a
sports event. A Google n-gram search of the word *whistleblower* shows that
it was rarely used in books or media until about 1970.[2] The use of the term
rose dramatically during an era where scandals from Vietnam to Watergate to
nuclear power were brought to light. The term has also been used pejorative-
ly to refer to the moral equivalent of a schoolyard tattletale, someone who
has snitched on or sold out their comrades or superiors.

Like so many concepts in sociology, the line between hero and snitch is a
matter of perspective. Whistleblowing is seen as an act of betrayal from the
perspective of the organization or individuals being exposed. At the same
time, whistleblowing is an act of courage in which one's reputation and
livelihood are placed at risk. In many cases, the motives of whistleblowers
are drawn into question, and they face ad hominem attacks and questions of
personal character.

Criminologist David Matza (Sykes and Matza, 1957) proposed several
neutralization techniques used by organizations and otherwise esteemed people engaging in white-collar crime. Condemning the condemner is the routine response of a government or organization when illegality is uncovered

(Simon, 2018). Whistleblowers may be vilified as agitators, as unpatriotic, or motivated by personal gain. In the contexts of good trouble, this mechanism diverts attention from the harmful behavior of an organization while aiming to discredit the truth-teller. This further mystifies the actions of elites and perpetuates the common belief that crime is an individual act.

To be clear, not every whistleblower is participating in good trouble. Some very famous whistleblowers have come forward for reasons that are not entirely authentic or altruistic. For example, consider Mark Felt, the deputy director of the FBI, who is better known as "Deep Throat." He is best known as the leaker of the details of the Watergate cover-up and other abuses of power by the Nixon administration to *Washington Post* reporter Bob Woodward (Felt & O'Connor, 2006). The information he provided Woodward proved pivotal in bringing down the Nixon administration for illegality and abuses of power. However, exposing corruption and preserving democratic values did not seem to be the primary motivation of his actions. In fact, he was convicted in the early 1980s for the civil rights violations of members of the Weather Underground (C. I. King, 2005). This conviction stemmed from illegal break-ins and searches of radical left and antiwar groups. Given his position in the FBI, it seems much more likely that Felt had a personal vendetta against Nixon because he was passed over for promotion to FBI director after the death of J. Edgar Hoover. Again, deviant heroes have complex biographies and contradictions, but considering the personal motives of Felt, his actions do not seem to rise to the standard of genuine good trouble.

Despite certain whistleblower protections, the most common institutional response is to move to fire them (Near and Miceli, 1985). Indeed, threats to economic security through the loss of a job, threats of blacklisting, or ending of a career can be enough to silence even steadfast opponents of unethical behavior. Yet, some deviants will persist, bringing knowledge to the public, and saying, in the words of Du Bois, "Things that you do not want to hear, but need to be told" (Du Bois, 2004).

Myron Glazer, in his account of ten prominent whistleblowers (Glazer, 1983), finds that they follow one of three distinct paths when attempting to reconcile their moral beliefs with intense pressure to conform. *Reluctant collaborators* may privately condemn the acts of an organization they are working with but do not speak out until they have separated from the organization. *Implicated protesters* speak out from within their organizations but otherwise go along with the harmful practices as a matter of conformity. Finally, *unbending resisters* are steadfast in their commitment to moral and ethical behavior, resulting in a public disclosure of the hazard and eventually retaliation on the part of the organization. The last of these three categories come closest to the operational definition of *deviant hero* used in this book.

The next section considers the biographies and plights of several famous (or infamous) whistleblowers. These straddle several industries and occupational groupings including policing (Serpico), clandestine services (Snowden), the military (Manning), tobacco (Wygant), accounting (Watkins), and atomic energy (Silkwood). Some of these individuals faced formal consequences or legal jeopardy, others were ostracized by comrades, several received threats of violence, and one was killed for her truth-telling.

Frank Serpico

One well-known "unbending resister" is former New York City police detective Frank Serpico. Serpico's duties included enforcing laws and regulations in the streets of Brooklyn, but during his patrols, he found that the most alarming violations of law were not in the streets but among the ranks of the police force. Serpico ran up against the culture of internal corruption and the police force's "blue code of silence" that conceals it. These unwritten rules of solidarity shield police departments from outside scrutiny, especially in the case of officer misconduct (Westley, 1970). While these norms are informal, they are quite powerful in socializing officers and shaping the character of a police force (Kappeler, Sluder, & Alpert, 1998). Neophyte officers are soon acclimatized into an ideology and a culture that demands high levels of conformity to police norms and values. The resulting social environment of a police department has been called *deviant conformity*, which relies on the extreme commitment of its members to ensure compliance with potentially repressive practices. Such a description may be applied to the department Frank Serpico joined in the 1960s.

According to Peter Maas's popular biography *Serpico* (1973), the young rookie cop was torn between a police culture that permitted minor corruption, gratuities, and bribes and formal regulations that precluded these activities. For example, officers in his precinct were known to "shop" for free items in stores and ask for gratuities from restaurants and shopkeepers. Other cops were more aggressive in clearly crossing ethical lines, participating in shakedowns of businesses and people involved in vice crimes.

Serpico resisted and opposed the culture of bribery in his precinct. His refusal to take a bribe or gratuity made fellow officers suspicious, and they sought to marginalize him. Serpico eventually reported the widespread corruption he observed in the NYPD to his superiors (Maas, 1973) but he was ignored and labeled a "snitch." During an undercover drug bust that went wrong, Serpico was shot in the face by an unknown assailant and left to die in an apartment complex by fellow officers. He survived his wounds and went on to challenge the blue code or, as it is also known, blue wall of silence. Shortly after the shooting in 1970, Serpico testified about police corruption to the Knapp Commission, where he said the following about police culture and corruption:

I hope that police officers in the future will not experience the same frustration and anxiety that I was subjected to for the past five years at the hands of my superiors because of my attempt to report corruption. I was made to feel that I had burdened them with an unwanted task. The problem is that the atmosphere does not yet exist in which an honest police officer can act without fear of ridicule or reprisal from fellow officers. Police corruption cannot exist unless it is at least tolerated at higher levels in the department. Therefore, the most important result that can come from these hearings is a conviction by police officers that the department will change. In order to ensure this an independent, permanent investigative body dealing with police corruption, like this commission, is essential. ("Excerpts from the Testimony by Serpico," 1971)

Serpico rejected the term *whistleblower* as disparaging to people who speak up against corruption in a culture of silence (Cooper, 2013). In a possible nod to Paul Revere, a hero of the American Revolution, Serpico prefers the term *lamplighter,* arguing that "injustice can't prevail when the light of justice is shining on it" (Bekiempis, 2015). Just as the scientific revolution sought to free humanity from the yoke of the traditions of the Dark Ages, lamplighters, through their deviance, demand accountability from corporations and government and press for honesty from politicians, thereby serving both truth and the public interest.

Coleen Rowley, Katharine Gun

The Sam Adams Award is given annually to a professional in the intelligence community who exhibits integrity and ethics. According to the award's website, it was created to honor someone who displays a commitment to the truth, regardless of the consequences (Sam Adams Associates for Integrity in Intelligence, n.d.). Dubbing it the "Corner-Brightener Candlestick Award," it was named for Samuel Adams, a CIA whistleblower during the Vietnam War who challenged the official underestimate of the strength of Vietcong soldiers. The name of the award, Corner-Brightener, conjures the Enlightenment thinkers and scientists of the scientific revolution, who also shed light on unillumined corners. The recipients of this award are something of a who's who in truth-telling and have faced serious legal jeopardy as a result. Recipients of the Sam Adams Award include Coleen Rowley, who in 2002 came forward about the FBI's mishandling of intelligence that may have prevented the September 11th attacks. Katharine Gun, who worked as a translator for a British intelligence agency, was honored a year later for leaking secrets that demonstrated the United States was engaged in illegally falsifying intelligence in the push for the 2003 invasion of Iraq. Gun was charged under the UK's Official Secrets Act, but eventually, the state dropped the charges.

Edward Snowden

The label "enemy of the state" is applied to both leakers and whistleblowers. One of the most famous of these leakers, and a Sam Adams Award winner, is Edward Snowden, an employee for a government contractor whose job as a security analyst gave him access to National Security Agency documents. These documents described how foreign and American electronic communications were being captured, monitored, and stored. After September 11th, the US government embarked on an expansive surveillance project, which included the interception and analysis of electronic communications abroad. Snowden leaked many documents proving that, among other things, the US government, in violation of the law, was spying on its citizens. These disclosures alerted the public and the press to mass global and domestic surveillance programs and a national security apparatus that operates in secrecy, independent of external controls and checks on accountability.

The leaks also marked Snowden as an enemy of the state by the US government. He became a global fugitive, fleeing the United States for Hong Kong and eventually Russia, where he continues to speak out, give interviews, and warn of a surveillance state. When asked about the motivations for his actions, Snowden has said that he "does not want to live in a world where everything we do is being recorded" (MacAskill, 2013). Later, he told an American television interviewer, "What is right is not always the same as what is legal." Snowden indicated a willingness to serve time for his actions so long as it didn't deter others from coming forward, and offered the following reflection:

> If you're volunteering yourself to be used as a negative example, if you're volunteering to spend a lifetime in prison, rather than spend a time in prison, a short period, where you'll come out, you'll advocate, you'll emerge stronger and inspire other people to resist these policies – are you doing good or are you doing bad? (Williams, 2014).

As of this writing, Snowden has been living in temporary asylum in Russia since 2013. He is still wanted by the United States on charges of espionage.

Chelsea Manning

Another "enemy of the state," Chelsea Manning, walked out of Fort Leavenworth military prison in May 2017. She had been released twenty-eight years early on a presidential pardon after spending seven years incarcerated for disclosing state secrets. When sentenced, she was known as Pvt. Bradley Manning. After Manning's conviction for violations of the Espionage Act, he announced that he transitioned his gender in the all-male military prison. Military prison life must be hard time for anyone, but Manning's transition to a woman undoubtedly placed additional hardship on her, in addition to the punishment for the crime of treason she had committed as Bradley. Highlighting this multitude of complexities and intersections in her biography, she is hailed as a hero by antiwar and antisecrecy advocates but is regarded as a traitor by her country and is rejected even by many in the transgender community.

Chelsea Manning was a pivotal case in the areas of digital sedition and demonstrated to democracies around the world how one low-level employee can wreak havoc on attempts to cover up state secrets. Manning's crimes are manifold. Foreshadowing Snowden, she disclosed state secrets, especially those related to military and diplomatic cables. These cables revealed video of the killing of unarmed insurgents and journalists and documented the fabrications of the U.S. government in the lead-up to the Iraq War.

Once in the hands of the military justice system, Manning endured "maximum custody" conditions that included solitary confinement. In a letter to her attorney, she said that she was forced to be nude and was harassed by guards. Manning was convicted under the Espionage Act, but only after she disclosed the crimes of the government that convicted her.

MORE TRUTH-TELLERS

Conformist science may do amazing things: It can cure cancer or it can be used to develop weapons of mass destruction and harmful consumer products. It can also assist, as it did in World War II, the social engineering of a Holocaust. Deviant truth-tellers may expose deceptive practices that have deadly consequences. For example, we know that it was because of whistle-blower Jeffry Wygant that tobacco companies deliberately manipulated information about the addictive properties of cigarettes. Wygant's retelling of his story starts from the moment he was fired from his job at the Brown and Williamson Tobacco Company because he "knew too much" (Brenner, 2004). His wife left him, and he started receiving threatening letters and phone calls.

Another such deviant truth-teller is consumer advocate Ralph Nader. Nader's phone was bugged and General Motors had him privately investigated after he published his book *Unsafe at Any Speed*, which was critical of an automobile industry that placed profits above the safety of its customers. In a similar spirit, Rachel Carson's exposé on the deadly practices of the chemical industry in *Silent Spring* resulted in attacks on her personal character and credentials by chemists with industry ties (Lear, 2009, 443–444).

Complex organizations present a context where wrongdoing may be absorbed into the culture as part of standard operating procedures. The pressure to conform can be overwhelming in profit-driven enterprises. Companies will often tell employees who are not toeing the corporate line that they are "rocking the boat" and not being a "team player." So, when Sherron Watkins, the highest-ranking female executive in the Enron Corporation, exposed the accounting fraud that was propping up the then seventh-largest company in the United States, she was told to mind her business if she wanted her career to advance.

Some truth-tellers have put their lives in jeopardy to alert the public to the truth. Karen Silkwood was a chemical technician hired to work in a Kerr-McGee Corporation plant that was making plutonium and other materials for the U.S. atomic energy and its nuclear efforts. She quickly became active in her union, participating in a strike and investigating grievances related to health and safety. Silkwood found numerous unsafe practices concerning the handling of radioactive materials. She herself was exposed to plutonium in her workplace. It was found in her home and in her body. She became a whistleblower and testified to the Atomic Energy Commission about the numerous violations. Three months after her testimony, she was killed in a car accident in which her vehicle appeared to be rammed from behind.

DEVIANT ART AS TRUTH-TELLING

Art can represent a movement or force that comes either on the leading edge or wake of social change. Indeed the raison d'être for art is to provoke an emotional response—it is a form of persuasion meant to challenge preconceived notions and inspire others to act. Thus, deviant artistic behavior can instigate the same type of subtle or rapid change that arises in science or politics. Art, performance, and creative expression can be viewed as another type of truth-telling reflecting the social conditions and changes out of which it arises.

Howard Becker, although noted primarily for his contributions to the sociology of deviance and qualitative methodologies, also wrote about art and the social contexts from which artistic movements emerge (Becker, 1974). Becker argues that art is a form of collective action, with meaning derived not just from the artist but from the consumer, producer, stage manager, costume designer, etc. This cooperative or collaborative aspect of art both facilitates its production and restrains its range of expression.

Becker proposed that art could be studied in the same way sociologists study any other occupation. Art was simply an institution with organizing structures and individuals interacting within social constraints and boundaries. In his more recent book, *What about Mozart? What about Murder?*, he argues that art, like deviance, is part of a labeling process (Becker, 2014). What we take for granted as being art, or, more specifically, good art, does not have an objective component but rather is determined by the collective.

Experts in aesthetics and art history can simply debate what has been labeled as such. Just as Kuhn (1970) demonstrated that paradigm shifts can transform the understanding of truth in the scientific community, changes in the artistic community can shift the understanding of art.

Just as it does in science, innovation in art may go in fits and starts, punctuated by rapid changes in development. Slight changes in accepted style or gross deviations of technique may challenge establishment ideas about what constitutes artistic expression: a subtle change in the way a string is plucked, producing a new and unexpected sound, or a new brushstroke morphing into a new genre. Druann Heckert (1989), in fact, referred to impressionism as a form of positive deviance. The impressionists freely brushed colors and did not observe contours and depictions that were considered appropriate at the time. They were considered radicals who violated the established rules of painting. Impressionism was at first rejected by respected peers, shunned by the public, and widely panned by critics as a debased form, unbecoming of the great French masters. Only later did the impressionists become praised and valued as great artists.

As Heckert (1989) observes, impressionists were originally labeled "negative deviants" and then elevated to a "positive deviant" status over time. Ultimately, impressionism changed the field of painting, influencing other artistic fields such as music and literature. It also gave rise to subsequent movements that challenged orthodoxies in art.

Art has long been a locus of counterculture. New movements in art, cinema, and music are almost always met by an ensuing backlash. Rock and roll was dismissed as an annoying fad by the older generation (as was hip-hop) (Griffith, 1986). Nowadays digital photography is still marginalized (O'Hagan, 2014). In short, like any other processes of rule construction and normalization, artistic expression cycles through periods of rejection and acceptance, with the possibility of an iterative effect. Individual artists may challenge norms or conventions of the art world and may also push back on the norms and conventions of society. While one does not have to be successful to be a deviant hero, establishing a new style of expression that overturns conventional wisdom helps canonize those who get into good trouble.

Deviant artists have long been subject to condemnation and censorship. For instance, Diego Rivera was commissioned to paint the mural *Man at the Crossroads* in the lobby of Rockefeller Center, in New York City, but the painting was destroyed after he refused to remove a depiction of Vladimir Lenin. Andres Serrano's 1987 photograph, *Immersion,* which depicts a crucifix submerged in urine, resulted in his losing funding and receiving death threats. On a more sinister level, the state may label artists as subversives, effectively criminalizing forms of expression. Nazi Germany declared most forms of modern art to be corrupted by Jewish and Marxist influences as "degenerate" and a category they applied to visual art forms such as impressionism, cubism, and surrealism, but also to musical styles as well, especially African American forms of expression like jazz and swing.

Just as impressionism challenged artistic standards and conceptions of art in the nineteenth century, contemporary artistic movements have similarly been labeled "deviant." Hip-hop emerged through a cultural exchange between Caribbean immigrants and disenfranchised youth in New York (Chang, 2005). The hip-hop genre revolutionized the recording industry as well as the entire mainstream concept of "music." Like other movements of creative expression, both the lyrics and style drew criticism and resistance. For instance, the criminal justice system, especially the police, are a frequent theme in the hip-hop genre. N.W.A were arrested in Detroit after the police rushed the stage during their performance of "Fuck the Police." Lamar's album, *DAMN*, which features lyrics critical of police, led a well-known television commentator, Geraldo Rivera, to exclaim, "This is why I say that hip-hop has done more damage to young African Americans than racism in recent years" (Leight, Reeves, & Lee, 2017). Rivera's remarks reflect a common refrain in the mainstream that sees hip-hop as promoting violence and anti-cop sentiment. Despite much criticism, especially from white conservatives, defenders of hip-hop argue that the violent narrative is simply a reflection of a racist social reality. Labeled as deviant by a status quo social order, hip-hop's challenge to racism makes rap a revolutionary and emancipatory form of expression that is necessarily a kind of good trouble.

To be clear, there are reasons to question values promoted under hip-hop that seem to glorify misogyny and getting rich at the expense of others. For instance, feminist author bell hooks challenged the pioneering hip-hop genre of "gangsta rap" as actually reinforcing capitalist and sexist norms in society.

> The sexist, misogynist, patriarchal ways of thinking and behaving that are glorified in gangsta rap are a reflection of the prevailing values in our society, values created and sustained by white supremacist capitalist patriarchy. As the crudest and most brutal expression of sexism, misogynistic attitudes tend to be portrayed by the dominant culture as an expression of male deviance. In reality they are part of a sexist continuum, necessary for the maintenance of patriarchal social order. (hooks, 1994, 28)

For hooks, it is no accident that the best-selling hip-hop genre is one that constructs a narrative of exploitation of others and sexist oppression. In light of hooks's critique, some might say that hip-hop may not be a medium of good trouble at all. Although it clearly speaks a truth in describing racism and everyday interactions that blacks have with the criminal justice system, gangsta rap contains lyrical elements that reinforce capitalist values and patriarchal misogyny. Nonetheless, hip-hop remains an important form and style of music, not because of its misogyny but for its provocation of whites and the criminal justice system.

Entertainers in film and television may also seek good trouble in promotion of a cause or by being on the wrong side of the political winds. In the 1950s, many actors, screenwriters, and directors were blacklisted as a part of the McCarthyite Red Scare. Acting great Charlie Chaplin was deported because of his association with communism. In the 1990s, the television show *Murphy Brown* poked the culture wars through the depiction of the namesake character's decision to become a single mother. Comedic entertainers may also get into good trouble by using satire, wit, and wisdom . . . another form of truth-telling to persuade a mass audience of an injustice.

Literary greats have often faced informal and formal sanctions for their fictional works. Many of these authors are revered as major contributors to various literary canons. Others are lesser known pulp novelists who nonetheless stood up for the right to publish freely. At first glance, fiction writers may not be truth-tellers in a literal sense, per Henry James's well-known postulate that a novel "is in its broadest definition a personal, a direct impression of life" (1884, 510). Efforts to limit artistic truth have surfaced in a variety of contexts. Censorship of the arts, in the broadest sense, attempts to control creative expression and define the limits of artistic activity. More specifically, censorship aims to suppress discourse that certain segments of society deem impermissible. It may be used to suppress dissent in a totalitarian regime or ban a performance deemed obscene by a democratic government. When creators or distributors of a censored work resist and disseminate the work anyway, they may find that they have gotten into good trouble.

From science, to industry to art and music, truth-telling is fertile ground for the growth of good trouble. It goes without saying that this is also true in education. Everyone in the field of education serves, or should serve, as a truth-teller, and that may cause trouble. Currently, as at times in the past, the academy is under scrutiny from politicians and pundits who politicize truth and fact. Consider, for instance, the comments of a legislator about publicly funded universities in Arizona:

> Why does a kid go to a major university these days? A lot of Republicans would say they go there to get brainwashed and learn how to become activists and basically go out in the world and cause trouble. (quoted in Sulivan and Jordan, 2017)

If knowing the "truth" is a cause for trouble, then all of those in the academy are potential troublemakers. Through scientific inquiry, creative expression, and lamplighting as whistleblowers, truth-tellers in seemingly divergent, unrelated areas can challenge authority and the status quo by revealing an objective truth. In other cases, such as through art and creativity, truth-telling is through the medium. Stories told through fiction illuminate real-world realities that have been discursively obscured. The revelations through art unconceal these powerful relationships while inviting criticism. As this chapter has demonstrated, truth-tellers such as these may find themselves in personal and legal jeopardy, censored and condemned, but their words, actions, and artistic expression represent an important type of creative nonconformity.

NOTES

1. http://www.phrases.org.uk/meanings/whistle-blower.html
2. https://books.google.com/ngrams/graph?content=whistleblower&year_start=1800&year_end=2000&corpus=15&smoothing=3&share=&direct_url=t1%3B%2Cwhistleblower%3B%2Cc0

Chapter Eight

Deviant Peacemakers, Lovers, and Dreamers

Driving south from the University of Idaho to the state capital, Boise, on Highway 95, a motorist will approach the five-mile-long grade of White Bird Hill. The grade descends from the windswept Camas Prairie and into a valley carved by the untamed Salmon River of No Return. From the summit, you glimpse the Seven Devils, which crown Hells Canyon, the deepest gorge in North America. East of that region, the Nez Perce were resettled after being removed from their ancestral homelands. When gold was discovered in 1860 and white settlers moved in, the U.S. Army was called in to defend them. Violent conflict ensued almost immediately. In 1877 a Nez Perce truce party was attacked by a vigilante, Arthur Chapman (M. H. Brown, 1967). The Nez Perce quickly counterattacked and killed several settlers, outmaneuvering the U.S. Army at White Bird. This incident sparked the Nez Perce war and the famous retreat of Chief Joseph and the Nez Perce (McDermott, 1978). The entire tribe were fugitives, and Chief Joseph was deemed an "enemy of the state." Joseph's biography, from being born into a tribe deemed "outlaw," to his famous surrender at Bear Paw, serves as a narrative on peacemaking as a form of deviant heroism.

Chief Joseph

Chief Joseph was born as Hin-mah-too-yah-lat-kekt (Thunder Rolling Down a Mountain) into the Wallowa band of the Nez Perce in northeastern Oregon. His father converted to Christianity and changed his name to Joseph (the Elder), as did his son. When white settlers began moving into the area, the federal government sought to nullify the Treaty of Walla Walla, which granted limited sovereignty to tribes in exchange for land concessions (Oregon Historical Society, n.d.). Some Nez Perce signed while others did not, dividing the tribe between "treaty" and "non-treaty" bands. When Joseph became chief in 1871 he sought peaceful and sometimes conciliatory relations with the new settlers. At the same time, he questioned the premise of the manifest destiny that whites took for granted, which effectively subjugated and criminalized the native American population.

> I have asked some of the great white chiefs where they get their authority to say to the Indian that he shall stay in one place, while he sees white men going where they please. They can not tell me. (Chief Joseph, 1879, 417)

Joseph's band refused to settle into lands mandated, under broken treaties, by the US Army. After White Bird, Joseph and the Wallowa band of the Nez Perce were forced, as fugitives and enemies of the state, on an evacuation for their lives and freedom. Chief Joseph's retreat was tactically brilliant, as General Howard gave chase to capture the "rogue band of Indians." The retreat crossed the forbidding Bitterroot Range, traversing Yellowstone National Park, eventually heading north in pursuit of asylum in Canada with Sitting Bull of the Lakota. Two other regiments joined Howard as the U.S. Army tried to head off the Nez Perce before they could reach sanctuary. Captured thirty miles from the Canadian border, Joseph surrendered and said he would "fight no more forever." The Nez Perce were among the last of the indigenous tribes to be fully "subdued" and "relocated," but the process followed a familiar path. Declared an "enemy of the state," the indigenous populations were effectively criminalized at birth and subject to official violence from the government and vigilante violence from settlers.

Famous and heroic chiefs such as Crazy Horse, Geronimo, Tecumseh, Captain Jack, Sitting Bull, and Red Cloud were all deemed outlaws or enemies and subject to violent subjugation. Many retaliated with violence but were ultimately defeated and subjugated. The tragedy of the Native Americans represents another chapter in the story of whole populations that have been declared "criminal" and whose heroes resisted subjugation. For the United States, the westward expansion from sea to shining sea was marked by broken treaties and warfare against an entire race of people.

Along with slavery and expropriation of native lands, aggression and warfare punctuate most chapters in American history. These themes have impacted a multitude of social institutions. For instance, in his era, Mills expressed trepidation about the vested interests entwined in the establishment of the military-industrial complex, an alliance between the power elite of government and industry with the military that was unencumbered by democratic control (1956). The theme of militarization has now crept into all major social institutions, including the criminal justice system, and the war metaphor is routinely applied to social problems, including criminological ones. These themes have undoubtedly impacted the delivery of justice in this country. As Kraska and Kappeler (1997) explain:

> Militarism influences many dimensions of social life, especially in societies such as the United States that place high value on military superiority. Just as the medicalization of social problems becomes intertwined with social think and problem construction outside the medical profession, so does militarization affect multiple dimensions of the construction of and reaction to social problems outside of the armed services. (2–3)

Accordingly, the criminal justice system has embraced the language and methods of war and fights "wars on crime," "wars on terrorism," and "wars on drugs." At the same time, police and prisons are encouraged to embrace the tactics and language of the military, with the establishment of "boot camps" for convicts and paramilitary-style policing. Yet dissent has always shadowed the tendencies of violence and militarism. Often, these peacemakers themselves are criminalized or at least marginalized. Before considering several important peacemakers, it is useful to consider how systems of war and peace are incorporated into a sociological understanding of matters of crime and justice.

PEACEMAKING IN CRIMINOLOGY

Violence is a common state response to the existence of crime in society. Despite the emergence of alternative paths and restorative justice options, it is both convenient and politically expedient for the state to exercise power, as it did with the Indian Removal Act of 1830 through the forceful control of the body. In the United States, mass incarceration, police violence, and the death penalty all remain entrenched elements of a reactive justice system as it responds to crime in society. This is often the case with good trouble as well. As King's *Letter from Birmingham Jail* illustrates, nonviolent direct action has been routinely met with a violent response. Yet, MLK and many others have been steadfast in proposing that nonviolence can remedy injustices supported by violence. Other peacemakers, from Gandhi to Thoreau and from Chavez to Mandela, have demonstrated how nonviolent good trouble can beget restorative justice—that is, reconciliation with those violated and rehabilitation of the institutions that perpetuated a wrong.

Peacemaking criminology is an obscure and often marginalized subfield in criminology (Wozniak, 2002) that emerged as an effort to completely rethink matters of crime and justice. Focusing on restorative justice and alternative methods, peacemaking criminology proposes peace-oriented solutions to crime. Tied to several radical movements in criminology, it is more of a movement dedicated to principles of social justice than a clear subfield within the discipline. Criminologists embracing a peacemaking approach to criminology have argued that love and empathy have been long neglected in Western concepts of crime and justice (DeValve, 2017). Peacemaking criminology emerged to question the assumptions of violence, racism, inequality, and suffering that traditional criminology takes for granted in formulating assumptions of crime. The criminal justice system, especially in the United States, is premised on retribution—on meeting brutal acts and affronts to society with a similarly severe response. Besides deprivation of liberty, retribution is an oft-cited reason for the treatment of the condemned. Yet, crime and injustice persist. Despite the increasing sophistication of crime control technologies, crimes continue and conflicts between police and communities remain (Wolf and DeAngelis, 2011).

Asserting that the American criminal justice system is premised on violence as a means of social control, Pepinsky and Quinney (1991), by proposing peacemaking criminology, sought to radically reconceptualize the entire approach to criminology. Drawing on works ranging from Marxism and feminism to Hindu and Buddhist concepts of compassion and suffering, the essays collected in their edited volume point to modest steps that can be taken in formulating a more humane approach to criminal justice. Their premise is that the suffering and pain an individual may suffer under unjust social circumstances are often projected into acts of violence on others (Quinney, 1991). In line with critical approaches to criminology, peacemaking criminology emphasizes how inequality and power differentials produce a social structure that is inherently criminogenic.

In contrast to major theories about crime, peacemaking criminology is more of a proposed response to crime than an explanation as to why or how crime occurs. It urges a multicultural understanding of systems of crime and peace and an implementation of restorative justice—the restoration of the social bond between the community and offender. The Navajo system of justice, for example, relies on peacemakers and embraces the spirit of more traditional and less punitive forms of crime control (Nielsen & Zion, 2005). Peacemaking criminology aims to incorporate alternative perspectives of crime and deterrence, such as indigenous traditions, to question the taken-for-granted character of Western systems of criminal justice. In addition, an important, yet neglected subfield in criminology has called for a reoriented perspective of the rebel in criminal justice. For instance, Michael DeValve has urged a reorientation of the criminal justice system to incorporate the idea of rebellion as an action that is guided by a sense of love and of duty (DeValve, 2017). Moving forward from this peacemaking approach to criminology, it is useful to consider principled rebels who have been motivated by love to seek a more peaceful and just world.

Juveniles in Good Trouble

Given these teachings of peacemaking in criminology, the remainder of this chapter focuses on peacemakers and juveniles who have been labeled traitors, delinquents, and illegals by the state, individuals who resisted violence or were criminalized through no fault of their own. It points to flaws in a justice system relying on violence and enforcing inequality. Each case considered here demonstrates how the progress of humanity needs to be catalyzed by those who seek good trouble.

Children enter a world rife with conflict, and in their innocence, "grownup" problems seem silly; for them, the solutions to our seemingly complex problems suddenly seem apparent. A child's perception can illuminate just how ridiculous the roots of violence and world conflict often are. But children's lives can also be punctuated with fear and confusion about issues that they do not understand. Children of the 1920s heard about the spread of fascism in Europe, baby boomers can recall with bewilderment the absurd "duck and cover" school drills of the 1950s and 1960s against a nuclear blast, generation Xers can recall Cold War threats of nuclear annihilation with an arsenal capable of destroying the world five times over, and the childhood of millennials was marked by the shadow of post-9/11 hysteria. Profiled here are juveniles who were born into extremely oppressive normative environments that scarred a generation of children including the Taliban and the Nazis. In other cases, immigration law may make a child a criminal by no other choice.

You don't usually think of a deviant fifteen-year-old when you imagine a Nobel Peace Prize laureate. A deviant juvenile is more likely to evoke the image of a truant than a girl who was shot because she demanded the right to go to school. Her age, her cause, and the violent response to her actions provide one of the more remarkable living examples of someone who got into good trouble, was violently attacked, lived, and shook the world. It is a truly remarkable biography for someone who, in most advance democracies, would not have been old enough to vote.

Malala was born in the war-torn Khyber region of the Swat Valley of Pakistan to a family that was impoverished and displaced but believed in education. Malala's autobiography, *I Am Malala*, depicts a loving family life, despite being surrounded by violence (Yousafzai, 2013). Her father founded a chain of schools for children, including refugees, but these schools, and their commitment to educating girls, aggravated the Taliban fighters who were coming over the porous border with Afghanistan.

By the mid-2000s the Taliban had taken control of Swat. The extreme version of Islamic law they imposed was particularly cruel to women and young girls. As the Taliban gained control of the area, they forbade women and girls from being out in public and began destroying schools. The former prime minister, Benazir Bhutto, Pakistan's first female head of state, was assassinated in 2008; that year, the Taliban destroyed more than four hundred schools. During the violence, her father spoke out against the devastation and received death threats. At the age of ten, Malala began writing for a BBC blog under a pseudonym, passing handwritten notes to a reporter to upload on the Internet. She also began to speak more brazenly in public about the need for girls to have an education. Given the Taliban's belief in the inferior status of women and children, as well as their willingness to use violence to enforce their misogynistic dogma, this was both bold and extremely dangerous.

Despite threats, Malala persisted in her belief in justice and education, continuing to defy the Taliban. Her blog morphed into a larger public platform where she continued to bear witness to atrocities and suppression of education. In 2008, she gave a public speech in Peshawar entitled "How Dare the Taliban Take Away My Basic Right to Education?"

By late 2009, the Taliban were blowing up or closing schools through the Peshawar region. Her family became displaced, but her cries for education grew louder. Profiled and interviewed on television and recognized by world leaders, Malala's profile grew. So did the ire of the Taliban, who sought to silence her voice. While seated on a school bus, a Talib boarded, shouted her name, and shot her in the head. She survived and was brought to the United Kingdom for rehabilitation and has since become a luminary and inspiration to young and old alike.

The strength of her defiance of the Taliban is rivaled only by her commitment to peace and justice. Consider the words she told Jon Stewart as a guest on his popular American satire and talk show when asked about the threats she received from the Taliban:

> I started thinking about that, and I used to think that the Talib would come, and he would just kill me. But then I said, "If he comes, what would you do, Malala?" then I would reply to myself, "Malala, just take a shoe and hit him." But then I said, "If you hit a Talib with your shoe, then there would be no difference between you and the Talib. You must not treat others with cruelty and that much harshly, you must fight others but through peace and through dialogue and through education." Then I said I will tell him how important education is and that "I even want education for your children as well." And I will tell him, "That's what I want to tell you, now do what you want." (2013)

Malala's inspirational bravery and defiance of the Taliban show how a young girl's deviance was not only good, but necessary, a burden children should be exempted from but are not.

Other juveniles have been in good trouble that they did not seek. The *Diary of Anne Frank* portrays the horrors of living as a Jew under Nazi occupation through the eyes of thirteen-year-old Anne. After the Nazis invaded the Netherlands in 1940, by decree all Jews were to report to a work camp. Anne's family went into hiding to elude capture and probably death. Her family was illegally helped by several employees of a company that Anne's father worked for, most notably Meip Gies, who hid them in Amsterdam. Once in hiding, Anne began to write down her experiences. Her now famous diary is a timeless account of the hopes and dreams of an adolescent girl. It also recounts the daily struggles of living in hiding. Here she contemplates living in a social structure gone awry:

> It's difficult in times like these: ideals, dreams and cherished hopes rise within us, only to be crushed by grim reality. It's a wonder I haven't abandoned all my ideals, they seem so absurd and impractical. Yet I cling to them because I still believe, in spite of everything, that people are truly good at heart. (1947, 237)

Anne and her family were eventually found and deported to a concentration camp. Of eight in hiding, only her father survived the camps.

Lovers and Dreamers

In his memoir *Born a Crime* (2016), television personality Trevor Noah reflects on what it was like growing up as a biracial child under the South African apartheid regime. While the book is intended as humor, Noah also conveys the isolation and humiliation he endured as a biracial child in a country where miscegenation laws effectively criminalized him from birth. In a tribute to his remarkable mother, Noah recounts how black families pay a "black tax," meaning that blacks "spend all of their time trying to fix the problems of the past" (Noah, 2016). Noah's memoir is a useful reminder of how entire people are effectively criminalized at birth. Throughout most of the history of the United States, entire classes of people have been "born a criminal." Historically, this includes Native Americans and the plight of enslaved backs detailed in Chapter 4. More recently, we have another class of born criminals, childhood "illegal aliens."

Cesare Lombroso, known as the father of criminology, was an early proponent of positivism in the social sciences and developed the idea that criminals could be identified through physiological characteristics such as skull shapes and other phenotypical observations (1911). Nowadays his ideas are regarded as absurd by most credible criminologists, but the concept of the "born criminal" persists in popular culture as well as modern biology. While this book is not an attempt to wade into this debate, it does acknowledge that there are in fact, "born" criminals—but it is through labeling, not because of biological predispositions. As Anne Frank's biography demonstrates, not being born into the right religion, or lacking the correct paperwork, can make somebody illegal. A more modern instance involves undocumented immigrants and refugees, who are routinely labeled "illegal aliens," even as farmers and other industries depend on them for cheap labor.

In the United States, the descendants of undocumented immigrants, called "Dreamers," have become the center of a political debate. Dreamers are those who arrived as children in the US without proper documentation. In an appeal to give amnesty to the childhood arrivals, the Deferred Action for Childhood Arrivals (DACA) program was instituted under the Obama administration, granting Dreamers temporary amnesty and legal status. The program has since become a political football. Critics of DACA bemoan an amnesty program that "rewards" people who are in the country illegally. Supporters of the program say that it simply grants paperwork to people who have lived most of their lives here and offers them a path to citizenship. The debate exposes the wide political chasm in the US and quickly devolves into heated discussions of unrelated matters of immigration and foreign policy.

Many of these Dreamers are heroes in the conventional sense. For instance, thousands of undocumented children have gone on to serve in the military. Others, such as Jesus Contreras, a Houston area paramedic, worked tirelessly for several weeks after Hurricane Harvey, helping diabetics, elderly, and people trapped in their homes (Arkin, 2017). Contras was brought into the US illegally by his mother when he was six years old and faces deportation to a country that he barely knows. In all, there are eight hundred thousand "Dreamers" facing similar circumstances. Simply having the courage to live and thrive in a country that has deemed them illegal gives us the right to call them "deviant heroes."

Deportations have inspired other forms of good trouble in the US and elsewhere. For instance, it was reported in late 2017 that German airline pilots refused to fly planes carrying asylum seekers who were being deported back to Afghanistan (Welle, 2017). In the United States, several mayors have declared their cities "sanctuary cities" and refused to cooperate with Immigration and Customs Enforcement raids. At the U.S.-Mexican border, some Americans are providing humanitarian aid to people who attempt to cross the border illegally. In all the above, motivations of compassion and love presented a necessary context for good trouble.

Martin Luther King instructed his followers that "hate cannot drive out hate: only love can do that". Psychologist Eric Fromm asserted that romantic love is not natural but is achieved through discipline and overcoming narcissism (Fromm, 1956, 13). He wrote that "love is not primarily a relationship to a specific person; it is an attitude, an ordination of character which determines the relatedness of the person to the whole world as a whole, not toward one object of love." Fromm argued that our most intimate relationships, our experience of love, are shaped by social forces. Love, Fromm believed, is a force in itself, but one that intersects with history and other social forces.

Criminalizing Love

The love between the aptly named Mildred and Richard Loving came up against social forces in the state of Virginia, which criminalized their romantic relationship. The Lovings were arrested in their own bedroom and tried under Virginia's antimiscegenation statute. Like Nazi Germany and apartheid South Africa, the United States has had explicit antimiscegenation laws dating back to the days of slavery. Mildred and Richard lived as exiles away from Virginia while their court case, *Loving v. Virginia*, proceeded. Although the Supreme Court was reluctant to hear the case, they unanimously overturned the Lovings' conviction.

Love has been criminalized in other contexts as well. Twenty years ago, every state prohibited same-sex marriage. In fact, it was not until *Lawrence v. Texas* in 2003 that laws prohibiting consensual relations between same-sex partners were struck down. Up until that time, homosexuals faced homophobic violence and intimidation from both the police and the public. Those who openly expressed their love for one another were denied employment, despised, chastised, and even killed. Yet they persisted. The Stonewall riots against police raids on a gay tavern in New York City were a mass action and open defiance of norms and laws against the LGBT community. As with other movements, confrontations with the police catalyzed a movement and led to efforts to normalize same-sex couples. In 2015, *Obergefell v. Hodges* affirmed that people have the fundamental right to marry, effectively legalizing same-sex marriage in the United States.

Brownie Mary Rathbun

In other cases, compassion for others has been a driving motivation for people breaking the law. In some cases, this compassion has led to a much broader legal movement. For instance, my students are intrigued by the story of a seventy-eight-year-old woman named Mary Rathbun of San Francisco. AIDS hit her city hard in the 1980s and 1990s and gay men in her community began to get sick, suffer and die. Few treatments were available to treat the disease and symptoms. Cannabis, though illegal in California then, alleviated several symptoms associated with HIV. Rathbun began baking cookies and brownies, laced with cannabis, and distributing them at San Francisco General Hospital. Living only on social security, she bought the ingredients with her own money. Her efforts won her the name "Brownie Mary" and she was adored as the Florence Nightingale of medical marijuana (Sawyer, 2017). Despite the altruism behind her efforts, she was arrested for distributing a controlled substance. She was ultimately released, but her arrest prompted a movement to legalize marijuana for medicinal uses. As of 2018, thirty states have some form of legal medicinal cannabis and nine others have legalized it outright. Rathbun rejected the label hero, but her efforts have decriminalized those who use marijuana medicinally and sparked a broader discussion of what if anything constitutes a just war on drugs.

From immigrants to same-sex couples, the law has sought to intercede in the human bond of love. While love may not always conquer all, the strength to love is a powerful force against violence and bigotry.

War

A full discussion of lovers and peacemakers cannot take place without considering the anthesis of love and peace: war, a context were the worst of human behavior is readily seen. "War crimes" and the acts of those who are simply "following orders" have resulted in innumerable suffering and horrors. Sociologist Max Weber famously theorized the state as a "human community that has a monopoly on the legitimate use of violence within a given territory" (Watters and Waters 2015, 136). It follows that the state will construct war heroes to legitimize its conduct. Every militarized state honors such heroes, while labeling those who might resist as traitors. Here, it is worth considering several of these so-called traitors and how they have gotten into good trouble.

Conscientiously objecting from participation in the military or otherwise refusing military service may be undertaken because of political views, religious conviction, or other moral objections. At various times in history, individuals doing so may open themselves up to court martial, imprisonment, and execution. Although conscientious objectors are now protected under the United Nations Universal Declaration of Human Rights (UN, 2012), such protections are relatively new and not always followed.

Many early Christians refused to join the Roman army. One of the first known conscientious objectors was Maximilian, who refused to enlist in the army on religious grounds (Gettleman, 1985), an act that resulted in his beheading in AD 295 (Alston, 2002). Maximilian was canonized and has served as an inspiration for other Christians who have declined military service. While Christianity has obviously changed its views about official violence, many people have continued to refuse to engage in violence on behalf of the state for religious reasons. Quakers, Seventh Day Adventists, and Amish, for example, restrict their members from joining the military. Other religious traditions, such as Islam, may prohibit their followers from participating in wars that are determined to be "unjust." In this way, following the rules of one socializing institution (religion) places members at odds with the rules of another (the state).

The Jedi Master Yoda said, "Great warrior? Wars not make one great." Yet armed conflict seeks to honor valor and heroes. Dereliction of duty, absence without leave, and refusal to follow orders are all serious military crimes, as is "draft dodging" or intervening in "war crimes." Depending on the context, those who resist violence can be either deviant or heroic, and sometimes both. For instance, conscientious objector Desmond Doss served in the army as a noncombatant during WWII, and because of his valor in rescuing wounded soldiers, was awarded the Medal of Honor, the only conscientious objector to do so.

Sometimes heroes are manufactured to cloak the lies and suffering that accompany warfare. Moved by the September 11th attack, Pat Tillman gave up an NFL contract to fight as an army ranger against the Taliban (Krakauer, 2009). His move was lauded by many, and he served as a seemingly perfect "all-American" image to bolster the army's recruitment. Tillman was a hero for sure, but not for the reasons the army wanted him to be. For instance, in a direct refutation of the aphorism that there are supposedly "no atheists in foxholes," Tillman was an atheist known to read Islamic, Hindu, and Buddhist religious texts for their literary and historical significance. After serving in Iraq, he was deployed to Afghanistan, where he was killed in a hail of bullets from his own unit. The cause of his death was not enemy fire but fratricide. The army attempted to cover up the details, fabricating a narrative that Tillman died valorously fighting the Taliban. Tillman's family pressed for the truth for four years, until the army finally admitted it had lied about this death.

Others have resisted conscription or refused to serve or follow orders. Nicaraguan immigrant Camilo Mejía funded his college education by enlisting in the U.S. Army. Before he had a chance to finish college, he was deployed to Iraq. In his autobiography, *The Road from Ar Ramadi* (2008), Mejía recounts the mental tension and inner conflict he experienced by participating in what he felt was an illegal and unethical war. Calling US foreign policy an "imperial dragon that devours its own soldiers and Iraqi civilians for the sake of profits" he realized he could no longer passively conform to his orders and duties as a solider (223). While on leave in the US he decided it was no longer conscionable to participate in a war he determined was about oil and based on lies (Mejía, 2008). His application for conscientious objector status was denied, and he was convicted of desertion in a court-martial. Mejía was dishonorably discharged and spent a year in a military prison (Shetterly, 2009). He actions were clearly illegal, and in the context of military service, treason. Yet his questioning of American violence served as a prelude for the perception of the American war in Iraq. About the time of his release from prison in 2005, the American public had finally grown weary of the war and began to accept that the war in Iraq was made under false pretenses.

In other parts of the world, deviant peacemakers have etched their defiance into the conscience of generations. Recall the image of Tiananmen Square in 1989 (FRONTLINE, 2006). Communism was on the verge of collapse in Europe and Russia, and it seemed that China could be the next country to embrace democracy. Over one million students occupied Tiananmen Square demanding liberty. The People's Liberation Army was called in to crush the demonstration. A lone man stood in the street before a column of tanks. Known only as "Tank Man" he stood his ground for twenty-two minutes, holding up the advance of the largest army in the world, until he was whisked away by some people in plain clothes. The world has yet to learn his real name. It is possible, given the Chinese justice system at the time, that Tank Man was executed. It is also possible he was pardoned—but the global community has yet to know. I hope the world will someday learn Tank Man's name. When we do, it will show that even the most ironclad regimes have cracks that allow justice to permeate.

The film, *Schindler's List,* depicted the brutality and inhumanity of the Nazi regime, but it also familiarized many with the silent and underground resistance to the regime and the Holocaust. Oscar Schindler was a deviant German who helped twelve hundred Jews avoid gas chambers and concentration camps. At the same time, there were many other "silent partners" in opposition to fascism. The White Rose Movement was an informal underground organization in Germany that opposed the Nazis and the wars they were fighting. It was active at the University of Munich, where members distributed anti-Nazi pamphlets that contained messages such as this:

> Nothing is so unworthy of a nation as allowing itself to be governed without opposition by a clique that has yielded to base instinct. . . . Western civilization must defend itself against fascism and offer passive resistance, before the nation's last young man has given his blood on some battlefield. (found at Biography Online, n.d.)

Twenty-one-year-old Sophie Scholl was moved by these pamphlets and began distributing them, along with other antiwar leaflets. She was arrested, beaten, and brought before a show trial where she interrupted the judge: "Somebody, after all, had to make a start. What we wrote and said is also believed by many others. They just don't dare express themselves as we did."

Scholl and her brother were executed by guillotine on February 22, 1943.

Many others around the world got into necessary trouble opposing violence and promoting peaceful noncompliance. Mahatma Gandhi is most revered for his philosophy of nonviolence and concepts of passive resistance. His activism began in apartheid South Africa; from there, he became involved in the anti-colonial movement against the British in India and was a key figure in that country's struggle for independence.

While much of the opposition to colonialism was violent (e.g., Ho Chi Minh, Castro, Guevarra), Gandhi was most famous for crafting a model of nonviolence and noncooperation for which he was imprisoned several times. Most famous was his Salt March, when thousands of Indians marched to the

Arabian Sea to harvest salt in defiance of the salt taxes imposed by the British. He, along with sixty thousand other Indians, were arrested for simply gathering salt from the sea. His movement became a massive organization, the Indian National Congress, which laid the groundwork for independence. Gandhi's nonviolence in action was a model of good trouble that inspired many others, including Martin Luther King.

Besides Malala, other Nobel laureates have graced the world stage as deviant heroes for peace. Nelson Mandela spent most of his life challenging the system of apartheid in South Africa. Because of his efforts, he was arrested and tried for crimes against the all-white government he did not recognize, crimes that included serious offenses such as treason and lesser ones, like instigating strikes. For his work through the African National Congress to include all South Africans in the political process, Mandela was incarcerated for the better part of three decades on a conviction for sabotage.

> Whatever sentence Your Worship sees fit to impose upon me for the crime for which I have been convicted before this court, may it rest assured that when my sentence has been completed I will still be moved, as men are always moved, by their conscience; I will still be moved by my dislike of the race discrimination against my people when I come out from serving my sentence, to take up again, as best I can, the struggle for the removal of those injustices until they are finally abolished once and for all. (Mandela, 1994, 50)

As the case of Mandela demonstrates, founders of modern democracies or movements against inequality are often those who have been formerly declared "enemies of the republic," "subversives," or "traitors." Some have fought against racism, while others have challenged sexist norms. Norm-breaking is one of the few social phenomena that is a cultural universal; some kind of deviant behavior exists in nearly every society. It happens in both permissive societies and oppressive societies. It happens in homogenous cultures as well as in the highly diverse. Good trouble for peace may occur in any context where violence and militarism are normalized.

Deviant Athletes

The Olympic Games and "sports diplomacy" are readily known as venues where peace and international reconciliation are promoted. Sports can also be a forum for peaceful protest and good trouble. Recall those images from the 1968 Olympics, when Tommie Smith and Juan Carlos, while being awarded the silver and gold medals, respectively, raised their fists and bowed their heads to protest racism at home and the war in Vietnam. Historically, sports and athletic competition can be settings in which deviant heroes challenge biases that surround the playing field, upending assumed inferiorities in front of a wide audience.

The same is true of gender biases, where women have been shut out of sports competitions deemed masculine. Sports has many heroes, but in rare cases like these, an athlete may risk everything to challenge an injustice and become a deviant hero.

Good trouble in sports is a type of peacemaking that deserves special attention because of the ability of athletics to impact a broad audience. Nelson Mandela understood this when, as newly elected president, he needed to give his new nation a reason to unite and move past the scars and bitterness of apartheid. Mandela understood the potential power that sports have to overcome inequality and racism. He surmised that sports are a transformative and connecting experience when he entered the stadium of a nearly all-white crowd for a rugby match to cheer on the national rugby team. Mandela knew the symbolic importance of this in attempting to peacefully unite a fractured nation torn by racist violence and an apartheid regime.

> Sport has the power to change the world. It has the power to inspire. It has the power to unite people in a way that little else does. It speaks to youth in a language they understand. Sport can create hope where once there was only despair. (Mandela 2011, 348)

Pioneers who broke the color line, such as Jessie Owens and Jackie Robinson, are rightly canonized not just for their athletic achievements but their bravery in competing before a skeptical or openly hostile audience. Far from home, in a hostile arena amid antagonistic officials, Owens humiliated the white supremacists of National Socialism while demonstrating the power of a multiracial Olympic team. Jackie Robinson was belittled and isolated by the racism of teammates and fans only to overcome prejudice and carve a path for integration in other American social institutions. In both cases, the norms of the games presumed the whiteness of the athlete—until a deviant changed the rules.

Sports, like education, can be a transformative and emancipatory endeavor. Like other institutional values, sports are full of contradictions; the focus on teamwork and rules reinforces conformist principles, while the nationalism that surrounds most mass events stokes jingoism and exclusion. At the same time, sports rely on transparency and fairness. As such, they can serve as a venue where tensions are negotiated, refined, and then resolved. In some cases, good trouble may change a sport and affect the society as a whole.

Sports is a socializing institution. Besides the pages of formal rules and regulations that players must abide by, participants and spectators are expected to follow informal norms as well, like standing up for the national anthem. To succeed in sports, an athlete must be focused and disciplined. Several studies in the sociology of deviance have focused on the issue of overconformity in sports and training or performing beyond accepted limits.

For instance, athletes may embrace an exaggerated adherence to sport ethics (Nixon, 1992) or overcondition themselves to meet uncriticized norms and exaggerated images of an athlete that the culture presents (Ewald and Jibou, 1985). This has been called a form of "positive deviance," an antithesis to hyper-conformity (Hughes and Coakley, 1991). Pushing beyond the operational definition of positive deviance, amateur athletes may begin to train beyond accepted limits for students, others may resort to performance-enhancing drugs. In short, there is much pressure on athletes to conform to standards of competition, so it can be notable when an athlete breaks an accepted norm to make a social statement.

The impact of sport on cultures around the world is undeniable. Sport heroes such as Michael Jordan or Usain Bolt are instantly recognized by youth around the world. As sports is reflective of larger social values, where heroes are made and champions celebrated, there are many celebrated instances where athletes have gotten into good trouble. Sports have long been an institution where barriers are broken. Billie Jean King challenged the sexism in tennis by playing, and defeating, Wimbledon champion and male chauvinist Bobby Riggs. Then there is Kathrine Switzer, who ran in the Boston Marathon in 1967, a race deemed too demanding for female athletes. Switzer was physically pushed off the course and had her number forcibly removed by race officials.

In other cases, champions may jeopardize a title or a chance to go professional or risk their popularity to resist an injustice or promote a cause that they believe to be moral. Olympic gold medalist and boxer Muhammad Ali was stripped of his boxing title and threatened with imprisonment when he refused to be drafted into the Vietnam War.

> I will not disgrace my religion, my people or myself by becoming a tool to enslave those who are fighting for their own justice, freedom and equality. If I thought the war was going to bring freedom and equality to 22 million of my people they wouldn't have to draft me, I'd join tomorrow. I have nothing to lose by standing up for my beliefs. So I'll go to jail, so what? We've been in jail for 400 years. (quoted in Shetterly 2009, 23)

Besides legal jeopardy for refusing induction into the army, Ali was stripped of his boxing titles and not allowed to compete. It may seem like a contradiction that Ali, a professional fighter, was a deviant hero of peace, but all heroes have contradictions and flaws.

Good Trouble Betrayed

Even the greatest people have flaws. Our heroes may fail us; some do not personally live up to ideals that they espouse, or they may make inconsistent decisions; others have personal faults that prevent them from having their widest impact. King's marital infidelity is sometimes mentioned as a weakness in character and was used to delegitimize his cause or, at least, question his legacy. Similarly, Gandhi, during his work as an attorney in South Africa, did not question apartheid and may have even believed in it (Desai & Vahed, 2015). There are many instances of deviant heroes, once recognized as right or just, who make concessions to power that disappoint their constituency. Mandela embraced white Afrikaners in his government, Arafat gave concessions to the Israelis, and Malcolm X changed his stance on whites being allies in the struggle for civil rights. Such compromises may be seen as a betrayal by a core constituency, but were made once a challenge to a norm was established. Other times, deviant heroes who were thought of as peacemakers turn out not to be after all, betraying their supposed cause.

The case of Aung San Suu Kyi, the longtime advocate of democracy in Myanmar, has important ramifications in this regard. Like India, Myanmar was part of the British Empire, but it was administered separately, as the country of Burma (Central Intelligence Agency, n.d.). After British rule, Burma was a constitutional democracy, but military rule ensued in 1962.

Suu Kyi's biography, *The Lady and the Peacock* (Popham, 2012), describes an extraordinary deviant hero, one who was brave and selfless as she engaged in nonviolent dissent against the military junta. Her father, who had founded the modern Burmese army, was assassinated shortly after independence in 1947. Despite personal tragedy, Suu Kyi was relatively privileged, with an influential mother, access to schooling, and the chance to live and travel abroad. In 1988, she returned and became active in the pro-democracy movement, which gained a large following—and a lot of trouble. The military government quickly targeted Suu Kyi and her followers, putting their lives at risk. Yet Suu Kyi remained committed to the principles of nonviolence pioneered by Gandhi and confirmed by her Buddhist beliefs. In an essay Suu Kyi penned before being placed on house arrest in 1989, she echoed the teachings of Gandhi, Thoreau, and Martin Luther King:

> The words "law and order" have so frequently been misused as an excuse for oppression that the very phrase has become suspect in countries which have known authoritarian rule. Some years ago a prominent Burmese author wrote an article on the notion of law and order as expressed by the official term *nyein-wut-pi-pyar*. One by one he analyzed the words, which literally mean "silent-crouched-crushed-flattened," and concluded that the whole made for an undesirable state of affairs, one which militated against the emergence of an articulate, energetic, progressive citizenry. There is no intrinsic virtue to law and order unless "law" is equated with justice and "order" with the discipline of a people satisfied that justice has been done. Law as an instrument of state oppression is a familiar feature of totalitarianism. (1991, 176–177).

In 1990, multiparty elections resulted in a victory of the National League for Democracy (NLD) led by Suu Kyi. Instead of handing over power to her, however, she was placed under house arrest. Even though in 1991 she was recognized with a Nobel Peace Prize, she was kept under arrest for long intervals for the next twenty years for her pro-democracy stances (Popham, 2012). Then, in 2011, there was a substantial opening of this isolated country, with political and economic reforms. The NLD won elections, and Suu Kyi was elected to the national legislature.

Her profile quickly rose, as she was especially bold in her opposition. In a majority Buddhist country, Suu Kyi carried an aura of supernatural prowess. When she was campaigning for election in 1989, a column of soldiers was ordered to shoot her and her compatriots along the side of a road. But she walked forward, daring them to kill her, and kept walking, right past the column of soldiers (Popham, 2012). General Than Shwe later targeted her in a failed assassination attempt (Popham, 2012, 361–62). Despite years of house arrest, Suu Kyi persisted and her country opened, embraced democracy, and elected Suu Kyi to a top political spot.

Had the story of Myanmar ended when it transitioned to democracy, Suu Kyi might have been just another example of a misbehaving woman making history, a genuine deviant hero. However, this was not the case. As Suu Kyi's country opened up to the world, it exposed an alarming mistreatment of a minority community. Myanmar is majority Buddhist with a small but significant Muslim minority. The stateless Rohingya Muslim minority in Myanmar had endured atrocities for decades, but the transition to democracy resulted in a widespread persecution of the Rohingya, to the point of genocide (Ibrahim, 2018). As Myanmar's heroine of democracy, Suu Kyi was in a position to stop or at least speak out against the atrocities of her compatriots. But she did not.

Suu Kyi is just one supposed "deviant hero" who betrayed the cause of peace and nonviolence. Sometimes, heroes are selected as emblematic of a larger cause, only to be torn down by changing norms or by a failure to act when they could have. Clearly, the test of history is necessary to fully discern what constitutes good trouble and what does not. Gandhi's nonviolent movement of necessary trouble against the British was clearly a classic case of deviant heroism and peacemaking; however, the Indian subcontinent is still marred by violent religious conflict and even the threat of a regional nuclear conflict.

The point of the case of Suu Kyi is that not only do deviant heroes have flaws, but sometimes they become part of the problem. One can only speculate on why a person is vocal on one issue but silent on another; however, prejudice and apathy seem to infect those who champion a righteous cause over injustice in one case and then look away in another. Good trouble is more than acting when it is convenient or aligning with a majority view; it is about being principled and taking a stand against injustice wherever it is found. While most of the deviants profiled in this book embody principles of peace, justice, and altruism, not all live up to the standards of a true hero over time. It may require the passage of time to identify genuine good trouble.

Criminal and Environmental Justice

The dual public issues of crime and the environment affect the personal lives of each of us. Crime, or the absence thereof, is a long-standing indicator of well-being for people and communities. Similarly, the quality of the environment is regularly mentioned as a barometer of overall living conditions. Crime and environmental degradation are more than mere blights on communities; they encapsulate central questions of human rights and the overall health of humanity, and both have rightfully received much attention by scholars, politicians, the media, and individual citizens since the 1970s. However, only recently have these two areas—crime and the environment—been strongly linked by sociologists and criminologists.

Like war, environmental degradation poses an existential threat to human existence. In the same spirit as other peacemakers, deviant heroes like Rachel Carson or James Hansen, whom we discussed in the previous chapter, champion the cause of the environment, violate norms, and break laws to raise awareness about ecology, climate change, and environmental injustice.

Civil disobedience in the defense of the environment follows a long tradition of direct action in the United States in the form of both individual, value-oriented action and collective acts of civil disobedience. The Underground Railroad illegally aided the escape of fugitive slaves. Sit-down strikes helped establish the right to collective bargaining. Sit-ins and nonviolent confrontation brought an end to state-enforced segregation in the South.

Militant environmentalists have used other tactics as well. Edward Abbey's 1975 novel, *The Monkey Wrench Gang*, depicts an American West scarred by development, its landscape littered with billboards and its rivers subdued with concrete and steel. Abbey portrays the actions of four ecologically minded deviants who engage in acts of sabotage aimed at protecting the environment. Such actions start with relatively minor crimes, such as toppling billboards littering the once picturesque Southwest, to attacking deserted construction equipment. The fictional activism of *The Monkey Wrench Gang* is said to have inspired several real-world movements and individuals to act in defense of the environment. Some of them are mired in controversy. For instance, the actions of the ecological group Earth First! founded in 1980 as a radical environmental advocacy group included publicity stunts such as unfurling a banner picturing a plastic crack down the face of Glen Canyon Dam. Other actions of Earth First! included dumping manure on a fish and game officer's desk, disabling construction equipment, chaining themselves to fences at the offices of extractive industries, and releasing cattle from a feedlot (Gorman, 1988). Later, they participated in direct action that included tree-sits and demonstrations. But the cause of environmental advocacy began to splinter and in some cases diverge from principles of nonviolence. In a more extreme vein, the Earth Liberation Front and a sister cause, the Animal Liberation Front, have used forms of sabotage that include arson as well as other methods that have risked people's lives. Due to their willingness to use violence and the potential for doing harm, these splinter movements represent a betrayal of good trouble. Instead, true good trouble in championing the cause of environmental justice would embrace methods and principles that are counter-hegemonic to the material and ideological roots of ecological destruction.

Returning to the idea of peacemaking criminology, criminologists McClanahan and Brisman (2015) have argued against the securitizing of climate change and issues of ecology. Action on climate and matters of ecology should be pursued not because of national security threats, but because ecology is a worthy goal in and of itself. A war-making approach to ecology (i.e., a war on climate change) is problematic because the proposed solutions mimic the ideologies and actions that contribute to ecological destruction in the first place. McClanahan and Brisman argue that framing environmental harm as an issue of "security" creates a material and discursive orientation that overlooks environmental harms that are rooted in capital accumulation and hegemonic security systems. In other words, environmental destruction happens due to a legal and normative environment that permits destruction of nature for profit. Instead, peacemaking criminology would incorporate concepts of peace and justice into a model for remediating environmental harms. Just as criminology must embrace matters of environmental justice in the lexicon of the field, environmental justice has much to learn from the principles of peacemaking criminology. Creating good trouble for the cause of the environment may be one way of demonstrating these principles.

Lone acts of civil disobedience can have profound impacts on the public's perception of social problems. While small acts of deviance may be largely symbolic, they can galvanize a movement or stir a larger debate about a problem, with the act of good trouble engrained in the cultural lexicon. This was the case for Julia "Butterfly" Hill, who ascended a thousand-year-old redwood tree named Luna to protest logging in the Headwaters Forest of Northern California. The redwood was scheduled to be cut as part of a clearcut by Pacific Lumber Company. Hill sat in the tree for 738 days and refused to come down until the tree and surrounding forest were protected. Technically, her crime was trespassing, and she was panned for being a stinky hippy who was costing logging jobs, but it was an act of good trouble that roused awareness for the cause of environmental preservation. In 2018, several Appalachian women have been taking turns camping out in forests and trees, in defiance of local authorities, to prevent and bring awareness to the encroachment and spoiling of wildlands by energy and pipeline companies (Philip, 2018).

The Dakota Access Pipeline (DAP) was announced in June 2014. The project, a twelve-hundred-mile-long pipeline that connects shale oil fields in North Dakota to refineries in Illinois, was touted as a critical infrastructure project that brought jobs and fostered energy independence. The project relied on government subsidies and the condemnation of private land under eminent domain. It traverses ecologically sensitive areas, including the Missouri River, and passes through the ancestral land of the Sioux, disturbing culturally significant archeological sites. The project appeared to violate environmental law, property rights, antiquities acts, and in particular, two treaties with the Sioux. In a series of lawsuits, courts declared the project legal and lawful. The last part of the DAP passed just north of the Standing Rock Indian Reservation on the west bank of the Missouri River. There, in September 2016, protesters used their bodies to prevent the completion of the project. The police informed them that they were trespassing, but the number of protesters grew as people began to filter in from across the country.

By all accounts, the protesters were completely peaceful but refused to leave. Private security workers used attack dogs to intimidate them, and six protesters and one horse were attacked by the dogs. The actions of the security workers were filmed and circulated on social media and in full view of sheriff deputies. By October, National Guard arrived on behalf of the pipeline company, and soldiers and armed police forcefully cleared an encampment. More protesters arrived, but the fall weather began to set in on the Dakotas. In below-freezing weather, police used water cannons on the protesters, but a few persisted and vowed to stay through the winter.

During the protest, on November 8, 2016, the United States elected a new president. Through the winter, the number of protesters gradually decreased, until their numbers were so small they were easily evicted by police and the National Guard. By February of 2017, a series of executive orders expedited an environmental review. When the pipeline was completed and started to flow by April 2017, the stock price of Energy Transfer Partners, the main contractor in a consortium of oil companies associated with the pipeline, hit an all-time high.

This chapter has looked at issues of war and genocide, immigration, sports, anticolonialism, and environmentalism against the unifying concept that the peaceful use of good trouble may be a counter to violence. As an author, I am at a loss for words to properly conclude a chapter that has probed such a wide array of topics. Perhaps we should end with the words of Sitting Bull: *"What white man can say I ever stole his land or a penny of his money? Yet they say that I am a thief."*

III

Good Trouble and the Individual

Chapter Nine

Complicit Conformity

C. P. Snow wrote that "when you think of the long and gloomy history of man, you will find that far more, and far more hideous, crimes have been committed in the name of obedience than have ever been committed in the name of rebellion" (1971, 195). This chapter examines the anthesis of good trouble: complacent conformity.

The year 1968 was eventful and tragic in the United States. This was also true from the perspective of criminology. Martin Luther King Jr. and Bobby Kennedy were assassinated. The assassination of King sparked riots across several U.S. cities, including Chicago; Washington, D.C.; and Baltimore, provoking a heightened law enforcement response nationwide. Protests at the Democratic National Convention in Chicago triggered a police riot that used unrestrained violence against demonstrators. The subsequent legitimation crisis in policing marked the beginning of the end of the reform era of policing, which was marked by the bureaucratization and professionalization of the police force (for instance, see Williams & Murphy, 1990). Amid rising crime rates, Richard Nixon was elected, in part, on a platform of "law and order." His running mate, Spiro Agnew, was also fond of the phrase. Both would eventually resign in disgrace, in different circumstances, over their own criminal conduct. Elsewhere in the world in 1968, civil unrest in France saw general strikes and student occupations; in Czechoslovakia, the Prague Spring was an open protest against Soviet domination of the region. Mexico City hosted the 1968 Olympic Games, where Tommie Smith and Juan Carlos gave their black power salute from the medal podium as the American national anthem was played. In March of that year, in a small Vietnam hamlet known as My Lai, four U.S. soldiers in the platoon Charlie "C" Company massacred several hundred women, children, and old men, a war crime in defense of which soldiers claimed they were "following orders." The American public would not learn of it for almost eighteen more months.

Investigative journalist Seymour Hersh first broke the story of the My Lai Massacre to the American public in late 1969. He described U.S. soldiers entering My Lai with "guns blazin," shooting people at random, without any reasonable explanation for the motive (Hersh, 1970). The first-person accounts of the massacre were horrific and included the murder of a nursing baby, the rape of a child, bayonetting an old woman in the back, and indiscriminate killing of unarmed civilians. However, the subsequent investigation of the massacre found that the killing was not random at all but was done with intent on clear orders from a commanding officer, Lieutenant William Calley, with the apparent consent of his commanding officer, Captain Ernest Medina (Hersh, 1972). Charges were brought against several enlisted soldiers and officers in a military court-martial, but Calley was the only one convicted. He was charged with the murder of 102 people and convicted on twenty-two of those counts. While Calley was a war criminal who gave the orders, it was the complicit conformity of his subordinates that enabled the massacre to occur. The massacre was described as quite routine and part of their everyday actions as a soldier. One soldier, Kenneth Hodges of "C" Company described the massacre like this:

> I feel that they were able to carry out the assigned task, the orders that meant killing small kids, killing women, because they were trained that way. They were trained that when you get into combat, it's either you or the enemy. (Hersh, 1970, 99–100)

While My Lai was a clear war crime, the soldiers who banally massacred defenseless civilians were following orders, conforming to what was asked of them by a commanding officer. How could ordinary soldiers commit such atrocities? While norms, rules, and laws are generally thought to protect people from harm, ensure general tranquility, and enable the functioning of society, all too often conformity causes the opposite. In fact, it is everyday complicit conformity that has enabled some of the most horrific acts.

The context of war and militaristic regimes demonstrates where conformity can be especially problematic. The archetypical example is the case of Nazi Germany, where ordinary citizens engaged in the most egregious atrocities in the history of humanity. In warfare, the most horrific of collective human actions can be realized. In the most redundant form of military speak, "war crimes" have been observed in most major modern wars. From the Nanking massacre by Japanese troops to the sadism of Abu Ghraib by Americans in the Iraq War, "crimes of conformity" seem to be a hallmark of most armed conflict. Yet how could so many soldiers follow orders that would seemingly violate their own sense of right and wrong? In the case of

My Lai, as in other war crimes, following orders—conformity and obedience to authority—seems to be the driving rationale.

Academic literature on the My Lai Massacre suggests echoes of the German Holocaust and other genocides where obedience and conformity were a precursor to horrific acts. Kelman and Hamilton, in their book *Crimes of Obedience* (1989), provide a social-psychological analysis of responses to authority and conformity in situations where individuals are faced with committing a crime. Looking into the dynamics of the My Lai Massacre and the ensuing cover-up and response, they propose a framework to identify a sanctioned massacre as a crime of conformity (16–20). First, this includes the authorization by a higher authority, where soldiers do not just what was required, but are complicit in conducting actions that are not expressly forbidden. This gives soldiers implicit permission to act out in ways that are not explicitly prohibited. Secondly, the act is committed in the otherwise routine tasks of soldiers on "search and destroy missions." The atrocities are thus a normalized behavior in the context of what soldiers are ordered to do. Lastly, a collective dehumanization of others enables complicit conformists to justify their conduct not just against an enemy but an unarmed civilian population. In short, conformity, a dynamic social-psychological process of authority, socialization, and internalization, can be devastating to the human species.

COMPLICIT CONFORMITY DEFINED

This chapter is a problematization of conformity, establishing that while agreement and compliance with norms may be necessary for the everyday functioning of a society, conformity can also be a reactionary and destructive social force. Conformity is not always a positive social force ensuring harmony and tranquility; thus, a study of conformity must include its psychosocial aspects and relationship to authority. In describing the pervasiveness of complicit conformity, this chapter will detail several cases where conformity has been especially problematic.

Up to this point, we have celebrated the nonconformist words and practices of people who have demonstrated the necessity and immense social value of deviance and crime. Such a tribute must draw attention not only to the usefulness of deviance but also to the problem of conformity. Sometimes entire groups and societies can go "bad." In small-group dynamics, bullying is a classic example of disdainful behavior involving conformity, as is gang rape. On a more macro-level, history is full of instances of collective compliance that resulted in mass suffering, violence, and death. In many cases, an entire society can represent injustice, as in the case of Nazi Germany or the

Jim Crow South. On a meso-level, group manifestations of this problem include Abu Ghraib prison and the My Lai Massacre.

As detailed in earlier chapters, the basic assumption of psychology and sociology is that rebels, those who depart from the status quo and disrupt loyalty and group cohesion, are inherently problematic. The forerunners of the positive deviance thesis challenge the premise that nonconformists are disdainful at worst or morally neutral at best. Thus far, this book has urged moving further, advocating that scholars consider deviance as a necessary force for good and social change. Therefore, such a salient conception must problematize the practice of conformity, at least in certain situations.

The full consideration of good trouble requires attention to its antithesis: *complicit conformity*. This type of conformity happens when socialization, obedience, and desire to belong result in a dynamic that allows egregious and immoral actions to occur. The typology constructed in chapter 2 identifies complicit conformity happening when norms are followed resulting in a negative or detrimental social context. Complicit conformity can occur either in a small group, a medium-sized organization, or an entire society. Some of the worst chapters in the history of humanity may be attributed to the powerful social force of conformity. The commission of genocide requires a large-scale collective process of deference to authority and a denial of the humanity of the victims.

Examples of complicit conformity are found in a variety of contexts, ranging from smoking and doing drugs, to doing nothing while someone else is bullied, to war crimes such as My Lai. Conformity can represent a socially negative and destructive character, as it involves asking individuals to give up critical thinking and participate in a negative behavior. Complicit conformity represents the worst aspects of obedience, socialization, and the human disposition to do what is asked of you. More than simply acquiescing, complicit conformity is actively submitting to and going along with something detrimental and harmful to others. Given the pervasiveness and large scope of complicit conformity, it is useful to consider how both sociology and psychology approach this issue.

THE SOCIOLOGY OF CONFORMITY

A recurring theme in my teaching and scholarship related to crime and deviance is that most people, most of the time, conform with the rules, norms, and laws that their society has established for its members. This represents a key aspect of the process of socialization, the process by which people learn social norms and expectations and acceptable forms of behavior. Generally, conforming to rules that establish shared moral frameworks and ensure social harmony is typically considered a good thing. Once an individual has internalized the rules and norms of her society, conformity follows easily. However, when those norms are unjust, conformity becomes problematic. The ease with which individuals may accept unjust or immoral norms is shocking. From the killing fields of Cambodia to an American-run prison in Iraq, history is full of horrific instances of individuals violating their own notions of right and wrong because they were authorized, ordered, or simply pressured into the act.

The classical premise of sociology is that humans are social animals. While we each have unique characteristics and traits, sociology argues that we are largely shaped by social factors. Indeed, the underlying assumption of the sociological imagination is that individuals are intricately entwined with their social structure. Personal troubles are always enmeshed in larger social issues. Having a sociological imagination confers the ability to understand how such troubles are based in structural and historical processes. We are all products of a complex web of interrelationships with which we become acquainted through the process of socialization. Durkheim argued in his famous *Rules of the Sociological Method* (1966) that social structure is the dominant force in shaping the behavior of the individual. For Durkheim "social facts" communicated ways of acting and thinking. These facts are what hemmed seemingly individual characteristics to larger social structures.

The socialization process enables social reproduction, which gives societies structural continuity over a long period of time, connecting different generations of people to one another. A dynamic process, socialization starts in infancy and continues throughout the life course. Agents of socialization are various social institutions, such as the family, education, media, politics, etc. that communicate shared meanings and values. While socialization is a sociological process, *internalization* is a psychological process through which people, as they come into contact with these shared meanings and norms, integrate and accept them as their own.

Socialization into a culture or society is dependent on acceptance of its rules and norms. Conformity is the key in a successful socialization. Seldom do people resist socialization; it is largely regarded as a passive, subconscious process. However, humans are capable of acting back on their society and resisting socialization. This act of agency may be termed *nonconformity* or *deviance*.

Even though the concept of socialization is assumed to be one of the principles most foundational to the discipline of sociology, relatively little attention is paid to the process and problem of conformity, compared to deviance and rule violation. For example, a search of peer-reviewed journals in sociology over a three-year period ending in 2016 found just 172 articles with the subject heading "conformity." This compares to 1,852 articles under the subject heading "deviance."[1] Similarly, a further 2,657 articles were found under the subject heading "crime."

Despite socialization and conformity, with group cohesiveness being a key premise in the development of the academic discipline of sociology, clearly noncompliance remains a much more popular area of study in the field. The overemphasis on nonconformity in the sociology of deviance led one sociologist to call out the subfield as theoretically "impoverished" and overfocused on "sluts, nuts, and perverts" at the expense of rigorous social inquiry of power relations and the crimes of the well-off (Liazos, 1972). Nevertheless, conformity through socialization remains a central concept in the development of micro, meso, and macro understandings of human behavior and interaction.

THE SOCIAL PSYCHOLOGY OF CONFORMITY

Socialization is a powerful process needed to integrate members of a society into a community through some kind of shared cultural and normative framework. All members of a social group undergo socialization. The process is seldom reflected upon, let alone resisted, but anyone who belongs or wants to belong to a social group is typically expected to submit to socialization and to conform to the group's norms. The family, media, schools, and economic institutions communicate these various norms and beliefs to the individual who then, through the psychological process of internalization, makes them his or her own. Though psychology and sociology differ on explaining the process by which socialization mechanisms work on the psyche, the two disciplines agree that what is involved is a powerful adaptive process that requires group members to play by certain "ground rules" to ensure cohesiveness.

Perhaps more than in sociology, it is implicitly assumed in psychology that rule violation is a detrimental behavior that may undermine group cohesiveness (Jetten and Hornsey, 2011, 6–9). In contrast to sociology, which seems to focus on deviance over conformity, psychology is said to have a "conformity bias" that overemphasizes the process of obedience and authority while disregarding the countervailing evidence of dissent in groups, both large and small (Moscovici & Faucheux, 1972). This perspective wrongly affirms that psychological forces are irresistible to individuals and that changing normative contexts is an insurmountable task. The conformity bias gives an ahistorical and pessimistic worldview of humans as being incapable of challenging and changing status quo situations. Although the pressure to conform is a powerful psychological force, clearly people choose not to conform all the time.

Why is conformity seen as the default disposition of individuals in groups large and small? In traditional psychology, group members are thought to conform for one of two reasons (Deutsch & Gerard, 1955). First, when norms are ambiguous or circumstances uncertain, people look to others as a guide to appropriate behavior. This dynamic is seen during freshman orientation of new students at a university, or when one is sent abroad to a new culture for the first time. Second, psychologists understand that conformity is a powerful mechanism that individuals employ to fit in, obtain approval, and avoid punishment and social isolation. This process provides for both assimilation and influence over norms.

The literature on the problem of conformity and authority generally follows three general historical events. First, scholars have used it to explain the mass appeal of fascist regimes in the 1930s. For example, the work of Adorno and other members of the Frankfurt School relied on Freudian psychoanalysis and dialectical materialism to probe the role of anxiety and repression in causing submissiveness to authority figures. Later, conformity studies of the 1960s sought to explain the social-psychological roots and process of compliance. These studies included the Asch conformity project, the Milgram experiments, and the Zimbardo prison study, which are considered "classic" examples of the power of conformity to trump internalized notions of right and wrong. Lastly, more recent research from the 1990s and 2000s examined individual case studies of the pressure to conform in scandals related to authority and conformity, such as political scandals, systemic corporate wrongdoing, and sanctioned violence. Each of the eras in which these studies were done—the 1930s, the 1960s, and the 1970s—points to humans' willingness not only to conform to authority but to commit shocking atrocities in violation of their own moral values, simply to satiate authority figures or satisfy a need to belong.

Obedience and Authoritarianism

During the era of the Nazis, Germans are estimated to have killed six million Jews. Like My Lai, the Nazi Holocaust was not a random, senseless event. The killing of Jews had great meaning to the perpetrators and those who orchestrated the genocide. The Holocaust happened through an elaborate orchestration of bureaucracy, ideology, authority, obedience, and conformity. Historian Christopher Browning published *Ordinary Men* (1992) about the Nazi police Battalion 101 that participated in deportations and massacres of Jews. He argued that conformity, through obedience to authority and submission to group pressure, was the driving force in people committing heinous acts of violence. The book stands in contrast to other historical accounts, such as *Hitler's Willing Executioners* (Goldhagen, 1996), that focused on German anti-Semitism and its ideology of cruelty that was justified as right and necessary. This ethos of brutality made ordinary Germans murder not just with impunity but also enthusiasm. Both contrasting theses of the Holocaust problematize either conformity or socialization into ideology as precursors to the most horrific mass acts that humans have yet engaged in.

Several members of the Frankfurt School give some insight into the problem of conformity. Adorno, in his work *The Authoritarian Personality* (1950), sought to understand the attraction of fascism and authoritarianism for ordinary citizens. Using surveys, he identified various personality traits in these individuals, including conventionalism, submission, projection, and aggression, as well as other characteristics. Adorno and his colleagues found that people who scored high on an authoritarian test were predisposed to embracing right-wing ideology and were much more supportive of authoritarian and fascist governments. Adorno's explanations were rooted in Freudian models of adolescent development that focused on parenting and repressed sexual desires. Other members of the Frankfurt School further probed the psychology of authority and obedience. In his critique of capitalist consumer culture in *One-Dimensional Man* (1991), Marcuse argues that the reliance on technology and overly bureaucratic social control systems creates a manipulation of needs by powerful interests that precludes the emergence of opposing ideologies to challenge the status quo (8).

Early psychological insights into this problem are fraught with controversy. The insights into authority of the Frankfurt School are derived in part from the work of Sigmund Freud. Freud asserted that people submitted to authority to free themselves from the anxiety of the id-ego conflict. In his seminal work, *Civilization and Its Discontents* (1962), he argued that the tension between society's demands (civilization) and one's biological instincts (id impulses), create conflicts in the subconscious that generate anxiety.

Because "civilization is built up upon a renunciation of instinct," Freud argued that to ensure the overall concord and mutual benefit of the human species, human autonomy must capitulate to the needs of society. Ultimately this ceding of individual drives to the needs of a civilized society creates a conflict between the animal-like instincts (id) of humans and the socializing process of society (super ego). For Freud, humans ultimately submitted to authority to free themselves of anxiety.

Eric Fromm criticized Freudian psychoanalysis for advancing a dialectic that was overly limiting in explaining human behavior. Rather than the tension between animal instincts and the demands of civilization that underpinned most of Freud's ideas, Fromm felt there was more nuance in how the human personality is derived. In *Escape from Freedom*, Fromm argued that humans tended to gravitate toward overconformity and authoritarianism because of the tendency of freedom to create angst, self-doubt, and feelings of being unsafe.

Freedom, though it has brought him independence and rationality, has made him isolated and, thereby, anxious and powerless. This isolation is unbearable and the alternatives he is confronted with are either to escape from the burden of his freedom into new dependencies and submission, or to advance the full realization of positive freedom which is based upon the uniqueness and individuality of man (Fromm, 1941, ix–x)

Drawing from a more sociological insight, in his *Art of Loving* Fromm lamented the illusions of conformity, which conceal subconscious motivations without much reflection on an individual's part:

Most people are not even aware of their need to conform. They live under the illusion that they follow their own ideas and inclinations, that they are individualists, that they have arrived at their opinion as the result of their own thinking—and that it just happens that their ideas are the same as those of the majority. (Fromm 1953, 11)

Conformity Studies

The power of the majority to stoke inhumane behavior and silence dissenting viewpoints is well documented in social-psychological conformity studies. Several of these studies are worth revisiting, as they offer a telling glimpse of the power that complacent conformity has on an individual. The Milgram experiments, the Asch conformity project, and the Zimbardo prison studies at Stanford University are the classic mainstays found in almost any psychology textbook. Although some subsequent researchers have refuted or failed to replicate their original findings, they remain an important indicator of how powerful and brutal conformity can be.

THE MILGRAM STUDY

One of the most famous (or infamous) psychological studies on conformity sought to determine if an ordinary person would commit horrifying acts, such as the kind seen in the Nazi Holocaust, simply because they were ordered to do so by an authority figure. Yale psychologist Stanley Milgram became interested in this question after reading common defenses used by Nazi war criminals to justify their actions (Milgram, 1974). During the Nuremberg trials, Nazi officers often said they were only "following orders" to justify their horrific actions. Milgram designed an experiment in the early 1960s to see if he could get ordinary people to do terrible things if ordered to by an authority figure.

Participants were local males who answered a newspaper ad looking for volunteers. The volunteers were assigned the role of "teacher" and introduced to a "learner" who was in on the experiment. The teachers were told to help the learners memorize lists by administering a series of electric shocks when they gave a wrong answer. Put in front of an imposing electrical board with switches that ranged from mild to severe, they were told to increase the level each time the learner made an error (Milgram, 1974, 3–4). The teachers followed the instructions and initiated shocks of increasing intensity. The learners could be heard screaming in the other room (but could not be seen by the teacher). However, the learner was simply acting and was not hooked to any shock generator. As the learner got more answers wrong or resisted, the teacher was told by the researcher that "the experiment requires you to continue." Milgram found that nearly two-thirds of "teachers" would shock to the death; when ordered to do so by an authority figure who "assumed full responsibility." The Milgram experiments demonstrated how astonishingly easy it is to induce people to commit a crime of conformity.

THE ASCH CONFORMITY PROJECT

The second of the conformity studies is the tamest of the three, but the results were profound and showed the willingness of an individual to renounce the evidence of his or her own eyes under pressure from a majority. In the classic experiment, Solomon Asch (1951) asked research subjects to complete a vision test in which they were to judge the length of a line and then compare it to three other lines. The object was simple—to match the line to the one that most closely matches its length—and the answer was obvious. When individuals completed the test by themselves, they answered correctly 99 percent of the time. Then, a test subject was placed in a group setting of three or more individuals. These individuals unanimously gave clearly incorrect answers and mocked and chastised the test subject for his or her (correct) answer. Under pressure from the group, the test subject was willing to change to the obviously wrong solution about a third of the time. This experiment has been replicated more than a hundred times in various contexts (Bond and Smith, 1996). Although these results point to considerable cross-cultural variability and some decline in overall levels of conformity, in each a significant proportion of people were willing to violate what their good senses told them and side with the majority.

A variety of methodological criticisms of the Asch studies have emerged over the past six decades (Bond and Smith, 1996; Scheufle and Moy, 2000). Meta-analyses have suggested bias in the clinical application of the results and wild variations on replication. Still, the original study and subsequent replications demonstrate the strength of normative pressure in maintaining silence and, ultimately, conformity despite a clear violation of one's own sanity. Irving Janis (1972) also noted the effect of group pressure and a desire for cohesiveness when groups are charged with a decision-making process.

Janis proposed "group think" as a dynamic where internal dissent is discouraged in favor of group harmony. Such a process of conformity has been cited as the reason behind the fatally flawed decision of engineers to launch the doomed space shuttle *Challenger* and as the explanation for support among presidential advisors for green-lighting the ill-conceived invasion of Iraq.

THE STANFORD PRISON EXPERIMENT

The last classic social-psychological study to probe the effect of authority and the possibility of complicit conformity is the Stanford Prison Experiment (Haney, Banks, and Zimbardo, 1973). Led by psychology professor Philip Zimbardo, the experiment, assigned the roles of prisoner and guard to twenty-four young men in a simulated prison environment in the basement of a Stanford University psychology building. The experiment describes abuse and degradation as the research subjects devolved into their role. The guards became sadistic, and the prisoners became compliant and passive subjects. According to Zimbardo (2004), with no training or supervision, behaviors became toxic almost immediately, and with no prompting other than the assigned role and uniform that went with it. The results suggest a depressing view that humans readily accept authority and conform when atrocities take place. The experiment has been used to explain genocide and other acts of complicity such as the torture of prisoners at the Abu Ghraib Prison in Iraq, when it was run by U.S. soldiers.

In sum, Milgram, Asch, and Zimbardo do show effects of the powerful (and diabolical) pressure to conform on group members, and how that pressure can stoke some of the worst behaviors humanity has to offer. In such situations, a deviant is desperately needed to redeem our species. Regularly cited in sociology and psychology readers, these studies problematize how conformity and obedience may be a negative phenomenon. Taken by themselves, these oft-cited experiments give students a bleak and depressing view of human nature, pointing out the extent to which we are victims of our own socialization and readily submit to authority and group pressure.

A casual observer of these classic studies may jump to conclusions and assert that people are sheep, but the reality is that conformity is much more complex than that. One person's sheep are another's team players. These widely cited and routinely debated studies are not mentioned here to suggest that humanity is doomed, or that the trappings of modernity have rendered humans mere automatons. Further, this is not meant to imply there is some banal evil wrapped up in a person's desire to conform and belong. On the contrary, the mere existence of deviance demonstrates otherwise. To be clear, conformity is brutal, but the ability of humans to resist inhumane orders—that is deviant heroism—can be our saving grace in such instances.

While sociology is critical to understanding the totality of the problem of complicit conformity, psychology offers important insights into this problem that are often left out of sociological understandings of crime and deviance. One of these insights is that complicit conformity is not necessarily a default psychological disposition. Jetten and Hornsey (2011) challenge the classic view of conformity in psychology by noting that deviance and dissent are regular and prevalent in small groups. For instance, they argue that scholarship on Asch and Milgram tends to overwhelmingly focus on the study participants who conformed, rather than the participants who never conformed, in any circumstance. Jetten and Hornsey argue that conformity is not a default disposition in a social psychological context. Not only do people regularly deviate from authority, but it is often encouraged in several small-group contexts.

Reconsidering Milgram, it is much more sensational to discuss the 63 percent of people who will shock to the death; far less mentioned is how few did, and resisted entirely. In fact, subsequent iterations of the Milgram experiment demonstrate a less overwhelming level of obedience with just a fraction following the order to shock to the death (Milgram, 1974). Efforts to replicate the study fail to confirm Milgram's initial findings with few going fully obedient (Burger, 2009). The key of conformity is not actually that humans submit to authority, but that they are willing to do it for some greater good. This is what the Milgram experiment actually demonstrates. When given a direct order, the subjects actually rebel, but it is before orders are given that they willingly (as long as the experimenter is seemingly a scientist) participate, because they see it as a necessary evil for the advancement of science, which is the ultimate good.

It seems that the dilemma between obedience and rebellion reflects a similar divide between deontology and utilitarianism. Are people motivated by duty and obligation or are people motivated by moral will. This philosophical divide is reflected in several of Kelman and Hamilton's (1989) conclusions on the My Lai Massacre where they conclude that conformity may be successfully challenged when a person or people have access to an alternate moral framework and an alternate authority figure (139). State authority, religious authority, and personal conviction may all be sources of legitimacy for deviant action or inaction. The availability of alternatives to established authority may either inoculate individuals against the pressure to conform or give the conformist an opportunity to recognize another way forward.

Moving beyond classic psychological studies of conformity, popular culture gives added insight into its power and how it may be overcome. The Hollywood film *Twelve Angry Men* dramatizes the jury deliberations in the trial of a person accused of homicide (Rose, 1955). All but one juror is certain that the defendant was guilty of the crime, but the lone dissenter has a reasonable doubt that the accused may have been falsely accused. Needing a unanimous decision to avoid a hung jury, the film portrays the eleven other jurors becoming at first irritated and later infuriated, demanding that the lone dissenter concede what is obvious to them. Over the course of the film, the dissenter begins to explain his reasoning, convincing more of the jurors of his potential innocence. The full deliberations expose prejudices among other jurors, as well as facts that were not in the trial. Their dialogue demonstrates the immense pressure and power conformity can have in a small-group process. While it would have been easier to reach the "obvious" conclusion, one lone dissenter turned a court verdict.

There are real-world examples of the power of complicit conformity as well. Following both psychological and sociological approaches, nonconformity is typically thought of as a criminogenic behavior. However, as has been seen in much of this chapter, conformity may also be criminogenic, especially in terms of large-scale crimes. The everyday complicity of individuals may enable the large-scale commissioning of crimes. In this instance, it is worth considering the fall of Enron, which in 2001 was the largest corporate crime ever committed.[2]

The documentary film, *Enron: The Smartest Men in the Room*, is a superb demonstration of how conformity may doom our species. The film chronicles the fall of a company that, at one time, was the seventh largest in the United States. While greed is often assumed to be at the heart of most scandals involving corporate and white-collar criminals, Enron's culture produced an organizational environment that thrived on deviant innovations but still relied on a corporate culture of conformity that discouraged questions of ethics or principle. This was evident not only in the senior leadership of the company but also in the energy traders that Enron relied on to make money by moving electricity around in a newly deregulated energy market. These traders sought to monopolize electric markets to charge the highest price possible, and then manufactured forced electrical outages to illegally spike prices.

Journalists Bethany McLean and Peter Elkind's (2003) book, by the same title as the documentary, chronicles the criminogenic culture at Enron that required a conformity act or guise to "be Enron" that at the same time was bent on corruption and fraud. Consider this excerpt portraying traders who were engaged in illegal activities (and knew it):

> In trying to be so smart, Enron's West Coast traders were doing something that was incredibly stupid. But inside the Enron cocoon they simply couldn't see that. The attitude was, "play by your own rules," says a former trader. "We all did it. We talked about it openly. It was at the school yard we lived in. The

energy markets were new, immature, unsupervised. We took pride in getting around the rules, it was a game." (275)

The documentary film situates the behavior of Enron's energy traders within archival footage from Milgram's experiments. The analysis is somewhat crude, but it shows how the Enron traders, just like Milgram's research subjects (or Zimbardo's prison actors), would behave unethically when a higher authority seemed to be authorizing their actions and deflecting accountability. Spliced between interviews with traders were the screams of the learners in Milgram's studies. On-camera interviews with the traders noted their knowledge of illegal behaviors, while rationalizing it with an "everybody is doing it" attitude. The entire company was built on illegality and required widespread compliance and blind trust in authority for large-scale corporate fraud to take place.

Preluding Enron's complete collapse, Sherron Watkins, a vice president for the company, discovered accounting irregularities and tried to the correct the problem. In an organizational culture dominated with "guys with spikes," she was a lone voice trying to right a wrong that had enmeshed the entire company. Not realizing the extent of the fraud, she alerted the senior executives, who hoped she would go away, but she persisted—and was ultimately vindicated. The pressure to conform in a high-pressure corporate culture must be immense. An individual who does not toe the corporate line will be accused of rocking the boat and jeopardizing the company and will perhaps be condemned. A whistleblower like Watkins is a rare type of hero.

When you have an ethical challenge, your life's never the same. You're either going to rise to it to try to stop the bad behavior, or you're going to rationalize why you are staying silent.

As the conformity studies indicate, rationalization is a powerful tool in perpetuating malfeasance. From My Lai to Enron, complicit conformity relies on a complex social-psychological interplay of flawed normative structures, pressure to conform, and a relationship to authority that accepts that authority as legitimate and the source of moral direction.

My Lai Revisited

Returning to the My Lai Massacre and the subsequent investigation and cover-up, it is quite notable that during the executions of unarmed civilians, several soldiers did not conform and refused to follow orders. For example, Pfc. James Joseph Dursi testified that he refused to fire and "just stood there" while others were screaming at him to shoot (Hammer, 1971:147) Another enlisted man, Ronald Grezeik, reported that while he initially obeyed orders, he refused Calley's orders to "finish them off" (Hammer, 1971, 150). The massacre was brought to light only through the persistence of Ron Ridenhour, who had heard of the killings and reported it to members of Congress once he was back home.

The most flagrant (and heroic) act of disobedience at My Lai came from a twenty-five-year-old warrant officer, Hugh Thompson, a Huey helicopter pilot. Thompson contested the ruthless killing of civilians and defied the higher-ranking Lieutenant Calley's orders. From the sky, he saw mothers shielding their children's bodies in a ditch (Kelman and Hamilton, 1989, 8). Landing in the carnage, Thompson put his own body between the defenseless Vietnamese and Calley's soldiers. In a direct affront to military protocol and the chain of command, he ordered his gunners to open fire on their fellow American soldiers if they continued to fire on the Vietnamese and stood his ground until rescue helicopters came to evacuate the civilians. Thompson later returned to the ditch where civilians were massacred to unearth a buried but unharmed child.

For his actions, Thompson was awarded the Distinguished Flying Cross for heroism, but it was, inaccurately, given for the "rescuing of children" hiding in a conflict between "Viet Cong and advancing friendly forces" (Hersh, 1970, 119)—a government lie and part of a larger cover-up by the military. Thompson's real heroism was *not* conforming, disobeying orders, breaking the chain of command, and stopping a war crime. It was an act of deviant heroism and good trouble for which he would not be officially recognized until thirty years later with the presentation of the Soldier's Medal.

My Lai is just one of many gruesome acts of conformity committed in the context of warfare. It underscores the problem of not just complicit conformity but how dangerous the ease of acquiescence to authority can be. Both psychology and sociology provide insight into how individuals internalize group norms and act out on pressures to conform. Typically, conformity is thought of as something good, a process that assures group cohesion and overall social solidarity.

This chapter demonstrated both the ease with which complicit conformity can take root and the horrors that it can cause. Complicit conformity has both sociological and psychological explanations, as we have seen: forces that shape social behavior may come either from within the individual, through internalized notions of morals, values, beliefs, and legitimacy, or through external forces that reward conformity and punish deviance. In the modern state system, obedience to authority is generally constructed as moral and socially honorable. However, conformity is not inherently noble, and the connivance of passive acquiescence has been demonstrated to quite possibly be the downfall of civilization. The archetypal examples of the problem of conformity are its sanctioning of massacres and genocide.

Fortunately, conformity is not the default disposition of individuals, as psychology and real-world examples show; people can and do resist conforming quite regularly for morally just reasons. These people, such as the dissenting juror, the whistleblower, and the man who stopped a war crime, are deviant heroes who found good trouble.

NOTES

1. Search of Sociological Abstracts on ProQuest, April 11, 2017.
2. In terms of total value, Enron remains the single largest case of corporate crime prosecuted. However, overall cost of the mortgage and securities fraud that precipitated the 2008 mortgage crisis undoubtedly eclipses that figure.

Chapter Ten

Good Trouble in Everyday Life

The previous chapter demonstrates how conformity can be a cruel and often brutal social phenomena. Because of our socialization and the stigma associated with deviance, the thought of standing out and going against the norms makes almost anyone uncomfortable, even in situations where conformity might lead to suffering. This phenomenon is replicated in seemingly mundane circumstances to potentially devastating effect. For example, many choking deaths are thought to happen simply because the victim is "too embarrassed" to ask for help (Goldhagen, 1996). Likewise, it is thought that many people die or suffer from heart attacks for the same reason. In a similar vein, there are instances of people needing help where nobody offers it. Despite the medical risks to the person in peril, not doing anything is "conformity." This chapter examines how the lessons of good trouble may be implemented in everyday life while revisiting several key points taken from the earlier chapters.

Good Trouble has pondered the viability of deviant heroism and the consequences of good trouble in various social contexts. The first chapter established that common and everyday understandings typically view crime and deviance as something that is bad or a product of larger "social problems." This commonsensical approach to the study of crime and deviance is reflected in most scholarship and theorizations of crime and deviance. Despite the adoption of constructivist definitions, scholarship tends to focus on deviance as either morally bad or at best morally neutral behavior. Yet, deviant behavior has been at the leading edge of important social changes. Chapter 2 demonstrated that not only is good deviance a plausible derivative of the common conception of deviance but that nonconformist behavior has driven positive social change. In various contexts, the violation of norms may be necessary to remedy unjust conditions or alter a social order that is out of touch with evolving social values. Similarly, while conformity is typically seen as positive and an outcome of socialization and internalization of social values, horrible atrocities have been committed through the everyday complicity of ordinary people to authority. Therefore, one can readily conclude that good trouble is necessary for the progress of humanity.

Subsequent chapters profiled people who got into good trouble who were also forerunners of positive social change. Many of these individuals are household names. For the cause of racial equality, women's liberation, workers' rights, scientific truth, artistic freedom, and the struggle for peace, heroic individuals challenged unjust social conditions by violating laws or breaking norms. In most cases, these individuals were subject to some kind of social control, both formal and informal. Nowadays, many of these people, such as Rosa Parks, or Nelson Mandela, are celebrated as heroes. Still others, such as Charles Darwin, or Emma Goldman, remain controversial, even to this day. Contemporary examples of famous deviant heroes have been variously honored with Nobel Prizes. Clearly some of the history's most renowned heroes have been deviants who found good trouble.

In most of the cases profiled in this book, the deviant hero had a macro-level impact, or was a person symbolic of a much larger movement. Yet the principles of deviant heroism may be applied on a micro-level, as well. The sociological imagination and the Millsian methodology followed in the formulation of this book seek to examine the interplay between an individual and his or her social structure. It demonstrates how personal thoughts, feelings, and motivations are shaped by a much larger social process. Society is both an enabling and constraining force. Society may act on the individual, but the individual can also act back on society.

This final chapter shows that the lessons of deviant heroism can be applied to everyday life and that good trouble is something anyone can engage in at some point, for example, when confronted with pressure to conform complicitly at the expense of the well-being of someone else. In other words, although most people, most of the time, conform, everybody is deviant at some point. Deviant heroism can be a part of everyday sociology and experienced by any individual.

Consider a recently published photo of Saffiyah Kahn, a British citizen of Pakistani ancestry, confronting angry demonstrators with a gentle smile and soft downward gaze (Perraudin, 2017). Kahn crossed a protest for the English Defense League (EDL), a far-right anti-immigrant group in the UK. According to the report, the EDL protest numbered a hundred or so people and featured some counterprotesters. EDL members began to harass a woman wearing a hajib when Kahn stepped in between the woman and the protesters. The image captures the power of an everyday pose to confront hatred.

A Reuters photographer in Baton Rouge photographed a similar image during a confrontation of police with a Black Lives Matter protester (BBC,

2016b). The photo shows Leshia Evans, a young black woman, calmly holding her ground, her dress whipping in the wind, as police officers approach her. Evans looks poised and is standing tall, while the officers look off balance, almost as if they are about to tumble. For Evans, holding her ground is both brave and defiant as officers move to arrest her. Like the image of Kahn, the photo of Evans's everyday deviant heroism became iconic—an everyday act of deviant heroism captured forever. How can the understanding of "everyday sociology" bring an interpretive framework to "viral" images such as these, images that depict seemingly ordinary people engaging in symbolic, but revolutionary acts of defiance?

EVERYDAY SOCIOLOGY

The "everydayness" of social interaction is often overlooked by sociologists, especially those who study macro-level phenomena. "Everyday sociology" has been proposed as a way to connect the salience of lived experience to the major theoretical underpinnings of sociology (Kalekin-Fishman, 2013). When the sociology of everyday life is practiced, it can uncover simple quirks and processes that govern day-to-day human interactions. It can highlight body language and nonverbalized queues humans give to create shared meanings and experiences. It can also be used to reveal power relationships and inequalities that govern various micro-level encounters between people.

To understand everyday interactions, the Canadian American sociologist Erving Goffman proposed a view of human action that utilizes a dramaturgical performance metaphor. Goffman suggested that we perform our roles as actors based on tenuous hermeneutic devices (Cuzzort & King, 1995). Humans engage on a dynamic interplay of symbolic interpretation where social cues are communicated explicitly through speech or more subtly through nonverbal responses. Front stage encounters are where formal interactions take place, whereas backstage, people develop their front stage demeanor and engage in informal interaction. For Goffman, norms act as a guide for human behavior, where the violation of norms resulted in some kind of sanction or negative social reaction (Goffman, 1971, 95). In the process of social interaction, humans exchange meaning based on a common interpretive framework.

For example, when an individual projects a definition of an interpersonal situation, and thereby makes an implicit or explicit claim to be a person of a particular kind, he or she automatically exerts a moral demand upon others, obliging them to value and treat him in the manner that persons of that kind have a right to expect (Goffman, 1959, 24). Thus, mutual understanding between two social actors is governed not just by shared symbolic meanings but by normative pleas through both the intentional and unintentional disclosure of information. Therefore, interaction is an iterative process where individuals act and react based on a shared repertoire of understanding. For a symbolic interactionist, social interaction can be understood as dramatic relations that are revealed through the intertwining of theory and empirical observation. This may be observed in the contentious construction of social problems (Best, 1995). For instance, successful social movements involve a situation where claims and counterclaims are advanced by vying social actors. A powerful social actor may be in a position to define normal social relations, but this may be contested through the violation of these norms. As Benford and Hunt (2003) note, there is always a "drama between proponents and antagonists as each seeks to establish its definitions of situations and imputations, to rebut and discredit their opponents' claims, and to inspire individuals to either engage in collective action or stand fast and not act upon others' problem claims" (154). Therefore, the dramatic interplay between norm creation and violation may be observed through understanding everyday social interactions as part of a larger drama between observing established norms and rebutting them.

As has been demonstrated in this book, much of the sociology of deviance is concerned with the unusual or uncommon. As such, most scholarship and theory in sociology have been developed to explain relatively rare events such as revolutions, paradigm shifts, and unusual and deviant behavior. Yet most social interaction is quite routine and usual and gives little cause to question. Even extraordinary, heroic, and deviant individuals spend most of their time doing commonplace activities. As such, everyday social life takes on a "natural" and taken-for-granted quality.

In the 1950s, sociologist Harrold Garfinkle sought to develop a method to understand and analyze commonplace interactions (1967). He was concerned with the dynamics of everyday life and how commonplace situations are negotiated by individuals. The study of seemingly mundane behaviors is filled with meaning and points to how social realities are constructed through day-to-day interaction. Garfinkle pioneered the use of ethnomethodology, the study of the methods people use to communicate shared meanings and solve problems. Simply, ethnomethodology is the study of everyday life (Garfinkle, 1967, 9). One timeless experiment derived from Garfinkle's ethnomethodology is the "breaching experiment," which gauges people's reactions to infractions of commonly accepted social rules (Haru, n.d.). Garfinkle would instruct his students to violate everyday norms for a set period of time in order to observe how people adapted to and rationalized the breaches: for example, he would instruct his students to act as lodger in their own home or haggle over the set prices on food at the grocery store. The observations and notes from such experiments formed the basis of his ethnomethodology that studied the everyday rules that govern meaning and lived experience.

The goal of breaching norms was not nefarious in intent; rather, the exercise violates social etiquette to good-naturedly demonstrate sociology in action.

Introducing Breaching Experiments in the Classroom

Breaching experiments are easy to replicate and are often assigned in social deviance classes. Popular examples include not smiling all day, haggling over the price of something at a grocery store, refusing to shake hands with someone, ordering something off-menu at a restaurant, standing backward in line or in an elevator. The norm infractions are intended to break rules without causing social trauma, to give students a chance to reflect on the existence of norms in everyday life and what it feels like to break them, and to understand the social reaction to norm violation from a sociological perspective. Students also gain an understanding of how norms are constructed temporarily and spatially, and how what may be deviant in one context is not in another. Since the intent of the experiment is supposed to be playful and not cause trauma to the observer, it also lends insight into how norms may be negotiated and violations may be repairable, with some kind of reconciliation after the breaching experiment is over. The experiment is also useful in teaching students the power of conformity and the strengths norms have in defining daily life. They also give cause for reflection about how, while breaking norms is uncomfortable, social interactions adapt as people seek harmonious interactions, stability, and common interactive contexts.

When I teach "deviant behavior," I have my students conduct their own breaching experiments and then write a short reflective paper about the experience. In acquainting students with the sociological imagination, the goal is to get students to move past the reactive approach to norm violations that dismisses them as "weird," or people "freaking out" about encountering something unfamiliar. The exercise always generates lively discussion, as students tend to be extremely creative about what norms they break. For instance, one student clucked like a chicken in front of a student union building for almost an hour. Others do lower-key norm breaches, such as talking to someone with their eyes closed. The point of the exercise is to get students to see how social norms are negotiated and to ponder the consequences of engaging in an innocuous but nonetheless deviant behavior. Ideally, they come to understand that even though society cannot be physically seen, norms and social reactions are very "real." Once students grasp the contextuality of norm violation in an everyday situation, the next step is to see how ordinary acts can move people.

Deviant Acts of Kindness

In a different kind of breaching experiment, two decades ago Jones proposed "random acts of kindness" in a pedagogical article reflecting on an exercise used to teach students about "positive deviance" (1998). This experiment served as a remedy to the association of deviance with negative behavior. In the article, Jones documents how students overcome the "weirdness" of acting deviant. In turning preconceptions of deviance around for the neophyte to sociology, she points out how behaviors that may be received positively may actually be deviant. For instance, buying a stranger coffee or helping someone stranded on the road may violate a norm, but may be received favorably (depending on the context of course).

To have students learn this concept by "doing positive deviance," she asked her students to commit twelve acts of random kindness over the course of the term and to journal and reflect on them. She notes how many were intimidated by the assignment and tended to direct unexpected helpful acts to friends and family. Others, however, got over their initial trepidation and approached strangers with a kind or helpful act, such as offering an umbrella, only to be refused by the potential recipient. Besides demonstrating the possibility of "positive deviance," the activity aimed to give students a first-person experience with acting deviant in a way that is neither morally impartial or socially detrimental.

Jones's article reported that not all acts of kindness were received positively. For instance, a black male student offered to help an elderly white woman carry her groceries. She refused his overture, and he reflected that she perceived him as a threat and possibly as a stereotype of young black males (Jones, 1998:183). This breaching experiment demonstrates, at the micro-level, the power of positive deviance as well as the reluctance and difficulty in violating norms, even if it is for a noble or altruistic act. It is a microcosm of the power of positive deviance in everyday life. The next step is to go from the positive deviance of random acts of kindness to good trouble, which can remedy the complicit conformity that seems commonplace in some hurtful or discriminatory situations. I have replicated the "random acts of kindness" assignment in my own class on a somewhat smaller scale, focused more as a breaching experiment in "good trouble." Over the course of a week, students were asked to identify a social situation in which someone was harmed or bullied, or a stranger needed help, and either interrupt the harmful interaction or bullying conversation or offer aid to the stranger. It might mean speaking out about gossip like fat shaming or simply helping a stranger lift some heavy items. In some instances, students have talked about interceding in conversations that are homophobic or racist (I usually assign the project over Thanksgiving break, which is a notorious venue for heated and contentious discussions about politics among family members).

The "good trouble" breaching assignment has had mixed success. As with the basic norm-breaching experience, some students talk about their initial feelings of "trepidation" or their reluctance to break norms. Others mention that they feel they have excluded themselves but still feel positive about breaking a norm that results in others not being harmed. Still others talk about how a hurtful conversation simply went "silent" or became "awkward." A few students admit, at least in terms of the assignment, that they were too shy to breach a norm, even if there was a hurtful conversation or possibility to help. Finally, some students reported that they did not encounter an opportunity to find "good trouble" in the course of the week.

As the "good trouble" breaching experiment comes on the heels of the lessons from Martin Luther King's letter, in terms of the students' course work, these lessons are worth revisiting. The letter enables an instructor to demonstrate multiple concepts that are central in studying the sociology of crime and deviance, including socialization, social control, norms, justice, ridicule, human agency, exclusion, social change, and above all, altruistic nonconformity.

Praising conformist heroes is easy, as is the condemnation of deviant villains. The deviant hero is more difficult to grasp both intellectually and morally as he or she challenges both moral and intellectual preconceptions. Devoting a section of a course to praise and pay tribute to deviance is likely to raise some eyebrows. Yet, recognizing that crime and deviance can represent a social and heroic good does much to enhance students' understanding of nonconformity, as well as their overall worldview. Through revisiting a well-known and historic text such as King's letter, students can appreciate the process of social change and, ideally, expand their concept of justice.

In many ways, the most important lesson that can be derived about deviant heroism is that it can be found on an individual level and in everyday life. While many famous people have changed or altered history through challenging norms, deviant heroism may be practiced by anyone, anywhere. My aim has been to teach students how they can practice heroic deviance in small-scale, micro-level situations. These are situations where they may not be arrested or face formal sanctions but might subject themselves to informal social control in the form of ostracism or social exclusion. To illustrate this point, I pose situations that students have probably encountered in their own lives, such as when someone is being bullied or a relative makes a racist or homophobic remark. The normative or conformist response to such situations would be to nod politely or say nothing. In contrast, the deviant response would be to interrupt and challenge the hateful or hurtful context of the conversation. On querying students, I find that nearly all of them admit to having been in such a situation. These are ideal "teachable moments," in which students can draw connections between abstract course concepts and their own life. I ask students to volunteer situations that they have been in where they have or could have practiced deviant heroism. It is in these situations that we can learn the most from deviant heroes and perhaps make our own individual social situations more loving, just, and equitable.

As Allan Johnson notes in his book *Privilege, Power and Difference* (2006), small, everyday changes to behavior can have wide-ranging consequences. Ultimately such changes may be disruptive, but can provoke larger changes in normative contexts.

> When you *openly* change how you participate in a system, you do more than change your own behavior; you also change how the system happens. When you change how a system happens, you change the social environment that shapes other people's behavior, which, in turn further changes how the system happens. And, when you do that you also help change the consequences that come out of the dynamic relationship between systems and individuals, including patterns of privilege and oppression. (143)

In other words, micro-level patterns of behavior can have macro-level consequences and vice versa. Johnson encourages individuals to "do something" when they see problems of oppression. This includes making noise even if it is uncomfortable and finding ways to withdraw from the paths of least resistance. He says that the key to withdrawing support involves an interruption of the "flow of business as usual (144). Small actions such as not laughing at a racist joke or challenging heterosexism in a single conversation, may not seem like much, but Johnson argues that resistance to action is a measure of power and a way to make a difference in everyday interactions.

CONCLUSION

This book has presented dilemmas with regard to how sociologists and criminologists should contemplate the question of heroic deviance or crimes that break unjust rules. From there, the book considered an operational definition of deviant heroes as people who in their own social context, violated evil or fought against unjust laws. Although not often mentioned in contemporary discussions of crime and deviance, there is much support for including the deviant hero in scholarly accounts of deviance dating back to the early founders of the discipline, such as Durkheim, Du Bois, and Gilman. Theoretically, the deviant hero could be incorporated into several traditions that are used to explain or understand deviant behavior. Subsequent chapters have shown how this might be possible by comparing the biographies of individuals who have made history by challenging unjust norms or laws of their historical epoch.

Good Trouble has been written in praise of and in tribute to the ethical criminal, a unique kind of deviant, the rare individual who risks everything and makes a difference and may even change the very social structure under which we live. The sociology of crime and deviance has much to gain by recognizing that theoretically crime can under certain circumstances represent a social good—even a heroic good. Revisiting some of the classical works of sociology has shown that there is support for this in the early development of the discipline, particularly in the works of Durkheim, Du Bois, and Gilman. Returning to these works yields a large depth of insight and understanding, and not about deviant behavior but the process of social change as well. There is also much to gain from a multidisciplinary perspective in our understanding of deviance and crime, particularly by incorporating the arts and humanities.

I would like to close by reemphasizing that anybody can practice deviant heroism to some degree by incorporating "everyday sociology" into their toolkit of communicative repertoires on a micro-social level. Gandhi practiced deviant heroism to challenge the colonialism of the most powerful empire in the world, and Martin Luther King's "crimes" challenged the evil system of racism and segregation in the most powerful empire of his time. Not everybody can sacrifice as much as these deviant heroes did, effectively changing the course of history. Yet, if more people were to embrace the principles of deviant heroism on an individual level, they might even, if only slightly, alter their own normative environments. A person may not be threatened with jail or assassination, but they may be asked to stand up to powerful informal forms of social control like ostracism, ridicule, or social isolation. Even a small act of heroic deviance can help make the world a better place.

Works Cited

Abbey, E. (1975). *The monkey wrench gang* (1st ed.). Philadelphia: Lippincott.

Adler, F. (1975). *Sisters in crime: the rise of the new female criminal*. New York: McGraw-Hill Book Company.

Adler, P., & Adler, P. (2015). *Constructions of deviance: Social power, context, and interaction*. Nelson Education.

Adler, W. (2012). *The man who never died: The life, times, and legacy of Joe Hill, American labor icon* (Paperback ed.). New York: Bloomsbury.

Adorno, T. W. (1950). *The Authoritarian personality,* (1st ed.). New York: Harper.

AFL-CIO. (n.d.-a). Joe Hill. AFL-CIO. Retrieved July 12, 2018, from https://aflcio.org/about/history/labor-history-people/joe-hill

AFL-CIO. (n.d.-b). Mother Jones. AFL-CIO. Retrieved July 12, 2018, from https://aflcio.org/about/history/labor-history-people/mother-jones

al-Sharif, M. (2017). *Daring to Drive.* Simon & Schuster.

Alexander, M. (2011). *The new Jim Crow: Mass incarceration in the age of colorblindness* (Revised edition / with a new foreword by Cornel West). New York: New Press.

Alston, R. (2002). *Soldier and Society in Roman Egypt: A Social History*. Routledge.

Anderson, E. (1992). *Streetwise: Race, Class, and Change in an Urban Community*. University of Chicago Press.

Arkin, D. (2017, September 1). They battled Harvey. Now Texas "Dreamers" face DACA's possible demise. Retrieved March 4, 2018, from https://www.nbcnews.com/storyline/hurricane-harvey/first-harvey-now-daca-peril-houston-area-dreamers-face-another-n798256

Asch, S. E. (1951). Effects of group pressure upon the modification and distortion of judgment. In H. Guetzkow (Ed.), *Groups, leadership and men* (pp. 177–190). Pittsburgh, PA: Carnegie Press.

Atwood, Kathryn (2011). *Women Heroes of World War II*. Chicago: Chicago Review Press.

Aung San Suu Kyi. (1991). *Freedom from fear: And other writings* (Viking ed.). New York: Viking.

Austin, C. J. (2008). *Up Against the Wall: Violence in the Making and Unmaking of the Black Panther Party*. University of Arkansas Press. Retrieved from https://muse.jhu.edu/book/12892

Barak, G. (2015). *Class, race, gender, and crime: the social realities of justice in America* (4th ed.). Lanham, MD: Rowman & Littlefield.

Barlow, D. H., & Durand, V. M. (2004). *Abnormal Psychology: An Integrative Approach*. Wadsworth.

Basinger, S. J. (2003). Regulating Slavery: Deck-Stacking and Credible Commitment in the Fugitive Slave Act of 1850. *Journal of Law, Economics, & Organization, 19*(2), 307–342.

BBC. (2016a). Baton Rouge killing: Black Lives Matter protest photo hailed as "legendary." BBC News. Retrieved March 4, 2018, from https://www.bbc.com/news/world-us-canada-36759711

BBC. (2016b, July 11). "Legendary" image of US protests emerges. *BBC News*. Retrieved from https://www.bbc.co.uk/news/world-us-canada-36759711

Becker, H. (1963). *Outsiders: studies in the sociology of deviance*. Free Press of Glencoe.

Becker, H. (1974). Art As Collective Action. *American Sociological Review, 39*(6), 767–776.

Becker, H. (2014). *What about Mozart? What about murder?: Reasoning from cases*. Chicago: The University of Chicago Press.

Beirne, P., & Hill, Joan. (1991). Comparative criminology: An annotated bibliography *Research and bibliographical guides in criminal justice ; no. 3*. New York: Greenwood Press.

Bekiempis, V. (2015, October 4). Famous NYPD "Lamplighter" Frank Serpico Gets Political. *Newsweek*. Retrieved from http://www.newsweek.com/frank-serpico-political-office-376355

Belknap, J. (2014). *The Invisible Woman: Gender, Crime, and Justice*. Cengage Learning.

Benford, R., & Hunt, S. (2003). Interactional dynamics in public problems marketplaces: Movements and the counterframing and reframing of public problems. In J. A. Holstein & G. Miller (Eds.), *Challenges and choices: constructionist perspectives on social problems* (pp. 153–186). Hawthorne, NY: Aldine de Gruyter.

Ben-Yehuda, N. (1990). Positive and negative deviance: More fuel for a controversy. *Deviant Behavior, 11*(3), 221–243.

Best, J. (1995). Constructionism in Context. In J. Best (Ed.), *Images of Issues: Typifying Contemporary Social Problems*. New York: Aldine de Gruyter.

Biography Online. (n.d.). Sophie Scholl Biography. Retrieved July 12, 2018, from https://www.biographyonline.net/women/sophie-scholl.html

Blakemore, E. (2016, December 1). John Lewis' Arrest Records Are Finally Uncovered. Retrieved Feb. 12, 2018, from https://www.smithsonianmag.com/smart-news/john-lewis-arrest-records-are-finally-uncovered-180961255/

Bond, R., & Smith, P. B. (1996). Culture and conformity: A meta-analysis of studies using Asch's (1952b, 1956) line judgment task. *Psychological Bulletin, 119*(1), 111–137.

Brennan, F. (2017). *Race Rights Reparations: Institutional Racism and The Law*. Routledge.

Brenner, M. (2004, April). Jeffrey Wigand: The Man Who Knew Too Much. *Vanity Fair*. Retrieved from https://www.vanityfair.com/magazine/1996/05/wigand199605

Brophy, A. L. (2013). *The Nat Turner Trials* (SSRN Scholarly Paper No. ID 2281519). Rochester, NY: Social Science Research Network. Retrieved from https://papers.ssrn.com/abstract=2281519

Brown, E. (2015, July 5). Texas officials: Schools should teach that slavery was 'side issue' to Civil War. *Washington Post*.

Brown, M. H. (1967). *The flight of the Nez Perce*. New York: GPPutnam's Sons.

Browning, C. R. (1992). *Ordinary men: Reserve Police Battalion 101 and the final solution in Poland* (1st ed.). New York: HarperCollins.

Buber, M. (1966). Thoreau and the Danish resistance. In J. H. Hicks (Ed.), *Thoreau in our season*. Amherst: University of Massachusetts Press.

Buber, M. (n.d.). *Man's Duty As Man from Thoreau in Our Season*. Amherst: University of Massachusetts Press.

Burger, J. (2009). Reflections on "Replicating Milgram." *American Psychologist, 64*(1), 20–27.

Burr, V. (2015). *Social Constructionism*. Routledge.

Camp, H. C. (1995). *Iron in Her Soul: Elizabeth Gurley Flynn and the American Left*. WSU Press.

Campbell, S. W. (1970). *The slave catchers: Enforcement of the Fugitive slave law, 1850–1860*. Chapel Hill: University of North Carolina Press.

Castro, J. S. (2016). *Eros and Revolution: The Critical Philosophy of Herbert Marcuse*. BRILL.

Central Intelligence Agency. (n.d.). The World Factbook—Central Intelligence Agency. Retrieved July 12, 2018, from https://www.cia.gov/library/publications/the-world-factbook/geos/bm.html

Chang, J. (2005). *Can't stop, won't stop: A history of the hip-hop generation* (1st ed.). New York: St. Martin's Press.

Chesler, E. (1992). *Woman of valor: Margaret Sanger and the birth control movement in America*. New York: Simon & Schuster.

Chief Joseph. (1879). An Indian's View of Indian Affairs. *North American Review, 128*(269), 412–433.

Church Committee. (1975). *The FBI, Cointelpro, and Martin Luther King, Jr.: Final Report of the Select Committee to Study Governmental Operations with Respect to Intelligence A*. Red and Black Publishers.

Clinard, M. B. (1974). *Sociology of deviant behavior* (4th ed.). New York: Holt, Rinehart and Winston.

Clinard, M., & Meier, R. (2007). *Sociology of Deviant Behavior*. Cengage Learning.

Clinton, C. (2004). *Harriet Tubman: the road to freedom* (1st ed.). Boston, MA: Little, Brown.

Cobb, J. (2016). The Matter of Black Lives. Retrieved Feb. 12, 2018, from https:// www.newyorker.com/magazine/2016/03/14/where-is-black-lives-matter-headed

Colbert, S. D. (2017). *Black Movements Performance and Cultural Politics*. New Brunswick, New Jersey: Rutgers University Press.

Conference on Professional Responsibility. (1972). *Whistle blowing: the report of the Conference on Professional Responsibility*. New York: Grossman Publishers.

Cooper, C. (2013, March 23). "To whistleblow is like a death sentence": five people who risked everything to speak out. *Independent*. Retrieved from https://www.independent.co.uk/news/people/profiles/to-whistleblow-is-like-a-death-sentence-five-people-who-risked-everything-to-speak-out-8542421.html

Coser, L. (1962a). *Communities in the Study of Social Conflict*. New York: The Free Press.

Coser, L. A. (1962b). Some Functions of Deviant Behavior and Normative Flexibility. *American Journal of Sociology, 68*(2), 172–181. https://doi.org/10.1086/223307

Cunningham, V. (2016, October 10). "The Birth of a Nation" Isn't Worth Defending. *New Yorker*.

Curra, J. (2013). *The Relativity of Deviance*. SAGE Publications.

Cuzzort, R. P., & King, E. W. (1995). *Twentieth-century social thought*. Harcourt Brace College Publishers.

Darwin, C. (1996). *The origin of species*. Oxford: Oxford University Press.

Davis, N. J. (1971). Homosexuality: The scene and its students. In J. M. Henslin & E. Sagarin (Eds.), *The Sociology of sex: An introductory reader* (Rev. ed., pp. 297–322). New York: Appleton-Century-Crofts.

DeAngelis, J., & Wolf, B. (2016). Perceived accountability and public attitudes toward local police. *Criminal Justice Studies, 29*(3), 232–252.

Debs, E. (1918). "Statement to the Court Upon Being Convicted of Violating the Sedition Act" Court Stenographer. Retrieved from https://www.marxists.org/archive/debs/works/1918/court.htm.

Debs, E. V. (1927). *Walls and bars*. Patterson Smith.

Dehlin, J. (n.d.). *488-490: Neil Ransom and Kate Kelly - After Kate's Excommunication*. Retrieved from https://www.mormonstories.org/podcast/neil-ransom-and-kate-kelly-after-kates-excommunication/

Desai, A., & Vahed, G. (2015). *The South African Gandhi: Stretcher-Bearer of Empire*. Stanford University Press.

Deutsch, M., & Gerard, H. B. (1955). A study of normative and informational social influences upon individual judgment. *The Journal of Abnormal and Social Psychology, 51*(3), 629–636.

DeValve, M. (2015). *A different justice: Love and the future of criminal justice practice in America*. Durham, North Carolina: Carolina Academic Press.

DeValve, M. (2017). O for a Muse of Fire: Rebellion as Sacrament. *Critical Criminology, 25*(1), 87–102.

Dilchert, S., Ones, D. S., & Krueger, R. F. (n.d.). Maladaptive Personality Constructs, Measures, and Work Behaviors. *Industrial and Organizational Psychology, 7*(1), 98–110.

Dobbs, M. (2005, June 20). Watergate and the Two Lives of Mark Felt. *Washington Post*. Retrieved from http://www.washingtonpost.com/wp-dyn/content/article/2005/06/19/AR2005061900699.html

Dodge, D. (1985). The Over-Negativized Conceptualization of Deviance: A Programmatic Exploration. *Deviant Behavio, 6*, 17–37.

Dotter, D. L., & Roebuck, J. B. (1988). The labeling approach re-examined: Interactionism and the components of deviance. *Deviant Behavior, 9*(1), 19–32.

Douglass, F. (1855). *My Bondage and My Freedom* . . . Miller, Orton & Mulligan.

Douglass, F. (1882). *The Life and Times of Frederick Douglass: From 1817–1882*. Christian Age Office.

Douglass, F. (1960). *Narrative of the life of Frederick Douglass: An American slave*. Cambridge, Mass.: Belknap Press.

Du Bois, W. E. B. (1899). *The Philadelphia Negro: A Social Study*. Published for the University.

Du Bois, W. E. B. (1903). *The Souls of Black Folk: Essays and Sketches*. A. C. McClurg & Company.

Du Bois, W. E. B. "The Value of Agitation," *Voice of the Negro,* 4 (March 1907), 109-10

Du Bois, W. E. B. (1909). *John Brown*. (American Crisis Biographies). Philadelphia: G.W. Jacobs and Company.

Du Bois, W. E. B. (1959). *The Crisis*. The Crisis Publishing Company, Inc.

Du Bois, W. E. B. (2004). *The Social Theory of W.E.B. Du Bois*. (P. Zuckerman, Ed.). Thousand Oaks: SAGE Publications, Inc.

Dunham, R. G., & Alpert, G. P. (2015). *Critical Issues in Policing: Contemporary Readings, Seventh Edition*. Waveland Press.

Dunn, K. (2004, November). Dr. Kinsey's Revolution. *The Atlantic*. Retrieved from https://www.theatlantic.com/magazine/archive/2004/11/dr-kinseys-revolution/303649/

Durkheim, É. (1933). *Émile Durkheim on The division of labor in society*. New York: Macmillan.

Durkheim, É. (1966). *The rules of sociological method*. (8th ed., translated by Sarah A. Solovay and John H. Mueller, and edited by George E. G. Catlin.). New York: Free Press.

Epstein, B. (1993). *Political Protest and Cultural Revolution: Nonviolent Direct Action in the 1970s and 1980s*. University of California Press.

Erikson, K. (1966). *Wayward Puritans: a study in the sociology of deviance*. New York: Wiley.

Erikson, K. T. (1962). Notes on the Sociology of Deviance. *Social Problems, 9*(4), 307–314.

Ewald, K., & Jiobu, R. M. (1985). Explaining Positive Deviance: Becker's Model and the Case of Runners and Bodybuilders. *Sociology of Sport Journal, 2*(2), 144–156.

Excerpts From the Testimony by Serpico. (1971, December 15). *The New York Times*. Retrieved from https://www.nytimes.com/1971/12/15/archives/excerpts-from-the-testimony-by-serpico.html

Faulkner, C. (2011). *Lucretia Mott's heresy: abolition and women's rights in nineteenth-century America*. Philadelphia: University of Pennsylvania Press.

Federal Bureau of Investigation. (1996). FBI File on Cesar Chavez and the United Farm Workers, 8. Retreived from https://vault.fbi.gov/Cesar%20Chavez.

Federici, S. (2004). *Caliban and the witch*. New York: Autonomedia.

Felt, M., & O'Connor, J. (2006). *Mark Felt: The Man Who Brought Down the White House*. PublicAffairs.

Ferrell, J., & Sanders, C. (1995). *Cultural criminology*. Boston: Northeastern University Press.

Ferrell, J. (1996). *Crimes of Style: Urban graffiti and the politics of criminality*. Boston: Northeastern University Press.

Fine, S. (1969). *Sit-down: the General Motors Strike of 1936–1937*. University of Michigan Press.

Fischer, E., & Marek, F. (1996). *How To Read Karl Marx*. NYU Press.

Flavin, J. (2009). *Our bodies, our crimes: the policing of women's reproduction in America*. New York: New York University Press.

Flynn, E. G. (1955). *I speak my own piece: autobiography of "The Rebel Girl."* Masses & Mainstream.

Foner, P. S. (1986). *May Day: A Short History of the International Workers' Holiday, 1886-1986*. International Publishers.

Foucault, M. (1963). *The Birth of the Clinic: An Archaeology of Medical Perception*. Vintage Books.

Foucault, M. (1965). *Madness and civilization: A history of insanity in the Age of Reason*. New York: Vintage Books.

Foucault, M. (1977). *Discipline and Punish: The Birth of the Prison*. Vintage Books.

Foucault, M. (1978). *The history of sexuality* (1st American ed.). New York: Pantheon Books.

Frank, A. (1947). *The Diary of a Young Girl*. Vividing Inc.

Frankel, T. (2017, October 4). Why gun violence research has been shut down for 20 years. *Washington Post*.

Freud, S. (1962). *Civilization and its discontents* (1st American ed.). New York: WWNorton.

Fromm, E. (1941). *Escape from freedom*. New York: Farrar & Rinehart, Inc.

Fromm, E. (1956). *The art of loving* ([First edition].). New York: Harper & Row Publishers.

FRONTLINE. (2006, April 11). the tank man. Retrieved from https://www.pbs.org/wgbh/pages/frontline/tankman/

Fryer, J., Roland G. (2016). *An Empirical Analysis of Racial Differences in Police Use of Force* (Working Paper No. 22399). National Bureau of Economic Research. https://doi.org/10.3386/w22399

Funari, V., & Query, J. (2000). *Live Nude Girls Unite!*[Documentary Film]. United States: First Run Features.

Gage, M. J. (Ed.). (1873). Kansas Leavenworth Times. *Susan B. Anthony Scrapbook*.

Garfinkel, H. (1967). *Studies in ethnomethodology*. Englewood Cliffs, N.J.: Prentice-Hall.

Gates (Jr.), H. L., & Yacovone, D. (2013). *The African Americans: Many Rivers to Cross*. SmileyBooks.

Gayle v. Browder, No. 352 U.S. 903 (1956).

Gettleman, M. E. (1985). *Vietnam and America: A Documented History*. Grove Press.

Gewirtz, P. (1996). On "I Know It When I See It." *The Yale Law Journal, 105*(4), 1023–1047.

Gilman, C. P. (1966). *Women and economics: a study of the economic relation between men and women as a factor in social evolution* (1st Harper torchbook ed.). New York: Harper Torchbooks.

Gilmore, G. E. (2018, January 20). Colin Kaepernick and the Myth of the 'Good' Protest. *The New York Times*.

Ginger, R. (1949). *The Bending Cross: A Biography of Eugene Victor Debs*. Rutgers University Press.

Glazer, M. (1983). Ten Whistleblowers and How They Fared. *The Hastings Center Report, 13*(6), 33–41. https://doi.org/10.2307/3560742

Godoy, M. (2017, September 17). Dolores Huerta: The Civil Rights Icon Who Showed Farmworkers "Sí Se Puede." Retrieved May 11, 2018, from https://www.npr.org/sections/thesalt/2017/09/17/551490281/dolores-huerta-the-civil-rights-icon-who-showed-farmworkers-si-se-puede

Goffman, E. (1959). *The presentation of self in everyday life* (Anchor books edition.). Garden City, NY: Doubleday.

Goffman, E. (1963). *Stigma; notes on the management of spoiled identity*. Prentice-Hall.

Goffman, E. (1971). *Relations in public; microstudies of the public order*. New York: Basic Books.

Goldhagen, D. J. (1996). *Hitler's willing executioners: ordinary Germans and the Holocaust* (1st ed.). New York: Knopf: Distributed by Random House.

Goldman, E, & Baginski, M. (1906). Mother Earth. *Mother Earth Journal, 1*(1), 1–4.

Goldman, E. (1916). "Emma Goldman Before the Bar." *Mother Earth*. 11(3).

Goldman, E. (1931). *Living My Life*. New York: Courier Corporation.

Goode, E. (1991). Positive deviance: A viable concept? *Deviant Behavior, 12*(3), 289–309.

Goode, E. (2015). *Deviant Behavior* (10th ed.). Routledge.

Goodstein, L. (2017, December 20). Mormons Expel Founder of Group Seeking Priesthood for Women. *The New York Times*.

Google. (2018). Google Ngram Viewer. Retrieved July 12, 2018, from https://books.google.com/ngrams/graph?content=whistleblower&year_start=1800&year_end=2000
&corpus=15&smoothing=3&share=&direct_url=t1%3B%2Cwhistleblower%3B%2Cc0

Gordon, A. (2012). *The Selected Papers of Elizabeth Cady Stanton and Susan B. Anthony: An Awful Hush, 1895 To 1906* (Vol. 2). Piscataway: Rutgers University Press.

Gorman, T. (1988, August 14). Earth First! Tactics in Fight to Save Planet Anger Some, Tickle Others. *Los Angeles Times*. Retrieved from http://articles.latimes.com/1988-08-14/local/me-906_1_earth-movers

Gorn, E. J. (2015). *Mother Jones: The Most Dangerous Woman in America*. Farrar, Straus and Giroux.

Gray, T. and Turner, N. (1831) "The Confessions of Nat Turner" *Zea E-Books in American Studies*.

Green, J. R. (2006). *Death in the Haymarket: A story of Chicago, the first labor movement, and the bombing that divided gilded age America* (1st ed.). New York: Pantheon Books.

Griffith, E. (1986, May 24). Rock "n" Roll, Now Age 30, Turns from Fad to Legacy. *Los Angeles Times*. Retrieved from http://articles.latimes.com/1986-05-24/local/me-7512_1_black-gospel-corporate-music-rock-n-roll

Gurstein, R. (1996). *The Repeal of Reticence: America's Cultural and Legal Struggles Over Free Speech, Obscenity, Sexual Liberation, and Modern Art*. Farrar, Straus and Giroux.

Guthrie, W. (1940). *Union Maid*. [Audio Recording]. Keynote Records. New York.

Guthrie, W. (1967). *This land is your land*. [Audio Recording].New York: Folkways Records. Audio.

Guttmacher, A. F. (2014). *Margaret Sanger: An Autobiography*. Elsevier

Haidt, J. (2013). *The Righteous Mind: Why Good People are Divided by Politics and Religion*. Vintage Books.

Hammer, R. (1971). *The court-martial of Lt. Calley*. New York: Coward, McCann & Geoghegan.

Haney, C., Banks, C., & Zimbardo, P. (1973). Interpersonal dynamics in a simulated prison. *International Journal of Criminology and Penology*, 1, 69-97.

Hansen, J. (2009). *Storms of My Grandchildren: The Truth about the Coming Climate Catastrophe and Our Last Chance to Save Humanity*. Bloomsbury Publishing USA.

Harper, I. (1899). *The Life and Work of Susan B. Anthony* (Vol. 1). Kansas City, MO: Bowen-Merrill Company. Retrieved from http://archive.org/details/lifeandworksusa00unkngoog

Harris, L. H., Debbink, M., Martin, L., & Hassinger, J. (2011). Dynamics of stigma in abortion work: findings from a pilot study of the Providers Share Workshop. *Social Science & Medicine (1982)*, *73*(7), 1062–1070.

Hart, L. (2005). *Fatal Women: Lesbian Sexuality and the Mark of Aggression*. Routledge.

Haru, T. (n.d.). Breaching Experiment: Definition & Examples - Video & Lesson Transcript. Retrieved Aug. 9, 2018, from http://study.com/academy/lesson/breaching-experiment-definition-examples.html

Hashmi, S. H. (2002). *Islamic political ethics: civil society, pluralism, and conflict*. Princeton, NJ: Princeton University Press.

Hasian, M., & Flores, L. (2000). Mass Mediated Representations of the Susan Smith Trial. *Howard Journal of Communications*, *11*(3), 163–178.

Hays, A. (1936). *Joe Hill*. [Audio Recording]. Found at http://www.fortunecity.com/tinpan/parton/2/joehill.html

Heckert, A., & Heckert, D. M. (2002). a new typology of deviance: integrating normative and reactivist definitions of deviance. *Deviant Behavior*, *23*(5), 449–479.

Heckert, D. M. (1989). The relativity of positive deviance: The case of the French Impressionists. *Deviant Behavior*, *10*(2), 131–144.

Herington, M. J., & Fliert, E. van de. (2018). Positive Deviance in Theory and Practice: A Conceptual Review. *Deviant Behavior*, *39*(5), 664–678.

Hersh, S. M. (1970). *My lai 4: A report on the massacre and its aftermath*. Random House.

Hersh, S. M. (1972). *Cover-up: The Army's secret investigation of the massacre at My Lai 4*. Random House.

Hinton, S. E. (2006). *The outsiders* (Platinum edition.). New York: Speak.

Holstein, J. A., & Gubrium, J. F. (2013). *Handbook of Constructionist Research*. Guilford Publications.

Hooks, B. (1994). Sexism and Misogyny: Who Takes the Rap*Z Magazine. February*.. New York: Routledge.

Hooks, B. (2000). *Feminist Theory: From Margin to Center*. Pluto Press.

Hoose, P. (2010). *Claudette Colvin: Twice Toward Justice*. Macmillan.

Honey, M. (2007). *Going down Jericho Road: The Memphis strike, Martin Luther King's last campaign* (1st ed.). New York: W.W. Norton.

Horwitz, T. (2011). *Midnight Rising: John Brown and the Raid That Sparked the Civil War*. Henry Holt and Company.

Hughes, R., & Coakley, J. (1991). Positive deviance among athletes: The implications of overconformity to the sport ethic. *Sociology of sport journal*, 8(4), 307-325.

Humphrey, J. A., & Palmer, S. (2013). *Deviant Behavior: Patterns, Sources, and Control*. Springer Science & Business Media.

Ibrahim, A. (2018). *The Rohingyas: Inside Myanmar's Genocide*. Oxford University Press.

Inderbitzin, M., Bates, K. A., & Gainey, R. R. (2016). *Deviance and Social Control: A Sociological Perspective*. SAGE Publications.

Ings, S. (2017). *Stalin and the Scientists: A History of Triumph and Tragedy, 1905-1953*. Grove/Atlantic, Inc.

IWW. (n.d.). Lucy Parsons: Woman of Will | Industrial Workers of the World. Retrieved from https://www.iww.org/history/biography/LucyParsons/1

Jacobellis v. Ohio, No. 378 U.S. 184 (1964).

James, H. (1884). The Art of Fiction. *Longman's magazine, 1882-1905*, 4(23), 502–521.

Janis, I. (1972). *Victims of groupthink: A psychological study of foreign-policy decisions and fiascoes*. Boston. Houghton, Mifflin.

Jetten, J., & Hornsey, M. J. (2011). *Rebels in groups: Dissent, deviance, difference and defiance*. Chichester, West Sussex, UK; Malden, MA: Wiley-Blackwell. Retrieved from http://www.aspresolver.com/aspresolver.asp?PEXP;2110085

Jetten, J., & Hornsey, M. J. (2014). Deviance and Dissent in Groups. *Annual Review of Psychology*, 65(1), 461–485.

Johnson, A. G. (2006). *Privilege, power, and difference* (2nd ed.). Boston: McGraw-Hill.

Johnson, A. J. (2007). *The Scopes "Monkey Trial."* Detroit, MI: Omnigraphics.

Jones, A. L. (1998). Random Acts of Kindness: A Teaching Tool for Positive Deviance. *Teaching Sociology, 26*(3), 179–189.

Jones, M. (1925). The Autobiography of Mother Jones. Retrieved March 12, 2018, from https://www.marxists.org/subject/women/authors/jones/ch07.htm

Kalekin-Fishman, D. (2013). Sociology of everyday life. *Current Sociology, 61*(5–6), 714–732.

Kanagy, C. L., & Kraybill, D. B. (1999). *The Riddles of Human Society*. SAGE.

Kappeler, V. E., Sluder, R. D., & Alpert, G. P. (1998). *Forces of deviance: understanding the dark side of policing* (2nd ed.). Prospect Heights, IL: Waveland Press.

Kappeler, V., Sluder, R., & Alpert, G. P. (2015). Breeding Deviant Conformity: Police Ideology and Culture. In R. G. Dunham & G. P. Alpert (Eds.), *Critical Issues in Policing: Contemporary Readings, Seventh Edition* (pp. 79–105). Waveland Press.

Karlsen, C. F. (1987). *The devil in the shape of a woman: Witchcraft in colonial New England* (1st ed.). New York: Norton.

Katz, E. (2000). Sanger on Trial: The Brownsville Clinic Testimony. Retrieved March 21, 2018, from https://www.nyu.edu/projects/sanger/articles/sanger_on_trial.php

Katz, J. (1972). Deviance, Charisma, and Rule-Defined Behavior. *Social Problems, 20*(2), 186–202.

Kedmey, D. (2014, February 7). Those Two Pussy Riot Women? They're Not Actually in the Band Anymore. *Time*. Retrieved from http://time.com/5570/those-two-pussy-riot-girls-theyre-not-actually-in-the-band-anymore/

Kelman, H. C., & Hamilton, V. L. (1989). *Crimes of obedience: Toward a social psychology of authority and responsibility*. New Haven, CT: Yale University Press.

Kempadoo, K., & Doezema, J. (1998). *Global sex workers: Rights, resistance, and redefinition.* New York: Routledge.

Kersten, A. E. (2011). *Clarence Darrow: American iconoclast* (1st ed.). New York: Hill and Wang.

Khodorkovsky, M. (2012a, August 6). Khodorkovsky's Statement on the Pussy Riot "Trial." Retrieved July 12, 2018, from https://www.khodorkovsky.com/khodorkovskys-statement-on-the-pussy-riot-trial/

Khodorkovsky, M. (2012b, August 6). Pussy Riot trial: I've been there – how can these women endure it? *The Guardian.* Retrieved from https://www.theguardian.com/commentisfree/2012/aug/06/pussy-riot-trial-shame-russia

Kimeldorf, H. (1999). *Battling for American Labor: Wobblies, Craft Workers, and the Making of the Union Movement.* University of California Press.

King, C. I. (2005, June 4). Colbert I. King - Deep Throat's Other Legacy. Retrieved from http://www.washingtonpost.com/wp-dyn/content/article/2005/06/03/AR2005060301451.html

King, M. L. (1967, September). The Role of the Behavioral Scientist in the Civil Rights Movement. Retrieved Feb. 2, 2018, from http://www.apa.org/monitor/features/king-challenge.aspx

King, M. L. (1981). *Strength to love* (1st Fortress Press ed.). Philadelphia: Fortress Press.

King, M. L. (1963). Letter from Birmingham Jail. Pp 1–6. Found at http://web.cn.edu/kwheeler/documents/letter_birmingham_jail.pdf

Martin Luther King, Jr. Quotes. (n.d.). BrainyQuote.com. Retrieved April 17, 2019, from BrainyQuote.com Web site: https://www.brainyquote.com/quotes/martin_luther_king_jr_101472.

Krakauer, J. (2009). *Where men win glory: The odyssey of Pat Tillman* (1st ed., New York Times best sellers). New York: Doubleday.

Kraska, P., & Kappeler, V. (1997). Militarizing American Police: The Rise and Normalization of Paramilitary Units. *Social Problems, 44*(1), 1-18.

Kristof, N., & WuDunn, Sheryl. (2009). *Half the sky: Turning oppression into opportunity for women worldwide* (1st ed., New York Times best sellers). New York: Alfred A. Knopf.

Kuhn, T. S. (1970). *The structure of scientific revolutions* (2nd edition, enlarged.). Chicago: University of Chicago Press.

Kuhn, T. S. (2012). *The Structure of Scientific Revolutions: 50th Anniversary Edition.* University of Chicago Press.

Larson, K. C. (2004). *Bound for the Promised Land: Harriet Tubman, Portrait of an American Hero.* One World/Ballantine.

Lauer, C. (2015, April 24). Turkey Will Continue to Deny an Armenian Genocide. *Al Jazeera - America.* Retrieved from http://america.aljazeera.com/articles/2015/4/24/for-turks-acknowledging-an-armenian-genocide-undermines-national-identity.html

Lawrence v. Texas, No. 539 U.S. 558 (2003).

Lear, L. (2009). *Rachel Carson: Witness for Nature.* HMH.

Leight, E., Reeves, M., & Lee, C. (2017, April 15). Kendrick Lamar's 'Damn.': A Track-by-Track Guide – Rolling Stone. *Rolling Stone.*

Lemert, E. M. E. M. (1951). *Social pathology: A systematic approach to the theory of sociopathic behavior.* (1st ed.). New York: McGraw-Hill.

Lemert, E. M. (1966). *Human deviance, social problems, and social control.* Englewood Cliffs, NJ: Prentice-Hall.

Lengermann, P. M., & Niebrugge-Brantley, J. (1998). *The women founders: sociology and social theory, 1830–1930 : A text/reader.* Boston: McGraw-Hill.

Lepore, J. (2014). *The Secret History of Wonder Woman.* New York: Knopf.

Levin, J. (2017, August 18). The NFL's Billionaire Owners Are Too Late to Stop Colin Kaepernick. Retrieved July 12, 2018, from https://slate.com/sports/2017/08/colin-kaepernicks-protest-cost-him-his-job-but-started-a-movement.html

Levine, B. (n.d.). Choking: What You Need to Know to Save Lives (Including Your Own). Retrieved July 23, 2018, from http://www.grandparents.com/health-and-wellbeing/health/what-to-do-if-someone-is-choking

Levins, R. (1985). *The dialectical biologist.* Cambridge, MA: Harvard University Press.

Levy, J. E., & Chavez, C. (1975). *Cesar Chavez: autobiography of La Causa* (1st ed.). New York: Norton.

Lewis, J., & Aydin, A. (2013). *March: Book One*. Top Shelf Productions.

Liazos, A. (1972). The Poverty of the Sociology of Deviance: Nuts, Sluts, and Preverts. *Social Problems - SOC PROBL, 20*, 103–120.

Logan, D. A. (2002). *The hour and the woman: Harriet Martineau's "somewhat remarkable" life*. DeKalb: Northern Illinois University Press.

Lombroso, C., Ferrero, Guglielmo, Rafter, Nicole Hahn, & Gibson, Mary. (2004). *Criminal woman, the prostitute, and the normal woman* (E-Duke books scholarly collection). Durham: Duke University Press.

Lombroso, C., Gibson, Mary, & Rafter, Nicole Hahn. (2006). *Criminal man*. Durham, NC: Duke University Press.

Lombroso, G. (2016). *Criminal Man*. Youcanprint.

Loseke, D. R. (1999). *Thinking about social problems: an introduction to constructionist perspectives*. New York: Aldine de Gruyter.

Lovell, J. S. (2009). *Crimes of dissent: civil disobedience, criminal justice, and the politics of conscience*. New York: New York University Press.

Loving v. Virginia, No. 388 U.S. 1 (1967).

Lowney, K., & Best, J. (1995). Stalking Strangers and Lovers: Changing Media Typifications of a New Crime Problem. In J. Best (Ed.), *Images of issues: Typifying contemporary social problems* (2nd ed.). New York: Aldine de Gruyter.

Lukas, J. A. (1997). *Big Trouble: A Murder in a Small Western Town Sets Off a Struggle for the Soul of America*. Simon and Schuster.

Maas, P. (1973). *Serpico*. New York: Viking Press.

MacAskill, E. (2013, June 10). Edward Snowden, NSA files source: "If they want to get you, in time they will." *The Guardian*. Retrieved from https://www.theguardian.com/world/2013/jun/09/nsa-whistleblower-edward-snowden-why

Mackey, R., & Kates, G. (2012, March 7). Russian Riot Grrrls Jailed for "Punk Prayer." Retrieved July 12, 2018, from https://thelede.blogs.nytimes.com/2012/03/07/russian-riot-grrrls-jailed-for-punk-prayer/

Madison, E. (2018). *Reimagining journalism in a post-truth world: How late-night comedians, Internet trolls, and savvy reporters are transforming news*. Santa Barbara, CA: Praeger.

Maier, T. (2013). *Masters of Sex: The Life and Times of William Masters and Virginia Johnson, the Couple Who Taught America How to Love*. Basic Books.

Malala Yousafzai - The Daily Show with Jon Stewart (video clip). (2013, October 8). *The Daily Show with Jon Stewart*. Comedy Central. Retrieved from http://www.cc.com/video-clips/a335nz/the-daily-show-with-jon-stewart-malala-yousafzai

Mandela, N. (1994). *Long walk to freedom: The autobiography of Nelson Mandela*. (1st ed.). Boston: Little, Brown.

Mandela, N. (2011). *Nelson Mandela by himself: The authorised book of quotations*. Johannesburg: Pan Macmillan South Africa.

Mapping Police Violence. (2015). 2015 Police Violence Report. Retrieved March 17, 2018, from https://mappingpoliceviolence.org/2015/

Marcuse, H. (1991). *One-dimensional man: Studies in the ideology of advanced industrial society* (2nd ed.). Boston: Beacon Press.

Martineau, H. (1838). *How to Observe: Morals and Manners*. Harper.

Martineau, H. (1879). *Harriet Martineau's Autobiography . . .* Houghton, Osgood and Company.

Marx, K. (1889). *Capital: A Critical Analysis of Capitalist Production*. Appleton & Company.

McAdam, D. (1999). *Political Process and the Development of Black Insurgency, 1930–1970*. University of Chicago Press.

McCaghy, C. H., Capron, T. A., Jamieson, J. D., & Carey, S. H. H. (2010). *Deviant Behavior: Crime, Conflict, and Interest Groups*. Routledge.

McCarthy, J. D., & Zald, M. N. (1977). Resource Mobilization and Social Movements: A Partial Theory. *American Journal of Sociology, 82*(6), 1212–1241.

McClanahan, B., & Brisman, A. (2015). Climate Change and Peacemaking Criminology: Ecophilosophy, Peace and Security in the "War on Climate Change." *Critical Criminology*, *23*(4), 417–431.

McDermott, J. D. (1978). *Forlorn hope: the Battle of White Bird Canyon and the beginning of the Nez Perce War*. Boise: Idaho State Historical Society.

Mcgrain, P. (2016). Michael J. DeValve, ed. A Different Justice: Love and the Future of Criminal Justice Practice in America. Durham, NC: Carolina Academic Press, 2015. *Peace & Change*, *41*(2), 263–265.

McIntyre, L. C. (2018). *Post-truth*. Cambridge, MA: The MIT Press.

McLean, B., & Elkind, Peter. (2003). The smartest guys in the room: The amazing rise and scandalous fall of Enron. New York: Portfolio.

Mejía, C. (2008). *Road from Ar Ramadi: The Private Rebellion of Staff Sergeant Camilo Mejía : an Iraq War Memoir*. Haymarket Books.

Merton, R. K. (1968). *Social Theory and Social Structure*. Simon and Schuster.

Messer-Kruse, T. (2011). *The trial of the Haymarket Anarchists: Terrorism and justice in the Gilded Age* (1st ed.). New York: Palgrave Macmillan.

Milgram, S. (1974). *Obedience to authority: An experimental view* (1st ed.). New York: Harper & Row.

Million, J. (2003). *Woman's Voice, Woman's Place: Lucy Stone and the Birth of the Woman's Rights Movement*. Praeger.

Mills, C. (1956). *The power elite* (Galaxy book; GB-20). New York: Oxford University Press.

Mills, C. W. (1961). *The sociological imagination* (1st Evergreen ed.). New York: Grove Press.

Mitchell, J., Oakley, A., & Cott, N. F. (1986). *What is feminism?* Oxford, UK, Oxford: BBlackwell, Basil Blackwell.

Moore, J. (2017, March 22). "A form of punishment": Colin Kaepernick and the history of blackballing in sports. *The Guardian*. Retrieved from http://www.theguardian.com/sport/2017/mar/22/colin-kaepernick-blacklisted-history-sports

Morash, M. (2006). *Understanding gender, crime, and justice*. Thousand Oaks, CA: SAGE Publications.

Moscovici, S., & Faucheux, C. (1972). Social Influence, Conformity Bias, and the Study of Active Minorities. In L. Berkowitz (Ed.), *Advances in Experimental Social Psychology* (Vol. 6, pp. 149–202). Academic Press.

Moy, P., & Scheufele, D. A. (2000). Media Effects on Political and Social Trust. *Journalism & Mass Communication Quarterly*, *77*(4), 744–759. https://doi.org/10.1177/107769900007700403.

Nader, R. (1972). *Unsafe at any speed: the designed-in dangers of the American automobile* (Expanded ed.). New York: Grossman.

Near, J., & Miceli, M. (1985). Organizational Dissidence: The Case of Whistle-Blowing. *Journal of Business Ethics*, 4(1), 1-16.

Nielsen, M. O., & Zion, J. W. (2005). *Navajo Nation peacemaking: Living traditional justice*. Tucson: University of Arizona Press.

Nixon, H. L. (1992). A social network analysis of influences on athletes to play with pain and injuries. *Journal of sport and social issues*, 16(2), 127-135.

Noah, T. (2016). *Born a crime: Stories from a South African childhood* (1st ed.). New York: Spiegel & Grau.

Norrie, A. W. (1982). Marxism and the critique of criminal justice. *Contemporary Crises*, *6*(1), 59–73.

Oates, S. B. (1970). *To purge this land with blood: a biography of John Brown* (1st ed.). New York: Harper & Row.

Obergefell v. Hodges, No. 576 U.S. ___ (2015).

O'Hagan, S. (2014, December 11). Photography is art and always will be. *The Guardian*. Retrieved from http://www.theguardian.com/artanddesign/2014/dec/11/photography-is-art-sean-ohagan-jonathan-jones

Oregon Historical Society. (n.d.). Walla Walla Treaty Council 1855. Retrieved Feb. 1, 2018, from https://oregonencyclopedia.org/articles/walla_walla_treaty_council_1855/#.W0e8jC3MzUJ

Parsons, A. R., & Parsons, L. E. (1889). *Life of Albert R. Parsons, with Brief History of the Labor Movement in America*. L.E. Parsons.

Pepinsky, H. E., & Quinney, R. (1991). *Criminology as peacemaking*. Bloomington: Indiana University Press.

Perraudin, F. (2017, April 10). Photo of Saffiyah Khan defying EDL protester in Birmingham goes viral. *The Guardian*. Retrieved from http://www.theguardian.com/uk-news/2017/apr/09/birmingham-woman-standing-in-defiance-of-edl-protester-goes-viral

Philip, D. (n.d.). America's tree sitters risk lives on the front line. *The Guardian*. Retrieved May 9, 2018, from https://www.theguardian.com/environment/2018/may/26/tree-sitters-appalachian-oil-pipeline-virginia-west

Piott, S. L. (2014). *Americans in dissent: Thirteen influential social critics of the nineteenth century*. Lanham, Maryland: Lexington Books.

Piven, F. F., & Cloward, R. (1977). *Poor People's Movements: Why They Succeed, How They Fail*. Knopf Doubleday Publishing Group.

Pollack, A. (1998, December 1). Scientists Seek a New Movie Role: Hero, Not Villain. *The New York Times*.

Pollock, J. M. (2014). *Women's Crimes, Criminology, and Corrections*. Waveland Press.

Popham, P. (2012, March 29). 'The Lady and the Peacock': Peter Popham's Biography Reveals the Real Aung San Suu Kyi. *The Daily Beast*. Retrieved from https://www.thedailybeast.com/articles/2012/03/29/the-lady-and-the-peacock-peter-popham-s-biography-reveals-the-real-aung-san-suu-kyi

Posner, R. A. (2009). *Sex and Reason*. Cambridge, Massachusetts: Harvard University Press.

Quinney, R. (1970). *The social reality of crime*. Boston: Little, Brown.

Quinney, R. (1991). The way of peace: On crime, suffering, and service. In H. E. Pepinsky & R. Quinney (Eds.), *Criminology as peacemaking* (pp. 3-13). Bloomington: Indiana University Press.

Reiman, J., & Leighton, P. (2015). *The Rich Get Richer and the Poor Get Prison: A Reader (2-downloads)*. Routledge.

Reis, E. (1997). *Damned Women: Sinners and Witches in Puritan New England*. Cornell University Press.

Richardson, J. H. (2014, July 30). The Abortion Ministry of Dr. Willie Parker. Retrieved from https://www.esquire.com/features/abortion-ministry-of-dr-willie-parker-0914

Ritzer, G., & Stepnisky, J. (2016). *Classical Sociological Theory*. SAGE Publications.

Robinson, P. A. (1972, May 1). The Case for Dr. Kinsey. Retrieved from https://www.theatlantic.com/magazine/archive/1972/05/the-case-for-dr-kinsey/303645/

Roe v. Wade, No. 410 U.S. 113 (1973).

Rose, R. (1955). *Twelve angry men: A play in three acts*. Chicago: Dramatic PubCo.

Rosenfeld, Seth (2012). *Subversives: The FBI's War on Student Radicals, and Reagan's Rise to Power*. London: Macmillan.

Saad, L. (n.d.). "Most Admired" Poll Finds Americans Lack Major Heroes. Retrieved March 4, 2018, from https://news.gallup.com/poll/4282/Most-Admired-Poll-Finds-Americans-Lack-Major-Heroes.aspx

Sagarin, E. (1985). Positive deviance: An oxymoron. *Deviant Behavior, 6*(2). Retrieved from https://www.tandfonline.com/doi/abs/10.1080/01639625.1985.9967668

Salam, M. (2018, January 20). When Susan B. Anthony's 'Little Band of 9 Ladies' Voted Illegally. *The New York Times*. Retrieved from https://www.nytimes.com/2017/11/05/us/womens-rights-suffrage-susan-b-anthony.html

Sam Adams Associates for Integrity in Intelligence. (n.d.). Which Sam Adams? A More Recent Patriot - Sam Adams Associates for Integrity in Intelligence. Retrieved from http://samadamsaward.ch/history-of-the-sam-adams-award/

Sanger, M. (1970). *Margaret Sanger; an autobiography*. Elmsford N.Y.: Maxwell Reprint.

Santora, M., & Berendt, J. (2018, February 2). Poland Tries to Curb Holocaust Speech, and Israel Puts Up a Fight. *The New York Times*. Retrieved from https://www.nytimes.com/2018/02/01/world/europe/poland-israel-holocaust-law.html

Sawyer, N. (2017, April 19). The Legacy of Brownie Mary. *SF Weekly*. Retrieved from http://www.sfweekly.com/news/feature/the-legacy-of-brownie-mary/

Scarpitti, F. R., & McFarlane, P. T. (1975). *Deviance, action, reaction, interaction: Studies in positive and negative deviance* (1st ed.). Reading, MA: Addison-Wesley Pub. Co.

Seale, B., & Shames, S. (2016). *Power to the People: The World of the Black Panthers* (Edition Unstated). New York: Harry N. Abrams.

Shetterly, R. (2009). *Americans Who Tell the Truth*. Baker & Taylor, CATS.

Shetterly, R. (n.d.). Camilo Mejia. Retrieved March 1, 2018, from https://www.americanswhotellthetruth.org/portraits/camilo-mejia, /portraits/camilo-mejia

Shoenberger, N., Heckert, A., & Heckert, D. (2012). Techniques of Neutralization Theory and Positive Deviance. *Deviant Behavior, 33*(10), 774–791.

Simon, D. R. (2018). *Elite Deviance*. Routledge.

Spreitzer, G. M., & Sonenshein, S. (2004). Toward the Construct Definition of Positive Deviance. *American Behavioral Scientist, 47*(6), 828–847.

Stack, L. (2015, November 29). A Brief History of Deadly Attacks on Abortion Providers. *The New York Times*. Retrieved from https://www.nytimes.com/interactive/2015/11/29/us/30abortion-clinic-violence.html

Stephenson, W. (2017, February 13). Climate Disobedience in the Time of Trump. *The Nation*. Retrieved from https://www.thenation.com/article/climate-disobedience-in-the-time-of-trump/

Styron, W. (1967). *The Confessions of Nat Turner: A Novel*. Open Road Media.

Snow, C. (1971). *Public affairs*. London: Macmillan.

Sulivan, K., & Jordan, M. (2017, November 25). Elitists, crybabies and junky degrees: America's political divide on higher education. *Washington Post*. Retrieved from http://www.washingtonpost.com/sf/national/2017/11/25/elitists-crybabies-and-junky-degrees/

Sutherland, E. H. (1939). *Principles of criminology*. J. B. Lippincott.

Sutherland, E. H. (1983). *White collar crime: The uncut version*. New Haven: Yale University Press.

Sykes, G. M., & Matza, D. (1957). Techniques of neutralization: A theory of delinquency. *American Sociological Review, 22*, 664–670.

Tappan, P. W. (1947). Who is the Criminal? *American Sociological Review, 12*(1), 96–102.

Tarleton, J. (2011, March 25). Martin Luther King and Union Rights [Text]. Retrieved May 20, 2018, from http://www.psc-cuny.org/clarion/april-2011/martin-luther-king-and-union-rights

Tarrow, S. G. (2011). *Power in Movement: Social Movements and Contentious Politics*. Cambridge University Press.

Taylor, K.-Y. (2016). *From #BlackLivesMatter to Black Liberation*. Haymarket Books.

The Colbert Report - Series | Comedy Central Official Site | CC.com. (n.d.). Comedy Central. Retrieved from http://www.cc.com/shows/the-colbert-report

Theoharis, J. (2015). *The Rebellious Life of Mrs. Rosa Parks*. Beacon Press.

Thio, A. (1983). *Deviant behavior*. Houghton Mifflin Company.

Thoreau, H. D. (1849). *On the Duty of Civil Disobedience*. Read Books Ltd.

Tilly, C. (2004). *Social movements, 1768–2004*. Paradigm Publishers.

Tittle, C. R., & Paternoster, R. (2000). *Social Deviance and Crime: An Organizational and Theoretical Approach*. Roxbury Publishing Company.

Tucker, R. C. (1989). *The Marx-Engels Reader + Civilization and Its Discontents*. W W Norton & Company Incorporated.

Ulrich, L. T. (2007). *Well-behaved women seldom make history* (1st ed.). New York: Alfred AKnopf.

United Nations (Ed.). (2012). *Conscientious objection to military service*. New York : Geneva [Switzerland]: United Nations ; United Nations Human Rights, Office of the High Commissioner.

Vadera, A. K., Pratt, M. G., & Mishra, P. (2013). Constructive Deviance in Organizations: Integrating and Moving Forward. *Journal of Management, 39*(5), 1221–1276.

Walker, Samuel, Spohn, C., & DeLone, M. (2016). *The Color of Justice: Race, Ethnicity, and Crime in America*. Cengage Learning.

Walker, Shaun. (2014, February 19). Pussy Riot attacked with whips by Cossack militia at Sochi Olympics. *The Guardian*. Retrieved from https://www.theguardian.com/music/2014/feb/19/pussy-riot-attacked-whips-cossack-milita-sochi-winter-olympics

Walters, K., & Jarrell, R. (2013). *Blessed Peacemakers: 365 Extraordinary People Who Changed the World*. Wipf and Stock Publishers.

Waters, Tony, & Waters, Dagmar. (2015). *Weber's Rationalism and Modern Society: New Translations on Politics, Bureaucracy, and Social Stratification*. Springer.

Weber, M. (1946). *From Max Weber: Essays in sociology*. (H. Gerth & C. W. C. W. Mills, Eds.). New York: Oxford University Press.

Weber, M., Gerth, Hans, & Mills, C. Wright. (1946). *From Max Weber: Essays in sociology*. New York: Oxford University Press.

Welle, D. (2017, July 27). German pilots refuse to carry out deportations. Retrieved July 12, 2018, from http://m.dw.com/en/german-pilots-refuse-to-carry-out-deportations/a-41638832

Wells, H. G. (1920). *The outline of history, being a plain history of life and mankind. Written with the advice and editorial help of Ernest Barker [and others]*. New York Macmillan. Retrieved from http://archive.org/details/outlineofhistory01welluoft

West, B. (2003). Synergies in deviance: revisiting the positive deviance debate. *Electronic Journal of Sociology*, 7(4), 19.

Westley, W. A. (1970). *Violence and the police: A sociological study of law, custom, and morality*. Cambridge, MA: MIT Press.

Wilkins, L. T. (1964). *Social deviance: Social policy, action and research*. Englewood Cliffs, NJ: Prentice-Hall.

Williams, B. (2014, May 28). Edward Snowden's Motive Revealed: He Can "Sleep at Night." *NBC Nightly News*. Moscow, Russia: NBC. Retrieved from https://www.nbcnews.com/feature/edward-snowden-interview/edward-snowdens-motive-revealed-he-can-sleep-night-n116851

Williams, H., & Murphy, P. V. (1990). *The evolving strategy of police: a minority view*. Washington, D.C.]: USDepartment of Justice, Office of Justice Programs, National Institute of Justice.

Wolf, B., & De Angelis, J. (2011). Tasers, accountability, and less lethal force: Keying in on the contentious construction of police electroshock weapons. *International Journal of Criminology and Sociological Theory*, 4, 657–673.

Wolf, B., & Zuckerman, P. (2012). Deviant Heroes: Nonconformists as Agents of Justice and Social Change. *Deviant Behavior*, 33(8), 639–654.

Woot, T. D. (2011, November 26). Not Quite Speechless: Mother Jones. Retrieved Feb. 4, 2018, from http://not-quite-speechless.blogspot.com/2011/11/mother-jones.html

Wozniak, J. (2002, July 10). The Voices of Peacemaking Criminology: Insights into a Perspective with an Eye Toward Teaching. Retrieved July 12, 2018, from http://restorativejustice.org/rj-library/the-voices-of-peacemaking-criminology-insights-into-a-perspective-with-an-eye-toward-teaching/1875/

Wright, W. (2001). *The Wild West: The mythical cowboy and social theory*. Thousand Oaks, CA: SAGE.

X, M. (1973). *The Autobiography of Malcolm X*. Ballantine Books.

Young, R. F. (2005). *Dissent in America*. New York: Pearson Longman.

Young, R. F. (2015). *Dissent: the history of an American idea*. New York : London: New York University Press.

Yousafzai, M. (2013). *I am Malala: The girl who stood up for education and was shot by the Taliban* (First edition.). New York: Little, Brown, & Company.

Zahniser, J. D., & Fry, A. R. (2014). *Alice Paul: Claiming Power*. Oxford University Press.

Zimbardo, P. G. (2004). A situationist perspective on the psychology of evil: Understanding how good people are transformed into perpetrators. In A. G. Miller (Ed.), *The social psychology of good and evil* (pp. 21–50). New York, NY, US: The Guilford Press.

Zimmer, B. (2006). Language Log: The birth of truthiness? Retrieved May 3, 2018 from http://itre.cis.upenn.edu/~myl/languagelog/archives/002764.html

Zinn, H. (2005). *A people's history of the United States: 1492–present*. New York: Harper-Perennial.

Zuckerman, H. (1997). *Scientific Elite: Nobel Laureates in the United States*. Free Press.

Index

About the Author

Brian Wolf is an associate professor of criminology and sociology at the University of Idaho, where he also serves as chair of the department. His research covers the fields of deviant behavior, comparative criminology and social theory. Wolf has published works in journals such as *Deviant Behavior, Criminal Justice Studies, Radical Pedagogy,* and the *International Journal of Criminological Theory.* Wolf brings a broad international perspective to his research where he has conducted scholarship in South Asia, the Middle East, and Europe. A firm believer in experiential learning, he regularly brings students on justice-studies-themed, faculty-led study abroad trips.

CPSIA information can be obtained
at www.ICGtesting.com
Printed in the USA
LVHW040813020222
709989LV00010B/1227